THE
WOODCHUCK'S
GUIDE TO
GARDENING

By Ron Krupp

A Vermont Organic Gardener

Whetstone Books

Jennie Anderson of Hinsdale, New Hampshire, pushing wheel hoe.
Photo by Steve Hooper of the Keene Sentinel, Keene, New Hampshire, 1996.

> Gardening Book of the Year – 2002
> *The Christian Science Monitor*

Library of Congress Control No.: 2001 135508
ISBN 0-91573I-05-3
To order copies or review copies of the

Woodchuck's Guide to Gardening
Call 1-802-658-9974
e-mail: woodchuck37@hotmail.com
Ron Krupp
8 Lyons Avenue
South Burlington, Vermont 05403

Herb Users Be Aware: In the Spring section of the book, a chapter describes a number of healing plants, their medicinal properties, and how they can be used as home remedies. The author takes no responsibility for the use of these herbs and their remedies.

L. Brown & Sons Printing, Inc.
Barre, Vermont

Printed with soy based ink on recycled paper

DEDICATION

Yet the Rose has one powerful
virtue to boast,

Above all the flowers in the field,

When its leaves are all dead and
fine colours are lost,

Still how sweet a perfume
it will yield.

Isaac Watts 1674-1748

To my mother, Rosalie Fine, who loved
roses. She crossed the threshold on
December 5, 1999 in Louisville, Kentucky.
I miss her every day.

ACKNOWLEDGMENTS

A warm thanks to my friends: Antonia Mesurri, Ash Eames, Marilyn Maddison, Ken Susskind, Deborah Stuart, Julia Lynam, and Marian Halloran for their comments and patience. Thanks to Robert Maddison for his computer expertise and support. To Monica Marshall and Marcy Summers for their help with the material on Children and Gardening. To Richard Does who read over various chapters while we enjoyed breakfast at Friendly's Restaurant on Friday mornings. To Robert King who offered gardening advice and historical perspectives. Robert and I worked together at Hill and Dale Farm in Putney, Vermont, in the late 1960s. He is featured in a number of chapters in the book, e.g., cider making and root cellars.

I traded vegetables with my friend Peter Carlough for some early editing. A thanks also goes to Shay Totten of *The Vermont Times* and Betty Smith of Vermont Public Radio for having enough confidence in my work to make it go public.

A special thanks to Jessica Martinek for her sketches. Jessica is a nursing student at the University of Vermont, and this is her first book just as it is mine. Jamie Mittendorf is a neighbor who helped me develop the photographic elements in the book. I appreciate his photographs and professional support. Other acknowledgments go to Jim Flint, Robert King, Marilyn Maddison, and Steve Hooper of the *Keene Sentinel* in Keene, New Hampshire, for their photographs. Also, to the Special Collections Department of the Bailey-Howe Library at the University of Vermont and to the Tourism Department of the State of Vermont. A final thanks to Sally Sweetland of Waitsfield, Vermont, for her painting on the front cover, called Plant Peace. My gratitude also goes to Peter Gould of Whetstone Books. Additional thanks to Marcie Vallette of Hyde Park, Vermont, for artwork and layout design; and to Larry Brown of Barre, Vermont, for the printing of the book.

Last, but not least, I want to offer a word of appreciation to Linda Bland of Cahoots Writing Services of Cambridge, Vermont, who worked with me on the editing and publishing of the book. She brought me down to earth when I needed it and then raised me up.

PREFACE

I always figured gardening was like heaven—a place to grow plants in harmony with the natural world. *The Woodchuck's Guide to Gardening* visits a similar haven, from germinating seeds in spring to saving seeds in fall.

The goal of the book is to reconnect us to the four gardening cycles of the year through anecdotes and history, poetry and wit, politics, stories of children in the garden patch, and lots of down-to-earth organic gardening tips.

Woodchuck gardeners stand for thrift, practicality, and a connection to the earth and the cosmos. Growing vegetables, flowers, and fruits in colder climates takes ingenuity, patience, and a sense of humor because no one ever knows what the weather will be up to. This way of doing things not only represents a method but also a way of viewing life. Woodchuck gardeners like to say, "Keep it simple," "It depends," and "If it's not one thing, it's another." They are folks, young and old, who practice common sense organic gardening. Some even plant seeds by the moon or constellations, and stir up herbal brews and remedies.

The Woodchuck's Guide to Gardening takes the organic approach to growing plants. I have gardened for 35 years and have rarely used harmful chemicals in my garden. Simply put, they're not needed and are detrimental to the environment and your health. Using organic methods such as composting, companion planting, and crop rotations makes sense.

My wish is to give you a taste of the garden patch and encourage both young and old to discover the limitless world of the plant kingdom. After this, it's up to you.

MEDIEVAL POEM

Medieval wood calendars often illustrated the months of the year according to seasonal tasks. The following poem is a portrayal of the year that was chanted by children of the past. I have adapted it to a New England setting. (original author unknown)

March	It won't be long to start my toil
April	With spade and plough, I turn the soil
May	Here I set my seeds to spring
June	And listen as birds so sweetly sing
July	With my scythe the grass I mow
August	And here I shear my grains full low
September	And with my flail I earn my bread
October	And here I sow my wheat so red
November	As darkness enters, I kill the swine
December	And at Christmas, I drink the apple wine
January	By the fire, I warm my hands
February	And wonder and ponder, the snow-covered land.

CONTENTS

Part One: Spring

Part Two: Summer

Part Three: Autumn

Part Four: Winter

Part Five:
Children and Gardening

Photo by Jim Flint

HOW TO USE THIS BOOK

The Woodchuck's Guide to Gardening is divided into the four seasons: Spring, Summer, Autumn and Winter plus a special section on children and gardening.

The four Appendix Guides at the end of each season support the book the way a wooden stake holds up a tomato plant. The Appendix Guides provide technical information and commentaries. A glossary of common gardening terms is located at the end of the book, along with an index.

Starr Farm Community Garden. Photo by Jim Flint

PART ONE: SPRING

The Greenest of Seasons

Long nights of winter have fled,
snow still sits in patches of white,
rain will soon wash it away,
much to our delight.

Woodland plants push through the earth,
early blooms in the gentle air,
fairies dance in meadows sweet,
all without a care.

Then the green will suddenly appear,
birds their songs will sing,
streams will rise, boughs will burst,
now we know it's spring.

- Ron Krupp

P A R T   O N E
SPRING

CHAPTER 1

THE MAGIC OF GERMINATION AND BEYOND

Illustration by Jessica Martinek

Y ou might think after reading my poem I want to leap into spring by germinating seeds or turning the soil in the cold frame in my front yard. It's odd, but that's not the case. You see, once I get used to hibernating during the long dark months, leaping forth is no easy matter. I have become accustomed to burrowing in my winter's nest, all warm, snug, and secure. I know I need to let go, but I can't help it.

Yet even I am aware of a tension in the air. The spring sun rises higher each day and with it comes warmth. Yellow and purple crocuses push through the snow, ponds melt, lakes break up into ice floes, and pieces jingle and sing in the waves. And then, the final meltdown occurs, and mountain brooks run hard. The seeds under the leaf mulch on the forest floor begin to wake up after a long winter's rest. And I start the yearly cycle of germinating seeds in the confines of my home. But is this the case for most gardeners?

A Lost Art

Growing plants from seeds in spring was once an art and a must for the many souls who loved to till the earth, plant seeds, and care for plants. Today it's surprising how few gardeners grow their own plants

3

from seeds. Even those who stand to profit from doing so turn their backs on seed germination. They have come to depend on purchasing young plants from outside sources. Unfortunately many McSprawl-type stores limit themselves to just a couple of varieties, even though local nurseries and greenhouses offer more choices.

One advantage to growing plants from seed is that you can experiment with heirloom and rare varieties. You can share with other gardeners the seeds you raised and saved from the previous season. I love to start all my plants from seeds because it's my way of taking part in the full cycle of the year.

I launch the new gardening season by rummaging through seeds saved from previous years. The ritual of perusing garden catalogs already took place in winter; new seeds were ordered and have arrived in the mail. Before we begin to plant those seeds in the earth, let's learn about the magic and nature of seeds.

THE SECRETS OF SEEDS

A seed is a miracle waiting to happen: It comes prepackaged

Transplanting seedlings in greenhouse.
Special Collections, Bailey/Howe Library, University of Vermont.

4

with its own food supply and the vital genetic information needed to grow properly. If you soak a bean in water for a day or two then carefully open it, you can see the young plant at one end of the seed. It is tiny and delicate. You might notice the first few leaves, as well as the small, pointed root. The rest of the seed contains stored food for the young plant.

The progression of seed germination to seedling and on to growth of a young plant cannot proceed without the four Greek archetypal elements: earth, water, fire (light), and air.

Earth

For starting seeds indoors, the germination mixture's purpose is to provide good drainage, high water-holding capacity, and moderate amounts of mineral nutrients. Most gardeners use a soilless germination mix for starting seeds. These mixes comprise many natural ingredients including peat and sphagnum moss, vermiculite, washed sand, granite dust, perlite, and compost. Avoid using garden soil because it hardens into a dense, impenetrable mass. As soon as the plant has a root and green leaves, it can absorb its own food, but it still needs the nutrients in the germinating mix to grow.

The section below called Vermont is Going to Pot provides information on germinating mixes, potting mixes, and potting soils. These terms are used interchangeably.

Water

Germinating seeds need a moist but not soggy environment. If you squeeze the germination mix in your hand and water runs down your arm, it's too wet. If the mix is too dry, the seed loses whatever water it has absorbed, and dies. So be observant and careful; water depending on the feel of the mix. Once a week is a rule of thumb.

Fire

Every flower, vegetable, and herb seed has an optimal temperature for germination and a range within which germination occurs. Most seeds germinate when the soil temperature is 68-86 degrees Fahrenheit, although cool weather seeds such as lettuce, spinach, and

---

1. You will notice the word **Woodchuck** used throughout the book. It's there to connote thrift, practicality, and simplicity. See the Introduction for an explanation of the "Woodchuck Principle."

the Brassicas (cabbage, cauliflower, and broccoli) prefer it cooler. I start the Brassicas and lettuce out in the cold frame (described below) because they are cool weather plants. I always plant spinach outside and never transplant it, even though this can be done with plugs started in trays.

Many perennial flower seeds have to be frozen before they will germinate. Others have specific requirements for germination.

See Spring Appendix Guide 1 for books on seed starting and seed saving.

Light (part of the fire element)

Seeds don't need light to germinate. In fact, I usually cover the germination trays with wet newspapers to conserve water and hold the moisture and warmth. The seed has within it the ingredients necessary to germinate. Once the seedlings emerge, sunlight is required for growth.

Some gardeners use electrically heated rubber mats to speed up the germination process. These mats are placed under seed trays.

Indoor Lighting of Plants

Experts say young growing plants need 14 hours of indoor lighting in the spring. We all know that ain't possible in the northern tier of states. So what's a woodchuck gardener to do? Follow one of the woodchuck principles: Use what ya got:

I use 4-foot warm and cool fluorescent lights; these pretty much cover the color spectrum of plant growth. In addition I have some fluorescent "grow lights," specially designed to duplicate the full spectrum of the sun.

See Spring Appendix Guide 2 for specific information on selecting warm or cool fluorescent tubes, grow lights, and fixtures.

Sunlight

A woodchuck alternative light source has been around for millions of years. You guessed it, folks, it's called sunlight. Simply place the young plants next to a south-facing window; just be sure to turn them at least once a week to avoid their bending too much in one direction. If they continually reach for the light, they become leggy and weak. The plants may not look as green and strong as those under the fluorescent lights, but they catch up and do just fine in the garden.

Eventually, the small plants reach 6 to 8 inches. At this point, it's difficult to keep them growing under fluorescent lights or next to

> New seed is faithful.
> It roots deepest
> in the places
> that are
> most empty.
> - The Faithful Gardener by C.P. Estes

a sunny window because the lower leaves become hidden and don't get enough energy. This is when they need to be moved outside for short stints.

Remember, most annual flowers and vegetables only need four to eight weeks of growing inside after the first leaves appear, before moving them outside. You can move the plants outside for a couple of hours each day as long as it is warm-above 50 degrees-and there isn't a strong wind. As the weather warms up, leave them out longer.

The other alternative is to use a cold frame (see chapter 2), which works like a buffer zone or holding station. Cold frames provide young plants a protected environment before you plant them in the main garden.

Air

Germinating seeds and young seedlings need good circulation to prevent damping off, a common fungus disease of indoor plants. The best remedy is a fan run at low speed to keep air moving around the plants. Growing mixes can become contaminated with the fungus, but this doesn't usually occur with commercial mixes. You can sterilize homemade potting mixture by pouring boiling water slowly through it. One gallon of boiling water is sufficient for a standard-sized flat. You can also add one cup of white vinegar (5% acidity) to one quart of water and pour it through the potting mixture. I don't sterilize my mixes and find I only have damping off when air circulation is poor. Even then I only lose a couple of plants.

I can see this is getting a little complicated, just like life. Perfecting when to plant seeds, what type of potting mix to use, and how to care for young plants comes from the school of experience and hard knocks, plus some help from books and your gardening friends. Many tricks and techniques accompany spring gardening, but one thing is for sure: Watching seeds germinate is a miracle, and nurturing young seedlings is a joy as well as a source of meditation, though tedious it may well be at times.

VERMONT IS GOING TO POT

Many woodchuck gardeners have been telling me Vermont is going to "pot." They aren't referring to that material called hemp the Declaration of Independence was written on, or that popular weed called marijuana, which is the biggest cash crop in Vermont, California, and a few other states. What they're talking about is potting soils or what some call germinating mixes. More and more gardeners are raising their own plants from seeds, and that means they need lots of potting mix ingredients.

A number of Vermont companies are producing mixes.

See Spring Appendix Guide 3 for a description of the Foster Farm in Middlebury, Vermont; they not only use cow manure to make potting mixes and compost, but also use it to make methane gas for heat.

Potting Mix

Some mixes are used for germination, others for transplanting, still others for container gardening and potted plants. You want a mix that suits its purpose, can retain moisture, and has a texture suitable for seeds and roots.

The heavy organic matter in soilless mixes are sphagnum moss and peat, dug from peat bogs. The lightweight materials are vermiculite (mica) and perlite (volcanic glass); both are minerals mined from the earth. Lighter mixes for germinating purposes use more vermiculite and perlite and less peat and sphagnum moss. Heavier, coarser mixtures are used for houseplants and larger containers. Mixtures for transplanting fall somewhere in the middle.

Some biodynamic gardeners use spagnum moss, granite dust, washed sand, and compost in their mixes. The granite dust contains trace elements.

Even though vermiculite and perlite are natural substances mined from the earth, they are heated to make them blow up and expand. This is where the objection comes into play and why natural substances like washed sand and granite dust are used along with sphagnum moss and compost.

To make your own mixes, purchase peat or sphagnum moss that has been shredded or milled. Or buy it in a raw state, in which case you need to run the moss through a screen and sieve it yourself. Buy vermiculite or perlite in bulk and add in homemade compost.

A WOODCHUCK'S ALL-PURPOSE FORMULA

Fill a 5-gallon plastic bucket with peat or sphagnum moss and put it in a larger container; a wheelbarrow or garden cart is ideal to stir the formula up in. Add in a whole bucket of vermiculite and half a bucket of well broken down homemade compost. For outdoor containers (window boxes, whiskey barrels, buckets) use more compost (one whole bucket). You can also use this woodchuck formula for houseplants. As you have learned, recipes serve different purposes. Try experimenting.

Another option is to purchase commercial potting mixes like Pro-Mix, Peters Inc., or Grace products. I also recommend locally produced potting mixes, which can meet or exceed the performance of commercially based mixes. Make sure compost-based mixes are high in quality. Sufficient available nitrogen is a critical factor. Most commercial brands add water-soluble chemical fertilizers like Miracle Grow to their homemade mixes; I add a little extra compost to my mix and call it Woodchuck Grow.

Beware: Potting soils purchased from the Sprawl-Marts of the world can be poor in quality, containing too much soil. One day the term potting soil will be changed to potting mix because it's more appropriate. I prefer to buy local mixes or mix my own.

It's certainly fun to raise your own plants from seeds in the spring while the snow is still tickling your nose, and even better to enjoy the satisfaction of producing your own germination blends of soil. If more of us began to dally with mixes, it wouldn't be long before we would all be going to pot-in Vermont, then America, and even the world.

WOODCHUCK CONTAINERS AND MORE

You can use all manner of containers for seed germination and transplanting. Many people throw away black and green plastic trays and pots instead of reusing them. You can find these treasures at the recycling centers. Use plastic-coated milk cartons of all sizes by cutting off the top half. Try also the shallow wooden or styrofoam boxes florists call flats, 1-pound coffee cans, used clay and plastic flowerpots, cardboard egg cartons, white plastic yogurt containers, and the list goes on. If you are handy, scrounge slats of wood and make rectangular wooden flats: 2 feet long by 1 foot wide and at least 3 inches deep. These last for years if you take care of them.

Countless other commercial products include flats, wedge trays with 1/4" and 1/8" plug inserts, regular plastic trays, some with drain holes and others that hold water, plug trays, square and round pots, paper and peat containers, and paper pots that fan out into honeycomb shapes. One device even makes pots from newspapers.

A simple metal contraption creates cubes called soil blocks from a germination/compost mix. Seeds are planted in the cubes. Smaller cubes can be placed in larger cubes. Some companies mold cubes from soilless mixes. They are similar to the smaller Jiffy pellets, which are held together by a biodegradable plastic mesh in compressed peat. Seeds are planted into the cubes and pellets. Once the young plants are of sufficient size, you just transplant the whole cube or pellet into the garden. Learn more about these products by studying various garden supply catalogs such as Peaceful Valley, A.M. Leonard, Johnny's, Gardener's Supply, Mellinger's, and Fedco.

See Winter Appendix Guide 4 for a complete list of addresses, phone numbers, and web sites for garden tools, machines, nursery products, and supply companies. It's great winter reading.

SEEDS AREN'T CHEAP, BUT...

Seeds used to be passed down from one generation of farmers and gardeners to the next. In the latter half of the 19th century, the Shakers developed the first seed packets. During the Great Depression of the 1930s, seeds only cost five to ten cents per packet, but that was a lot of money in those days; many families saved seeds to conserve what little money they had. Things have changed: Last spring a friend of mine bought a package of melon seeds. There were supposed to be 15 seeds in the package; inside were only ten and, out of those, only five germinated. That's pretty expensive at $2.69 a pack. Here are some ways to buy vegetable and flower seeds that won't strain your pocketbook.

Woodchuck gardeners check out sales at local garden centers for deals on houseplants and seeds. Some garden centers offer last year's seeds at reduced prices in the spring: buy two get one free, or 50 percent off. Garden centers also have seed sales at the end of the gardening season.

Other ways you can conserve cash: Buy seeds in bulk and share with friends (see details below). Be frugal when you plant, only using the necessary number of seeds. Remember what vegetable, flower, and herb seeds did well the previous year and purchase them again.

Some seeds can only be stored for short periods of time and

others much longer. If you saved some seeds from last year, check the condition. Make sure there is no fungus in the storage containers.

Woodchuck Seed Tips

Ideal storage is to pack seeds in dry containers, like plastic or glass jars. Store the containers in dry, cool conditions. A cheesecloth bag full of dried milk soaks up moisture in the jar. It is best to change the cloth once a season.

With squash, cucumbers, and melons, it's kind of a hit-and-miss affair, depending on how they are stored; seeds in this family dry up quite easily.

Purchase carrot, beet, and spinach seed as fresh as possible.

The hardiest small seeds are marigolds, zinnias, cosmos, lettuce, and radish.

Bulk Seeds

Some great buys can be found in bulk seeds. For example, Peaceful Valley Farm Supply sells 16 ounces of Red Core Chantenay carrots for $7.00. Compare this with $4.00 an ounce at most farm stores. That's quite a savings. Go in with friends to purchase seeds in bulk.

Peaceful Valley Farm Supply
P.O. Box 2209, Grass Valley, CA 95945
(888) 784-1722 *www.groworganic.com*

Stokes, Burpee, Shumway's, Harris, and Fedco seed companies also sell seeds in bulk. In some cases, it's necessary to request their commercial catalog.

See Winter Appendix Guide 2 for a complete list of garden catalog addresses, phone numbers, and web sites. In Winter Appendix Guide 5 is a list of the better garden magazines, which provide a wealth of horticultural information.

Garden stores that sell bulk seed from the previous year are supposed to have it retested and list the germination rate on the tag. If it says 90 percent germination rate, that means nine out of ten seeds will germinate. Be aware that the seed testing centers use a controlled batch for germinating purposes. They ask each garden center to send a sample of seeds from each variety, but they don't test every sample; they may test a seed sample from garden center A and not from garden center B. The garden center B batch (not tested) may have been stored outside in a damp warehouse.

All that said, it's still hard to go wrong buying bulk seeds, especially beans, corn, and peas. Bulk corn and peas usually don't germinate more than 75-85 percent even though the claim on the tag may be higher. Remember, it's best to plant a little thicker in the spring and early summer because the germination rate can be lowered by cold and wet soil conditions.

The easiest way to check out the germination rates of corn, beans, and peas is to spread some of the older seeds on a very damp paper towel. Place another damp towel on top.

Cover them with a piece of plastic and place in a warm spot. In a few days, you will be able to see how well they germinate. If only 25 percent germinate, throw them out. If 50 percent germinate, double up when planting.

BEDDING PLANTS FOR LESS

Comparison Shopping

If you don't have as much money as you'd like to spend on flats of annual flowers, why not start your own bedding plants? (That's what the pros call annual flowers planted in mass quantities with impressive colors.) For example, you could buy a pack of petunia seeds at $2.15 for a hundred seeds. It would cost you about $33.30 to buy that many plants at a garden center. With zinnia seeds at $1.00 for a hundred, you'll save around $32.30. Of course I like to treat myself now and then to a six-pack of annuals at my favorite garden center.

When in Doubt, Read the Directions

Some perennial seeds need to be frozen and others need a dormancy period. Some need to be scraped and cut, others soaked, and certain perennial seeds have light and darkness requirements for germination.

Most annual flower seeds don't have any special requirements. They are easy to grow. Just follow the simplest of the woodchuck principles: Read the directions. Study the germination information and growing tips in the numerous gardening publications, magazines, and books, as well as my favorite flower catalog:

Stokes P.O. Box 548, Buffalo, N.Y. 14240

(800) 274-9238 *www.stokes.com*

Please Don't be Impatiens

Impatiens are the number one bedding plant sold at nurseries and for good reason: They bloom nonstop from the time you transplant them in early summer until frost. They come in many colors: lavender, burgundy, pink; and they come with star patterns and streaks. Impatiens are the best flowers to plant in shady spots.

Start impatiens by sprinkling seeds on the surface of a premoistened saturating medium like wet newspaper, or on top of a soilless mix in February. It's not necessary to cover the seeds because they are tiny and germinate easily.

Transplant the small seedlings into a soilless mix in plastic pots, plug trays, wooden and plastic flats-whatever is at hand. Just make sure there is good drainage. After three days of rest, place them under fluorescent hot and cold lights, grow lights, or in direct sunlight. Keep the soil moist and warm.

After the last frost in your area, plant the hardy little plants outside in rich, well-drained soil, in part or full shade. By the way, impatiens seeds cost about $3.15 for fifty seeds. You would pay $16.65 to purchase that many plants.

As you can see, there are ways to weed out the extra expense of gardening. Woodchuck gardeners can spot a bargain a mile away at a garden store. If a plant appears dead, a bag of fertilizer ripped, a clay pot chipped, ask the counter person if they are going to throw it out or what kind of deal they will make. The other way of saving money is to have the patience to wait for that tray of petunias to drop in price in a matter of weeks.

See Spring Appendix Guide 4 for a list of and information on Woodchuck Annual Flowers and Seed Starting Dates along with an explanation of the difference between annuals, biennials, and perennials.

Conclusion

Seeds are alive but sleeping during the winter months. With moisture, light, warmth, and a germinating mix, garden seeds awaken (germinate) after a long rest. Starting plants from seeds is a wonder-filled way to participate in the rites of early spring. Besides, every woodchuck gardener knows it's cheaper than buying plants at a garden center.

There isn't one right way to this business of seed starting. Gardeners of all shapes and sizes develop their own techniques. Most home gardeners have an assortment of techniques to germinate seeds, grow seedlings, and care for young plants. We all learn what works for us. Some home gardeners start all their plants from seeds, and others buy plants at the local greenhouse. And some do a little of both. It's great to have choices. I always seem to end up purchasing a few plants from the local nursery.

I entitled this chapter *The Magic of Germination and Beyond*. I now want to enter the "beyond" by moving from seeds and germination, to seedlings and young plants.

CHAPTER 2

EARLY SPRING PLANTING: INDOORS TO OUTDOORS

HINTS FROM A WOODCHUCK GARDENER

Start your pepper and eggplant seeds in trays from mid to late March, and tomato seeds from late March to early April. Onion, leek, and shallot seeds are begun in trays or pots in early March. Gardeners who live in colder pockets may want to start their seeds a little later, and those who live in warmer climates can start them earlier.

Experiments have shown that steady growth works better than slow growth with young seedlings and-believe it or not-plants grown later catch up with those started earlier. This may be because the sun is higher in the sky and the temperature in your home may be a little warmer later in the season. Nature has a way of balancing it all out, as long as we don't meddle with it too much.

Once the seeds germinate and grow into two-inch tomato, eggplant, and pepper seedlings, transplant them from the trays into 4" x 4" square, or 4" round plastic pots, or the bottoms of half-gallon milk cartons. Or come up with your own woodchuck containers. Place the pots into standard trays, which measure about 20 inches long by 10 1/2 inches wide.

Each tray holds eight pots with a plastic sheet on the bottom to hold water. These trays have holes in them. You can also use plastic trays with no holes in them that hold the excess water. In this case, the plastic sheets aren't necessary. By the way, it's a good idea to double up the trays; it provides strength so it's easier to carry them around. Lay the trays on a long wooden table next to a south-facing window or under fluorescent lights. Once the young vegetable plants are stronger, place them outside in late April in the cold frame to harden them off. Hardening off is a process of moving plants from an inside sheltered environment to an outside protected location to adapt them for their final planting into the garden.

Leave leek, shallot, and onion seedlings in their original trays or pots. Clip off the tops about every two weeks to encourage the bulbous part of the plant to grow.

From mid to late May, transplant the young tomato plants into the garden. By that time, the plant leaves are a healthy dark green and there is plenty of room in the pots for a strong stalk and root system. One common problem with growing tomatoes indoors is that they can become too leggy. If this happens, when planting them outside, lay them down horizontally and cover slowly with soil, bending the top of the plant vertically until it is upright. Be really careful not to break the stem. I always seem to break one or two.

Some tomato plants you buy from a local garden center come in small six-pack containers that don't provide much room for the roots to grow. Also, the stems can be weak and thin. My tomato plants suffer little shock when I place them in garden soil because they have plenty of space to form a sizeable root ball in their 4" by 4" pots.

If you wait till the first or second week of June, you can buy those six-packs inexpensively from local nurseries and greenhouses. Then you won't have to worry about grow lights, damping off, cold frames, and the rest. One woodchuck trick is to transplant a commercial six-pack of tomatoes that already have a small root ball into larger pots. This gives the roots room to spread. After a week or two, you can harden them off gradually outside. If you don't have a cold frame, just leave them on the porch in a sunny spot for a couple of hours per day, lengthening the time with each passing day.

I don't recommend putting eggplants, pepper plants, or tender annuals in your garden until Memorial Day or even later because they don't like cold soil. The key to growing these warm Mediterranean vegetables in summer is to have strong, healthy plants ready to place in your garden once the earth has warmed up. Some gardeners leave eggplants and peppers in containers because they love warm soil and are easy to water. Make sure there is good drainage.

I don't put my 65 tomato plants in my community garden plots all at once but stagger them out from mid-to late May. In case of frost, have covers available (hot-caps or gallon milk jugs whose bottoms have been cut off). It's a woodchuck paradox that gardeners who plant tomatoes at the end of May and early June have just as large a crop of red ripe fruit as an impulsive early planter like me. Successful woodchuck gardeners wait till Memorial Day to put out their tomato plants. They use common sense.

FLOWER SEEDS

Start flower seeds like impatiens and snapdragons in February, and others like marigolds in early April. Specific conditions are needed for certain perennial flower seeds like freezing them for a couple of days. Check the better seed catalogs like the ones from Stokes for good advice on starting flower seeds.

Once the flower seedlings emerge from wooden or plastic flats or trays, either transplant them into small pots or yogurt containers or leave them in the flats. Another option is to start the seeds directly in plug trays. Some plug trays have 24 cells, others have 48. Plugs are young plants grown from seeds in a one-piece plastic tray; the trays contain one-inch cells with a hole in the bottom of each. The tapered plugs pop out of the cells.

THE GREENHOUSE AND YOUR HOME

Commercial and home-style greenhouses produce the best plants because they provide plenty of heat and light. Large greenhouse operations control temperature with computerized heating and ventilation systems, heating mats for germination purposes, and other

appropriate greenhouse technologies. Some even have automated seed and plant transplanters, moisture controls, and so on.

Healthy greenhouse plants have a strong green look in the leaves along with thicker stems due to the combination of more light and higher temperatures. This is the advantage of a greenhouse operation and why it is hard to duplicate in the confines of your home. Cheaper greenhouse plants of the six-pack variety are shorter with

Young spring seedlings.

thinner stems and smaller root balls. They do okay in the garden; they just take a little longer to produce fruit.

The shortcoming of today's modern double-plastic greenhouses is they are extremely tight and don't allow much air flow compared with the older, leaky, glass greenhouses. This creates an unnatural environment for plants. Fungus, bacterial diseases, and insects are more of a problem with modern greenhouses. The question gardeners need to ask is, "What is good for the plant?" I am not against modern greenhouse design and materials, but they sometimes lack an understanding of the right environment for plant growth.

The ideal home garden includes a small affordable greenhouse where the gardener raises all plants from seed, and a cold frame where cold hardy seeds are started and young plants become strong as they adapt to the outside world. From there, it's on to the garden. Of course, most gardeners don't have a greenhouse, but many do use cold frames or what some call The Woodchuck's Greenhouse.

THE WOODCHUCK'S GREENHOUSE

Others may call this a cold frame, but I prefer the Woodchuck's Greenhouse. I couldn't live without a cold frame. I consider these wood and glass structures the magic boxes of the gardening world. Woodchuck Greenhouses are easy to build and maintain, and can be used in the spring, fall, and even in winter. Whatever name you prefer, these structures were common 30 years ago.

Once seeds germinate and grow into seedlings, my home has the look of a floral invasion. The only place left for them to go is into my cold frame. In his book *Four Seasons Harvest*, Elliot Coleman says gardeners should dedicate a monument to the cold frame. "It is the simplest, most flexible, and most successful low-tech tool for modifying the garden climate. It's simple because it is basically a wooden box with a glass, plastic, or fiberglass cover with no bottom that sits on top of the soil. The cold frame is flexible because it can be made as long or as tall as the gardener wishes. And it's successful because it is a tried-and-true garden aid that has been used in one form or another since ancient times (sheets of mica predated glass)." In the 1940s and '50s, cold frames were the foundation for the development of intensive commercial horticulture in the U.S.

Crop Protection from Cold, Moisture, and Wind
The cold frame's single layer of glass (or plastic) creates a micro-

climate that protects plants from wind as well as moisture and cold. It's the constant freezing and thawing in winter that does real damage to plants, such as strawberry plants. Wind is a problem too; it makes a cool day feel colder, removing heat quickly and evaporating moisture. The nighttime temperature inside a cold frame can be as much as twenty degrees warmer than outside.

Ron's Woodchuck Cold Frame

In front of my home, I built a 16-foot long, 5-foot wide cold frame that faces south. It's made from one-foot-wide wooden planks I scrounged. Old storm windows cover the frame. (Make sure there is no lead paint on the windows.) The official name for a cold frame's window or top covering is a *light*. Modern lights can be translucent material other than glass, such as plastic or fiberglass. Remember that if the lights are too lightweight, they may blow off. That's why some gardeners still prefer glass lights. You can always put a heavy piece of lumber to hold down the lights or use a hook and eye to connect the lights to the cold frame.

In late March, cover the entire cold frame with a large piece of plastic sheeting to warm up the soil. Remove the plastic, dig up the earth beneath it with a spade, and rake out the soil. Plant hardy vegetable seeds and cover the frame with lights. When the temperature is below 40 degrees Fahrenheit, keep the cold frame covered at night and during the day with lights. As the days lengthen, the sun rises

The ideal garden includes a cold frame.

Cold frames in early spring. Photo by Robert King.

higher in the sky, and it becomes warmer, lift the lights up gradually, using notched wooden sticks, for aeration and temperature control. Make sure to leave the frame completely open when there is a warm spring rain.

I designed my frame so the back wall is about 12 inches high and the front wall 8 inches high. The slight slope of about 20 degrees helps increase the effects of the sun and thus warms the frame.

In late March, I plant the cool-weather seeds of spinach, lettuce, radishes, and onion sets in the cold frame along with cabbage, broccoli, and cauliflower seeds. These last three are part of the Brassica family. Once the lettuce and Brassica seeds have germinated and grown into young plants of 2 to 3 inches high, I transplant them into flats or small peat pots. I then transplant these into my community garden plots from early to mid-May. These cool weather crops do better when started from seed in the cold frame than when started in my home.

Broccoli

Broccoli is a cool weather crop. Too much summer heat can cause premature formation of small heads (referred to as buttoning) and tough stems. Buttoning can also take place with cauliflower. That's why timing is so critical. By starting your own seedlings, you can have vigorous transplants when you need them. Early spring broccoli is best started 8 weeks before the last frost date, and late fall broccoli, 10 weeks before the last frost date. Some varieties have both central heads and sideshoots and others a single-yield head. Best broccoli varieties: Broccoli Raab, De Cicco, Green Goliath, Italian Green Sprouting, Packman, Purple Sprouting, and Waltham 29. Cook's Garden Seeds has a good selection.

By the time I plant peas in my garden in late April, I have begun to eat the radishes, scallions, lettuce, and spinach. These first spring cultivated greens are all raised in The Woodchuck's Greenhouse. By the way, I am still eating lettuce and spinach from the cold frame in late November and early December-from seeds planted in August.

A cold frame is a perfect place to help plants adjust to the cool spring nights and to extend the gardening season into fall. Cold frames are simple to build and easy to use. I even plant spinach in late August and let it sit all winter under lights in the cold frame. The spring brings the first spinach greens.

Pots of tomato, pepper, and eggplant in trays are placed in the cold frame from early to mid-May to harden them off. After a couple of weeks, they begin to develop stronger stems and darker leaves, and are ready to be planted in the garden. Some folks who live in the cooler spots plant pots of tomatoes, peppers, and eggplants directly into the cold frame and leave them there for the entire season.

For an explanation of common gardening terms like hardening off, soil Ph, acid and alkaline soils, bolting, plant varieties and cultivars, cover crops, and green manures, consult the glossary.

Maple Pie and Lost Mufflers

Spring comes quickly, by and by.
It brings with it
sugar snows and maple pie,
and dandelion greens, not so serene
and lost mufflers on muddy roads.
Did I forget the sounds of peepers and toads?

- Ron Krupp

CHAPTER 3
SPRING BLOOMS AND EDIBLES

In spring, nature holds her breath, waiting in solemnity for the rush of new life to unfold. The weather in Vermont is both subtle and dramatic with sugar snows, heavy rains, cold nights, and even some warm days. The grass turns from thatch brown to lighter shades of green, and the white blossoms of sugar maple buds dot the macadam roads. A little before dusk, the Green Mountains look like a field of purple heather as the green of the conifers and burgundy maple buds meld into the hillsides.

If the weather cooperates, you can harvest purple hyacinths, crocuses, and baby yellow daffodils from your front yard garden-all in time for Easter. Here are some tricks to help those young spring bulbs come up early: If the bulbs are planted next to the south-facing wall of your home, the foundation will warm the soil. Mulching bulbs in the fall protects them from the harsh winter elements. You can also break the cold spring winds with cedar hedges or a flat wooden board fence. Make sure your garden beds have a good southern exposure with lots of sun. Many spring bulbs just won't bloom early in northern gardens, but the methods mentioned above help them get an early start.

If you are intent on having early blooming bulbs, you can always buy them in a garden store and force them in the warmth of your home. A woodchuck alternative for Easter is to cut forsythia branches in early March. Force them to blossom by placing the stems in a vase full of water in full sunlight. Or plant wheat seeds in a wooden box to provide a nice flat "lawn" of young green grass to offset the yellow blossoms of the forsythia. All in all, it's wonderful to bring spring into your home while the trees are still bare.

See Chapter 29 in Winter Section on forcing forsythia and other woody stemmed plants, called Bringing in the Woodies.

Gardening, Foraging, and Observing

Woodchuck gardening also describes those gatherers who love to forage the meadows and wetlands for herbs, roots, and greens and who love to tap the sugar maple tree. The rule of thumb is 40 gallons of maple sap boil down to one gallon of the sweetest syrup in the world. Tap the sugar maple by boring with a hand drill into the outer

> Daffydown dilly
> Has come to town,
> In a yellow petticoat
> And a green gown.

Traditional English Rhyme

part of the tree two to three inches and then tapping in a metal spout. For more information, read the classic, *The Maple Sugar Book* by Helen and Scott Nearing (1950). You can also collect the sap of the white birch for a spring tonic after the maple sap stops running. Use the same tapping method as with the sugar maple. As soon as the young white birch leaves begin to form, stop tapping the tree for sap. Remember, this shortest of seasons in New England still has promises to keep, like picking wild ramps (what some call wild leeks or Easter onions), one of the first wild plants to appear in spring.

THE WOODLAND PLANTS

Some people just love to observe woodland plants in spring; I consider them gardeners just as much as the cultivated kind who plant vegetables and flowers.

One of my favorite springtime activities is to visit the young woodland plants in the forest near my home. I love to watch them arise from the snow melt and leaf litter in the forest. Woodland plants come out while the young tree leaves are still bundled up tight, waiting to spring out. During this time, a lot of light is still reaching the forest floor; once the tree leaves open up, the forest floor darkens and the woodland plants vanish until the following spring. The plants I am referring to are Dutchman's-breeches, bloodroot, wild ginger, hepatica, jack-in-the-pulpit, trout lily, spring beauty, May apple, Solomon's - seal, the trilliums, and the orchids that grow in protected woodland areas. Take the ephemeral bloodroot: Its large white flowers are enveloped in a single leaf so it appears the flower arises from the leaf. Like many early wildflowers, bloodroot must produce its blossoms from energy generated the previous year and stored in a bulb-like culm. And bloodroot must quickly get on with generating new energy because the flowers rarely last longer than a few days. Bloodroot gets its name from the orangish-red juice that flows from a cut root; this was used by Native Americans and pioneers as cloth dye. Be careful: The juice from the bloodroot can be toxic and produce a rash like poison ivy.

Let's not forget the trout lily with its drooping yellow blooms framed by a set of red-splotched leaves resembling trout markings.

And what about the loveliest of all spring blooms, the trilliums. Where I come from, you aren't supposed to pick 'em. In fact, one variety of trillium called Knodding is on the watch list for endangered plants. The three other common trilliums, white, painted, and red (sometimes called stinking Benjamin or nose bleed), should also be left alone. Painted trillium can easily die from transplanting just like the pink lady's-slipper. Tragically, white trillium have been all but collected out in the state of Maine.

The New England Wild Flower Society and others have made an extensive effort to urge sellers of woodland plants to grow them from seed or division rather than depleting native stands. Still more education is needed. When a drift of thousands of trillium covers a hillside, it's difficult to remember each plant required six years of growth from seed germination until bloom.

The appeal of woodland wildflowers, as with all perennials,

Trilliums in a woodland setting.

Trillium
and maple blossoms.
Photos by Jamie Mittendorf.

comes from the continuity of remembering the plant in its natural setting from one year to the next. Plants that link us to times past add to our pleasure in the present. Enjoy the hepaticas, Dutchman's breeches, and others by simply walking into the forest, finding your favorite place, and saying hello to your spring flower friends. Just make sure to stay on the forest paths; many stems, plants, shoots, and bulbs are hidden beneath the leaf mold awaiting their appointed time for emergence.

One woodchuck principle I follow is *Live with nature*. In other words, leave it alone. Eventually, some of the woodland plants will become endangered unless we stop messing around. If you are bent on planting them in your garden, purchase plants from a reputable nursery that raises them from seeds and division. You will pay more but simultaneously help ensure the survival of the wild species.

You can become a kid again by looking for woodland plants. Just when you think you won't find them, they appear. The first flowers will lift your spirits after a long cold winter. Spring is subtle in color compared to the power of autumn, but no less dramatic. To walk into the forest and meet thousands of white trillium is a sight to tickle your soul.

WHERE THE WILD EDIBLES GROW

Many gatherers also walk the wetlands and meadows to collect wild food and medicinal plants. Let's begin the story of wild edibles with May Nick and Ricketts Smith. And then move on to three collectors of wild plants in Vermont.

MAY NICK AND "SINGIN'"

In 1964, I was teaching in a one-room schoolhouse in eastern Kentucky. One day, I strolled over to see May Nick, a 60-year-old, cranky, white-haired woman. I called out for May and she yelled back, "Just sit a while and I'll be a-comin'." May Nick was a gatherer of wild plants. I often saw her up in the hills with her baskets, tromping around the forests, meadows, and wetlands. Soon May showed up with a basket of fresh spring mustard greens, which she fried up with lard, vinegar, and a little sugar. The greens were delicious.

Duthchman's Breeches
and Trout Lilies
in Red Rocks Park.
Photo by Jamie Mittendorf

One summer day I went over to Ricketts Smith's general store in Goosecreek. I wanted to talk with him. The old-timers who sat around the potbellied stove said he was out "singin'." I told them I never heard Ricketts sing-in church, school, or anywhere, for that matter. Soon Ricketts returned to tell me he had been out collecting ginseng, which he sent to China by way of some fellow from New York. I didn't believe him until years later when I found out it was true: There really is another way to go "singin'."

My first cultivated garden was near Goosecreek. One day my neighbors Mallie and Chrit Gambel drove their mule over with a plow and an apron full of seeds. From their generosity, my passion for plants began.

BARBARA'S THREE FAVORITE WILD GREENS

Barbara Nardozzi, my gardening friend and herbal guru, runs Bramblewood Gardens in Hinesburg, Vermont. She says, "for those who have endured the long northern winter months with colds and flus, for those whose immune systems have been stretched to the limit, there is light at the end of the tunnel and it's not called Florida: Believe it or not, it's called spring.

"When the last snow melt is almost gone, those first green shoots begin to burst. It's no accident nature is offering these new gifts of spring; they are absolutely packed with vitamins and minerals. Those hybrid cultivars, like store-bought lettuce, just don't offer the vitality of wild plants. This is all based on the assumption we are not separate from the cycle in nature, but part of it."

Barbara went on to tell me a 17th-century principle called the Doctrine of Signatures; it states that God created plants to cure human ailments and that the healing plant itself resembles whatever ailment it was meant to cure. One example is the dark, three-tipped leaf of the round-lobed hepatica; it is thought to cure liver ailments because of its resemblance to the human liver. The name hepatica is derived from the Greek hepar, meaning liver.

Barbara believes "We are asking for nourishment in spring, and since this is a time of reconnection, the plant kingdom is ready to make available the foods that will feed our bodily needs. There is, however, a difference between psychological or physical craving-like that for Ben & Jerry's ice cream-and real physiological needs, like a dog eating the first fresh grass, full of vitamins and minerals."

Violets, Nettles, and Dandelions

Barbara looks for her three favorite wild plants in early spring to incorporate into soups, salads, muffins, and casseroles. They bring nourishment to her family. One of the greens is violet leaves, which are very high in vitamin C. I also love to add the purple flowers of the violets to a salad full of other wild greens like dandelions.

And then there are the nettles, which have the most iron of any plant, though you must be extremely careful to only pick the tops because the other leaves sting. Sometimes even the top leaves give your tongue a little jolt. I can't wait to make a cream of nettle-potato soup because the nettles add a nut-like flavor. You can also eat them raw in salads.

Besides using nettles in the kitchen, I concoct a garden tea out of the nettle plants when they grow large. Just cut the plant about a foot off the ground and stuff it in a large barrel filled with water. Make sure to wear a good pair of gloves. The mixture needs to sit on its own for about ten days. The brew smells to high heaven, but the results are dynamic.

Use the "tea" to water garden plants. After a liberal soaking of nettle juice, I have seen carrot and other vegetable leaves turn from light to dark green in a matter of days. The nettle juice enlivens the plants with iron and other minerals. Warning: Stay away from friends after using the nettle tea in your garden because the smell lingers on your clothes. I can personally attest to this deterrent.

Nettle plant helps neighboring plants ward off disease. Experiments have shown that nettle planted near tomatoes helps them resist rotting and hold their juices longer. The nettle also stimulates humus formation. If you ever dig up the soil around a nettle plant, it will be rich and crumbly just like compost.

Barbara told me her family cannot live without her third favorite green, the dandelion. She said, "It's best, when cutting the young dandelions, carrots, and other vegetables, to leave room for new growth. I like young dandelions that grow at the edge of the woods because they are more tender and are a darker green than those that grow in full light. Remember, the leaves are less palatable as the plant grows older. After the blooms are gone, the leaves turn more bitter. A marinade of vinegar, sugar, and onions will take out the bitterness in a salad full of dandelions, nettles, and violets.

"Bitters stimulate the digestive and eliminative processes, and help your body get rid of toxins."

"Wild greens can be mixed (50-50) with fresh spinach for a salad or lasagna casserole." Barbara also uses young yellow dandelion petals in a muffin recipe. Include half a cup of petals for a standard recipe. Her kids are fast to notice those yellow streaks in the muffins.

See Spring Appendix Guide 6 for more information on dandelions, Hippocrates, and healing, along with a word of caution when harvesting wild plants.

LAMB'S-QUARTERS

Our second gatherer, Ann Pearce, loves to harvest lamb's-quarters at the Tommy Thompson Community Garden in Burlington, Vermont. To most people, lamb's-quarter is a weed, but to Ann it is a delicacy. The seeds of lamb's-quarters or amaranth were one of the first food plants gathered in the New World, predating maize. Ann uses the greens in fresh salads or in her famous quiche. She advises using only plants under a foot tall when the leaves are small and tender; this guideline also holds true for nettle, purslane, dandelion, and other wild greens. Not only do lamb's-quarters have a great nut-like taste, they are also healthy for you, being high in calcium and vitamins

A and C.

See Spring Appendix Guide 5 for Ann's Famous Lamb's-quarters Quiche Recipe.

THE GOOD WITCH ON THE HILL

Our final gatherer is Margaret Daniel, who collects wild greens, herbs, and roots. She lives on Christian Hill, high above the town of Bethel overlooking a panorama of the Green Mountain range in central Vermont. Around her home and garden she collects greens for salads, taps maple and white birch trees, brews herbal teas and tinctures, dries flowers, and picks berries. She also shares her knowledge with the children in the local elementary school. I call Margaret The Good Witch on the Hill. Let's travel with her through spring, autumn, and summer and learn about her three main home remedies:

Comfrey, St.-John's-wort and Calendula

Margaret told me you can make a tincture (alcohol, water, and herbs) from almost any medicinal plant like dandelion, echinacea, lavender, shepherd's purse, St.-John's-wort, nettle, horsetail, and chamomile. Echinacea is very popular these days as a help to the immune system. You can use the leaves, flowers, and roots in a tincture.

Comfrey is one of Margaret's favorite plants. It can be used internally or externally for broken bones, cuts, sores, and bruises. It's sometimes called knit bone because it penetrates and heals broken bones. Margaret makes up a comfrey tincture by digging up the young roots in the spring as soon as the first leaves appear. She then fills up a bucket of comfrey roots and washes them down with a hose. She scrubs the roots with a strong brush because they are pretty dirty, then rinses them off again and chops the roots into fine pieces.

See Spring Appendix Guide 6 for information on how to finish making a comfrey tincture and its many uses.

Years ago when I was a commercial vegetable grower, I sometimes cut myself. I would clean the wound, take some comfrey leaves, crush them up, and wrap the wound with the leaves and a clean cotton cloth. I was amazed how quickly the cut healed with little or no pain or redness. Comfrey's chemical constituent, allantoin, draws the tissue together and heals the wound. I wouldn't use it on a puncture wound because it would close it up too quickly.

Margaret also uses arnica, which does not grow wild in

Vermont. It is for bruises like a black and blue spot, while comfrey is more for deep healing. With arnica, use more caution. Comfrey is less toxic. You can purchase arnica seed and grow your own plants, which can be used in a salve or tincture.

St.-John's-wort and Calendula

Margaret's two other favorite home remedies are St.-John's-wort and calendula, both gathered in summer. They can be mixed in an oil or as a tincture. St.-John's-wort grows wild in Vermont, and calendula is an annual grown easily in your home garden. It even tends to reseed itself. They both have yellow flowers, and calendula also has orange flowers.

St.-John's-wort is used more than Prozac to treat mild depression in Germany. Calendula and St.-John's-wort can be applied externally either as a massage oil or internally at 1 tablespoon per day. St.-John's-wort is for the intestines, gas, nerves, and depression. Calendula is for skin. Use them as a massage oil; they penetrate your skin and enter your body that way.

See Spring Appendix Guide 6 on how to make the St.-John's-wort and calendula tinctures and oils.

Salad Greens

Margaret Daniel collects salad greens in the spring, including dandelions, nettles, and violets. The dandelion is Margaret's favorite salad green and the first one she eats raw in the spring. Her trick is to cut the leaves up very fine and then wash them in cold water. That way, they lose most of their bitterness. Later on, Margaret gathers lamb's-quarters, purslane, amaranth, and other greens to add to her salads. She seasons them with homemade dressings mixed with her own dried vegetable powders.

Margaret blanches the greens and freezes them along with other greens like lamb's-quarters, Swiss chard, and spinach. The dandelion can be cut close to ground level with a sharp knife, and it will grow back a number of times. Its roots can be eaten like carrots. They are sweet, not bitter; wait two to three years to get a good root size. Prepare dandelion roots by first scrubbing and then cutting them into little pieces; boil them up with the skin and eat them. You can even make dandelion wine.

See Spring Appendix Guide 6 for a recipe for dandelion wine.

The Drying Rack

When the heat of summer arrives, Margaret dries dandelion greens on a rack along with other greens such as parsley, onion greens, spinach, lamb's-quarters, turnip leaves, stinging nettle, plantain, and celery greens. She places the dried greens in airtight jars and later makes a vegetable powder from them to use in salads, soups, and casseroles. Many weed plants grow right in her vegetable garden. Margaret waits till they are 4 to 6 inches high, harvests the leaves, then pulls the weeds and places them in the compost. This method does not disturb the cultivated vegetable plants.

Morning, Evening, and House Teas

Margaret makes 3 quarts of fresh tea almost every day. As soon as the water comes to a boil, she places the herbs in a pot and then turns it off immediately. The herbal tea can be drunk hot or cold. Morning tea consists of stinging nettles, horsetail, yarrow, and-of most importance-comfrey. Evening teas are red clover, mint, raspberry, strawberry, and blackberry leaves. By the time fall arrives, Margaret has all her teas drying on racks in warm, airy attic spaces. Her house tea is made from beebalm and linden (basswood) leaves; it has a calming effect.

Illness

Margaret and her husband Ernst Daniel, who farmed in Europe and the U.S., raised their six children with the belief that hospitals were a last resort. As Margaret said, "I never waited for the children to get real sick. As soon as I noticed something out of balance, I would make a tea from comfrey, fennel, or chamomile. I basically used what was around me. In every part of the world there are healing plants, but I live on Christian Hill and I have almost everything I need right here: white birch sap, wild berries, apples, wild herbs, and weeds-especially dandelion, comfrey, St.-John's-wort and calendula."

Rhythms

As you might guess, Margaret is always walking about with several baskets in her arms, collecting herbs and weeds. She does not consider what she does work because she loves it. She doesn't need to plant many of the herbs she uses because they grow wild around her home. Her day follows certain rhythms, with peaks of activity in the morning and evening. One senses a peace within this activity. "This is what I love to do. I go out most every spring, summer, and fall day with my baskets and collect the wild things. When my children were young, they would just follow me around; there was always something to do."

If you stop by, Margaret might be putting together a fresh poultice for a friend, teaching a class, or most likely, collecting herbs. Margaret's life is never dull what with drying tea leaves, creating dried flower arrangements, preparing the next basket of plants for the kids, and making tinctures. It is the rhythm of her life. The story of The Good Witch on the Hill never seems to end.

A FINAL WOODCHUCK RULE OF THE WILD GREEN THUMB

Please go out with someone who knows the wild plants before you begin to gather them on your own. Develop a pathfinder consciousness: Pick only what you are sure of and what's needed, and don't go pulling the entire plant out of the ground. Many wild plants grow right in and around your garden, such as violets, dandelions, lamb's-quarters, and nettles. These are easy to identify and plentiful for salads. I am sure you can't wait to taste all of those nutritious spring greens, or how about some pine needle tea or rose hip jam? The world of wild food is endless.

CHAPTER 4

LATE SPRING GARDENING

RON'S VEGETABLE PLANTING TIPS

Soon early summer arrives and we can plant our spring peas and spinach and watch once more how "The Green Revolution" invades our world. "Lett-uce" move outside and sow our seeds into the earth. It "beets" me why more people don't garden. If they did, perhaps we would all "carr-ot" more about the earth.

To me, planting peas and spinach seeds is the real start to the spring gardening season. The seeds are sown in cool wet soil in late April, along with onion sets and potatoes. Of course, it all depends on how early you can till up the soil. The small home gardener with raised beds has an advantage because they can simply go out and dig up a bed or two and plant early spring vegetable seeds, sets, and tubers.

Peas

With so many varieties of peas out there, it's hard to know just which one to plant. There is the edible pod or snow pea, and the sugar snap pea, which is like a pregnant, edible-pod type. Or how about the traditional shelling pea that spills out those little green treasures we all love to eat? Have you ever eaten your own home-grown fresh green peas from the freezer on a cold February night?

Finally, there is the fragrant, flowering sweet pea with its palette of seductive shades, including pinks, whites, blues, and purples. Some peas grow as climbers and others stay closer to the ground. The key to planting peas is to put them in the ground as early as possible (mid- to late April and early to mid-May) because they don't do well when planted in early June.

If the soil is cold and wet, germination can be difficult. It's harder to germinate pea seeds in heavy clay as compared to a lighter silty or sandy loam soil. Mixing in some compost or soilless mix in the rows helps. Another woodchuck trick is to start pea seeds inside in peat pots, which come like ice-cube trays, all connected to one another. You can also start seeds in plug trays. Some gardeners buy pea seeds with a pinkish fungicide that protects them from cold, wet conditions. Organic gardeners don't use fungicides. If you use them, make sure to wash your hands.

Spinach

Spinach can be planted in rows by making a furrow with a heavy-duty, wide hoe. Once the young plants emerge from the earth, which may take longer than you expect, cultivate them with a sharp-edged half-moon or triangular hoe, then hill the soil up around the young plants with a heavy-duty, wide hoe. In a sense, it's a raised bed. When the spinach reaches maturity, pick the larger leaves just like lettuce and the plants will continue to produce new leaves. Plant spinach again in mid-August in your cold frame. Just leave them there and they will produce some greens for you in late fall. Some may even make it through the winter, depending on the severity of the weather, the variety you chose, and how well you cover the cold frame. I don't replant peas or spinach in my main garden in July because they don't like hot weather.

Learn about the nutritional value of spinach in the next chapter *The Green Revolution.*

How Raised Need Raised Beds Be

Raised beds (mounds of earth in various shapes and sizes, mixed with compost) are in vogue. But there are some misconceptions. You don't have to dig to China to create a raised bed, and they don't have to be a foot off the ground because that's a waste of time and energy. It's not necessary to dig deep into the earth unless the subsoil is compacted. In other words, double digging is not necessary on most soils.

Ron's Slightly Raised Bed, Made Easy

Measure out a 4-to-5-foot wide bed, let's say 25 feet long. On one side of the bed, using a long-handled pointed shovel, dig down and throw the soil into the middle of the bed. Do the exact same thing on the other side. Add compost and then rake all the organic materials and soil from the middle of the bed out to the two sides. Smooth the bed over with a rake a number of times, shaping and reshaping the bed.

Mark out rows in the bed with a hoe and plant your seedlings or seeds into the rows. You now have a slightly raised bed with a walkway on both sides. How many seeds or plants you place in the bed depends on what you plant. Five-foot-wide beds are ideal for lettuce. You can hoe down the weeds between the plants or use a hand cultivator without straining your back. Place young lettuce seedlings about a foot apart. Four-foot-wide beds are used for cucumber and summer squash, making a row down the center for the seeds.

Inch by Inch, Row by Row

If you don't want to build a raised bed, simply plant your seeds in the traditional row-by-row pattern. Carrots, tomatoes, potatoes, and other vegetables can be planted and hilled with a hoe; what you have then, in effect, is a slightly raised row without the time spent digging beds.

Excess moisture is released in a raised bed system. Building raised beds from sandy soil doesn't work that well during dry summers because the beds dry out rather quickly. On the other hand, digging a raised bed from a clay soil makes a lot of sense because clay holds more moisture and can inhibit the growth of plants if the soil is too wet. Adding compost to raised beds helps the plants grow in all types

Vermont gardeners from years gone by.
Photo from Special Collections, Bailey/Howe Library, University of Vermont.

of garden soils (sand, clay, or silt) or a combination of each called loam. Applying compost directly to the raised beds is an economical way of using compost versus spreading it over the whole garden.

The Floating Row Cover Syndrome
One method of helping young plants grow in the spring is to

cover them with floating row covers. Row covers are like small greenhouse quonset huts with metal hoops that hold a plastic mesh cover over the plants. The covering is made from spun polyester fibers. The covers help increase the soil temperature, protect the plants from insects such as flea beetles, and allow some moisture to enter. Row covers also protect early annuals that could get hit by a late frost.

Two woodchuck tricks: Use wooden clothes pins to hold the mesh to the metal hoops, and use discarded PVC plastic pipe as a substitute for metal hoops. Special u-shaped metal pins with flat rubbers hold the covers on the ground, or you can use wire coat hangers. Simply push the pins or hangers through the mesh into the earth to hold them in place. A new type of row cover apparatus acts like an accordion, which is easy to set in place and take down.

See Spring Appendix Guide 7 for more information on row covers.

In late April and early May, I transplant cabbage, broccoli, and cauliflower plants from my cold frame into wide beds in my main garden. Covering them with row covers protects them from the flea beetles that love to eat up young spring Brassicas; they are attracted to the mustard oils in the leaves. After two to three weeks, take off the row covers and cultivate around the plants with a sharp hoe. When the cucumbers and summer squash seeds have germinated and grown into young plants in mid-May, cover them with row covers to protect them from cucumber beetles. Remove the covers from early to mid-June depending on the number of beetles.

The Onion River

I do my spring planting at the Tommy Thompson Community Garden site located along the Winooski River (which means Onion River in Abenaki). The Winooski basin is considered the "banana belt" of flood plain soils in northern Vermont. The soil is a silty loam type, built up over hundreds of years of flooding. Gardeners who live in higher and cooler elevations need to plant later, as do those with heavy clay soils, which stay cooler and wetter longer.

You can tell if the soil is too wet to plant by simply reaching down and taking a lump of earth in your hand. If you squeeze the soil and the water gushes out, it's too wet to plant. If the soil feels pliable and a little moist in your hand, then it's dry enough to plant.

When I sow my second crop of beans and corn in June, the soil has warmed up, so I don't have to plant as thickly, nor cull as much as I did in the spring.

THE GREEN REVOLUTION

Lettuce, spinach, and Swiss chard are at the top of my chart when it comes to garden greens. Most greens thrive in cool spring and fall weather and therefore grow well in the climate of the north country. I grow spinach in the spring; lettuce in the spring, early summer, and fall; and chard throughout the growing season. Some gardeners extend the season by growing greens into November and later, in cold frames and unheated greenhouses.

See *The Vegetable Gardener's Bible* by E. Smith on extending the growing season with the use of row covers, raised beds, and unheated greenhouses.

Popeye's Special

Spinach is one of the most nutritious greens you can grow; raw spinach is very high in vitamin A, with very little being lost in the canning or freezing process. It also has lots of vitamin C, calcium, and iron. You can literally taste the minerals from fresh spinach harvested directly from the garden. It is one of the most versatile, tasty greens, served raw in salads, steamed, stir-fried with garlic and ginger, or chopped and added to soups, quiches, and casseroles.

Bloomsdale Longstanding is a favorite spinach variety of many gardeners. It has crinkled, dark green leaves and is slow to bolt. Winter Bloomsdale is a nice fall-harvested spinach.

Malabar Spinach Red Stem can be trained up a trellis or fence. The variety Space can be grown in an unheated greenhouse or cold frame in late fall and winter. By the way, New Zealand spinach is not a true spinach, but a green grown as a warm-weather substitute for spinach.

Poor Man's Spinach

Swiss chard is like a poor man's spinach. It will grow both in cool and warm temperatures. You can harvest much more chard than other greens because its large fleshy leaves grow back quickly after being cut and harvested, time after time. Chard is actually a bottomless beet that doesn't develop roots but rather large stalks with broad crisp leaves and plenty of minerals. Swiss chard comes in different colors: Varieties such as Fordhook Giant are green with white stems. Rhubarb and Ruby Chard have bright red stems with reddish-green leaves. The leaves and celery-like stalks of Swiss chard are a little tough so they need to be steamed or stir-fried. Add vinegar and garlic for a tangy dish.

The Queen of the Salad Bowl

Lettuce is synonymous with salad for people all over the earth. Of all the vegetables, lettuce is possibly the oldest and most popular. The Persians used it extensively as early as 550 B.C. The oldest English-language cookbook compiled in 1390 contains a watercress "salat." Iceberg lettuce remains the second most popular fresh vegetable in the U.S. after potatoes. It grows practically everywhere but prefers cooler temperatures of 50-60 degrees F. In Vermont, lettuce thrives in the cool spring and fall, even though certain varieties, like Green Ice, a crisphead type, grow in the hot summer with enough moisture. You can help shield lettuce from the sun by creating a sunscreen of cheesecloth placed six inches off the ground. Because lettuce is 95% water, it requires moist ground and well-fertilized soils high in nitrogen; the latter can be supplied with well-rotted compost. The soil and the leaves need to be thoroughly watered once a week, especially if there is little rain.

See Spring Appendix Guide 8 for different types of lettuce, their uses, and nutritional values. Also included is a description of late Autumn and winter lettuce.

The Newest Addition to the Green World: Mesclun

The latest green to hit the garden world is mesclun, a mixture of greens, herbs, and edible flowers. While seeming to be a newcomer, mesclun has been in American gardens since the 1600s. Back then the mix consisted of chicory, cress, rocket (arugula), chervil, and lettuce. Today, mesclun has made a garden comeback and includes all the above plus herbs and greens such as mustard, mache, dill, basil, parsley, fennel, endive, dandelion, radicchio, and more. Some greens have a peppery flavor like arugula, others are tart, and some taste nut-like such as mache. Make up your own mixes and create tangy or mild salads.

The Cook's Garden catalog offers an exceptionally good description of lettuce seeds and mesclun mixes. Shepherd Ogden of Cook's Garden is partly responsible for the popularity of this new or not-so-new salad mix phenomenon in the U.S.

Cook's Garden Seeds, P.O. Box 535, Londonderry, Vermont 05148 (800); 457-9703; *www.cooksgarden.com.*

A Gardener's Springtime Prayer

In northern New England, spring is the shortest of all seasons; it never really ends but jumps quickly into summer. To celebrate this event, let's end this season of hope with a prayer by my friend William Cleary of Burlington, Vermont.

Here are my hands, Spirit of Earth and Space
Mysterious Wisdom within and behind everything
that is and is promising,
Gardener ever ancient, ever new,
who fashioned out of these colossal explosions at our beginning
all the avenues to life, to its complexities,
and to the communion we are destined for.

Here are my hands.
Give them the skills of the midwife
to put order into expectations,
to coax along the natural forces of life and growth
that are already within the earth,
and to help wisely with the harvesting.

Here are my hands,
and here are my dreams
and my faith in the promise of your worldwide project:
the web of life with all it might become.
Yes, I will prepare the earth.

Yes, I will study its mysteries and test its possibilities.
Then, yes, I will choose seed,
set it on a promising place and its environs,
watering it above all, opening a way to the sun.

But only a midwife shall I be.
It is the seed that grows,
it is the earth and sun that urge on
and feed its growing forces,
it is you, Divine Gardener, who gives it its purpose
And then ultimately draws it toward its fulfillment.

Take these hands then, and put them to use
so that in the process of gardening
I myself may blossom anew. Amen.

Taken from *The Lively Garden Prayer Book*, by William Cleary.

CHAPTER 5

SPRING APPENDIX GUIDE

Spring Appendix Guide Number One

BOOKS ON SEED STARTING & SEED SAVING

- *The New Seed Starters Handbook* by Nancy Bubel. Rodale Press. If your seed packet doesn't tell you what you need to know, try this book.

- *Seed to Seed* by Suzanne Ashworth. Chelsea Green Publishing Co. General information and crop-by-crop instruction for the seed saver. Thorough and well researched, the best general guide for home seed savers.

- *Breed Your Own Vegetable Varieties* by Carol Deppe. Chelsea Green Publishing Co. As informative as Seed to Seed and more understandable to the layperson, especially when it comes to plant genetics.

- *The Seed Search* by Karen Platt. This book tells you where to buy over 40,000 seeds and gives their botanical names, seed houses, and exchanges all over the world.

- *Cornucopia, A Source Book of Edible Plants* by Stephen Fracciola Kampong Publishers. The book gives 1,300 worldwide sources for seeds and plants of some 3,000 different edibles including baby vegetables and rare tropical fruits.

- *Starting From Seed* by Karan Cutler. Brooklyn Botanical Gardens. Offers expert advice on how to grow hundreds of vegetables, herbs, and wildflowers from seed.

For a comprehensive list of garden seed catalogs, see the Winter Appendix Guide.

Spring Appendix Guide Number Two

WARM AND COOL FLUORESCENT TUBES, GROW LIGHTS, AND FIXTURES

Tubes, bulbs, lights: These terms are used interchangeably. Fluorescent lights come in warm, cool, or full-spectrum bulbs. The blue or cool colors help with growth, and the red or warm colors help with blooms. The most common are the cool fluorescent tubes in workshops, stores, homes, and factories. Cool bulbs sell for $2 to $3 and warm fluorescent bulbs sell for about $4. Combined, they cover a large part of the color spectrum of light. You can purchase the cool fluorescent bulbs at all hardware stores, but the warm lights can only be purchased at lighting stores or the large home centers like Home Depot.

Full-spectrum bulbs called *grow lights* are designed for plant growth. Some stores call them plant lights. They cover more of the spectrum (94%), but cost double the price of cool and warm lights. The better grow lights like Floralight Full-Spectrum bulbs last longer and cost about $12 per bulb. Less expensive brands sell for around $6. When it comes to cost, I like to follow the advice of my momma who used to say, "You better shop around." By the way, full-spectrum bulbs for seasonal effective disorder include the noon-day rays.

Some gardeners do not believe in the use of fluorescent bulbs for germination and plant growth. They prefer natural light in a greenhouse environment.

Fixtures and Light Stands

I have found the best size to be the 4-foot light fixtures widely used in workshops. Since light intensity is reduced at each end of any fluorescent tube, longer tubes give more useful light per foot. That's why I recommend four-foot long fixtures that hold a pair of tubes and will illuminate an area about 8 inches wide. Four-foot light fixtures sell for $10 to $20 depending on the quality. You can also find them at garage sales.

Build a simple fluorescent light stand using 2 x 4 wooden studs and plywood. An ideal home garden model has three tiers of lights that provide plenty of space for young seedlings. This model uses six 4-foot fluorescent lights and looks like a tall, wide bookshelf without the books. One woodchuck method is simply to hang light fixtures below a shelf next to a south-facing window. A table with trays of seedlings is placed below the lights.

Commercial indoor light gardens equipped with fixtures, stands, and lights can also be purchased from garden catalogs like Gardener's Supply. These lighting systems are lightweight, made of metal and plastic, come in all shapes and sizes, and last for years. They use various size bulbs. They are a good investment, but they don't come cheap.

Leave the lights on 14 hours a day, and keep them just 2 or 3 inches above the tops of the seedlings. If the distance is greater, the energy reaching the plants is reduced. To raise the lights as the seedlings grow, hang the fixture units with chains and make adjustments as necessary.

I start my seeds a little earlier than most gardeners because my main source of light is two south-facing windows along with two warm and cold fluorescent light units and a couple of grow lights. My home is also a little cooler than most, so room temperature is another factor to consider; plants grow more slowly in cooler temperatures. Another reason is that I used to be a commercial grower and starting seeds early is in my thumbs.

Spring Appendix Guide Number Three

FOSTER BROTHERS & THE STORY OF "MOO"

About a decade ago, Foster Brothers, a 1600-acre, 400-cow dairy farm in Middlebury, Vermont, started producing more than milk. They also make electricity from cow manure. This feat is achieved by using an anaerobic digester that uses bacteria to break down manure into methane gas. The gas is used as a clean source of fuel to provide electric power for the farm.

Foster Brothers took Yankee ingenuity even one step further by taking the manure used in the digester and separating the liquids from the solids. The liquids are used as a natural plant food to grow cow corn, and the solids are composted for many purposes.

This is where Vermont Natural Ag Products came in. They took over where the Fosters left off and added a number of ingredients to the compost. They developed the Moo products, which include Moo Mix, a professional potting mix; Moo Start, a germinating mix; Moo Doo, composted cow manure; and other products such as Moo Grow, Moo Dirt, and Moo Plus. Moo products comprise composted horse manure, soil, and peat moss.

Vermont Natural Ag Products is the second largest producer of potting mixes in New England. Their biggest customers are garden centers, but any woodchuck can go by in a truck and load up. You just gotta yell "Moo" real loud before you start.

Spring Appendix Guide Number Four

WOODCHUCK FLOWER SEED STARTING DATES & HELPFUL HINTS

The dates offered below are the earliest planting dates. You can plant later than stated depending on the location of your garden. It's best to plan ahead so your young plants don't get leggy and are difficult to transplant to the garden.

As with most things in life, experience is the best teacher. Check with garden friends and neighbors to find out when they start flower seeds and when they place the young plants in their gardens. Two woodchuck rules of thumb for northern gardeners: Err on the side of caution and plant a little later. And remember: The last frost usually occurs in late May.

JANUARY- FEBRUARY Sow seed for impatiens, petunias, coreopsis, dusty miller, begonias, and primrose. Snapdragons: Sow seeds in January, February, and early March. Geraniums: Sow seeds in January and February or about 12 weeks before planting out into garden. Salvias: Sow salvia, violets, violas, and lobelia in January or February because they need early germination. Salvia are the current rage with many different varieties; you wouldn't know it was a salvia with all the different pink, peach, deep purple, white, and orange colors. The blue salvia gigantica are three feet tall with beautiful spirals that look similar to French lavender.

FEBRUARY-MARCH Annual delphinium, foxglove, and dahlia seeds can be germinated in mid-February through March. Hybrid lisianthus are irresistible plants, somewhere between a rose and a poppy. They are used in arrangements for weddings. You can germinate them in wet napkins and transplant to flats. Start seeds in February and March. Statice, strawflowers, phlox seeds germinate in February and March.

MARCH-APRIL Ageratum, zinnias, cosmos, calendula, marigold: Start seeds in flats in March and early April.

The Difference Between Annuals, Biennials, and Perennials

ANNUAL An annual plant lives one year or less. The plant grows, blooms, produces seeds, and dies. Examples: marigolds, cosmos, basil, beans, sweet corn.

BIENNIAL Biennial plants require two years or more to complete their life cycle e.g., beets, carrots, parsnips, cabbage; they usually produce seed the second year if replanted. Here's a woodchuck biennial tip: Leave parsnips in the ground over winter and dig them up in the spring to eat. They are delicious. Sometimes, I leave a couple of parsnips in the ground to produce seeds; they create magnificent plants. Try this woodchuck tip, then see if any of your gardening friends can identify the parsnips.

PERENNIAL Perennial plants live an indefinite number of years. Examples of edible perennials are asparagus and rhubarb. Some examples of perennial flowers are black-eyed Susan, yarrow, purple coneflower, coreopsis, shasta daisy, delphinium, and evening primrose, which live for many years. Hardy perennials are plants able to winter over without artificial protection. Some not-so-hardy perennial herbs like basil are grown just as annuals. Perennials were the stars for years, but they needed a break from a decade of popularity. Perennials were overworked and needed time to rest while annuals took center stage.

Spring Appendix Guide Number Five

ANN'S LAMB'S-QUARTERS QUICHE RECIPE

Filling:

1 onion, chopped	1 large tomato, sliced
1 cup sliced mushrooms	3 eggs, beaten
1 or 2 cups lamb's-quarters, steamed for 2-4 minutes	1 cup milk
	A dash of salt
2 1/2 cups grated cheddar cheese	1 tablespoon dried parsley

Saute onion and mushrooms and place in whole wheat pastry crust. Add lamb's-quarters, followed by the tomatoes and cheese. Beat together the eggs, milk, salt, parsley, and pepper, then pour into the pie crust. Bake at 400 degrees for 20 minutes, then lower to 300 degrees and bake for another 20 minutes or until done.

Spring Appendix Guide Number Six

NOTES ON WILD MEDICINALS

Dandelions

The woodchuck gardener's response to calling dandelions a weed is "Give us this day, our daily illusion."

In truth, the dandelion is beneficial to the soil; its long taproot opens up and aerates the soil, and what could be more beautiful than green grass and yellow flowers? Resourceful Russian scientists found a dandelion species with enough latex to make rubber parts for tank tracks. By WWII's end, a quarter of a million Russian tanks rode on dandelion rubber.

Margaret's Dandelion Wine

Pour 5 qts. boiling water over 4 qts. of dandelion blossoms. Blossoms must be packed tightly in a 4-qt. measure.

Let stand for 24 hours. Squeeze through a cloth bag and add:

5 lbs. sugar
5 oranges, sliced with peels
1 lemon, sliced with peel
1 lb. seedless raisins
1 tablespoon yeast

Let stand for two weeks, stirring every day. Strain through cheesecloth twice. Let stand for two more weeks. When pouring, leave sludge on bottom.

Hippocrates

Barbara Nardozzi told me Hippocrates, the father of medicine, taught us to live by the principle that the body is a self-healer. He taught us we need to support this concept by moving out of the way and allowing the body to heal itself. This ancient belief is coming around again. Hippocrates also believed medicine can come from the food you eat; this is why wild plants are so critical for our health in the spring of the year when our nutritional stores are depleted. We need all the vitamins and minerals that can be mustered.

Words of Caution on Harvesting Wild Plants

Be careful when harvesting wild plants because it is becoming increasingly popular across the country. The collection of wild plants is known as wildcrafting; this is the art of identifying, harvesting, and preparing plants for medicine and food. Wildcrafting's surge in popularity, coupled with the widespread acceptance of many natural foods and medicines, has jump-started a hobby that can be lucrative.

Growth of this pastime has been so strong that some organizations are worried about its effect on plant populations. Traffic USA, a conservation program established to monitor trade in wild plants, put annual retail sales of plants and herbs at $1.6 billion in 1999.

Some groups are particularly concerned about populations of medicinal herbs such as ginseng, calendula, echinacea, goldenseal, and even St.-John's-wort, which grows wild along the roadsides and in the meadows in Vermont.

Herbalists believe wild ginseng can boost resistance to stress and commonly recommend echinacea as a cold and flu preventative. In Vermont, wild ginseng is rare, and to my knowledge, the only plant regulated, but only for commercial collectors.

Demand is growing as herb shops, restaurants, and grocery stores increasingly offer wild edibles and herbs. So please be careful how much you harvest in the wild even though I wouldn't worry about Barbara's three favorites: dandelions, nettles, and violets. They grow in abundance, especially in front of my house.

Respect, Care, and Caution

A lot of damage is done by applying a fast-food approach to the wilderness experience. Learn from experts and references where to walk in wild areas and what herbs to pick. Choosing plants and herbs along roadways can be dangerous because of car and truck exhaust fumes and heavy metals.

Always follow recommended dosages for using wild herbs and edibles. Too much of anything can be harmful to your organs. Remember, you can have the benefits of these wild herbs by purchasing products at local health food stores.

Comfrey, Calendula, and St.-John's-wort
Tinctures & Other Uses

- Make sure the comfrey roots are clean. If necessary use a potato peeler to ensure cleanliness.
- Fill a quart jar 1/3 full with pieces of comfrey.
- Add rubbing alcohol diluted with 1/3 water.

The comfrey solution needs to sit for 2 to 3 weeks, but it can be made in a week for emergency purposes. Shake it every day for ten days. It will probably get a little slimy. When done, pour the solution through cheesecloth or a fine metal mesh strainer. Bottle it up in glass or plastic, and store it in a cool place. It's now ready to use as a tincture. Margaret makes about 3 gallons a year. For her children's Christmas presents she sends them a quart of comfrey tincture. Her daughter Claudia uses the comfrey tincture to take away wrinkles. Some books say this works because comfrey generates skin and tissue.

It also takes care of bruises, sores, a finger caught in a door, almost any ache or pain. Margaret rubs whatever hurts with the comfrey tincture. In addition, she takes a piece of copper and lays it over the area where the tincture was used. Russian comfrey is #1 in her home.

For internal ailments, substitute cheap vodka for the alcohol in the recipe above. Take 15-20 drops, three times a day with a rubber dropper. The solution does eat up metal lids especially if they are rusty. To prevent this, put a piece of plastic or paper between the mixture and the lid. Margaret sometimes adds a few juniper berries, which help with rheumatism and are also good for your skin.

Calendula and St.-John's-wort Oils

Olive oil, while expensive, is always the best oil to use. Or you can always buy a cheaper cold-pressed type. It doesn't get rancid for 2 to 3 years when processed properly.

- Fill about 1/3 of a quart jar with buds and crushed yellow blossoms of St.-John's-wort, and only the blossoms of the calendula. Only take buds and flowers of St.-John's-wort as they are opening, not after they have fully opened. Also, do not pull plants out of the ground; there won't be any left if people keep doing this.
- Place the blossoms and buds in a plastic bag and crush and roll them with a rolling pin.
- Pour the mixture into a glass quart jar.
- Fill the jar with olive oil and let it sit in the sun for 4 to 6 weeks. The sun is critical in this process. A glass bottle full of crushed herbs and oil takes in the dynamic forces of the sun and transforms itself into a healing substance. Without the sun's energy, it does not work.
- Shake it daily. St.-John's-wort will turn red.
- If it becomes cloudy, pour it through a coffee filter.

Margaret makes up oil and herb concoctions separately. Once they are done, she can mix the oils together like lavender, chamomile, calendula, and so on. She also makes a separate home remedy from rosemary but only uses this in the morning as a waker-upper. Comfrey, St.-John's-wort, and calendula are her three basic home remedies, which are used for the bones and soreness, nerves, and skin, respectively. Salves are made up of herbs, olive oil, lanolin, beeswax, and rose water.

Spring Appendix Guide Number Seven

ROW COVERS

Row covers protect because most insects can't penetrate them, so plants aren't harmed by flea beatles, aphids, maggots, potato beetles, and other pests.

Row covers also allow sunlight and some water and air to pass through. Standard-weight row covers extend the early and late growing seasons with frost protection down to about 28 degrees F. You can plant crops one to two weeks earlier than usual, and extend the fall harvest two to three weeks, depending on how cold it gets. Covers aid germination by keeping soil moist. They protect from pounding rain and the surface crusting that follows.

The covers transmit 85% of sunlight. Soft polypropylene fibers are less abrasive to tender plants than polyester covers. The covers last about two seasons, three at most, because the sunlight weakens the fibers. Cost varies. You can order them from gardening supply catalogs or from local garden stores.

Covers can be cut to fit plants. They can be removed when temperatures rise consistently into the 70s. Taking off the row covers is a little time-consuming, but well worth it. Some new row covers are like accordions with hoops. They can be easily pushed together after use. You still need to water and weed about every two weeks, depending on the weather.

Spring Appendix Guide Number Eight

DIFFERENT TYPES OF LETTUCE
Spring, Summer, Early Fall Lettuce

- **LOOSELEAF**: 45-60 days to maturity. **ROYAL OAK LEAF, SALAD BOWL, BLACK-SEEDED SIMPSON**: 45-60 days. Very leafy, not much body.
- **BUTTERHEAD, BIBB** varieties, buttercrunch: 60-75 days. Velvety soft leaves with sweet and clean flavor. Grows well early and late in season.
- **CRISPHEAD**: 75+ days. **GREEN ICE, ICEBERG** types such as **GREAT**

LAKES and ITHACA. One of my favorites is Green Ice, which grows well throughout the growing season, even during the hot summer days as long as it is watered. Firm large leaves are perfect for sandwiches.

• ROMAINE: 75+ days. Romaine-cos varieties grow well early and late in the season.

Late Fall, Winter Lettuce

Most varieties of lettuce, if planted in an unheated greenhouse, cold frame, or under row covers will not make it through the late fall, winter, and early spring. However, a few will: North Pole, a small butterhead; Rougette du Midi, also known as Red Montpelier (red butterhead); Winter Density, a large, hardy cos-head; Rouge d'Hiver, a loose romaine head; and Winter Marvel, a winter-hardy lettuce with a fine butterhead. These varieties have been bred to cope with the short days and cool, wet conditions of late fall, and the cold of winter. They should be seeded down by late August. Cook's Garden Seeds has a good description of these plants.

It's always tricky to grow cold weather greens. You first have to decide if it's worth the time, energy, and some gelt to build the enclosures, cold frames, and greenhouses. When considering growing cool-weather plants, there is the question of whether too much nitrate is absorbed. The stress of cool soil conditions may cause winter hardy greens to take up more nitrates than during the summer. More studies are needed. The question has to do with balance in the garden patch. Perhaps we were meant to grow only what is in season. However, there will always be gardeners who want to push the garden envelope.

Nutritional Information

Looseleaf and romaine are comparatively high in vitamins A and C, and calcium. Butterhead contains only half as much of these nutrients, but is high in iron. Crisphead contains the lowest of all four due to the blanching effect of the tightly formed heads. In general, outer leaves are higher in nutritional value, as compared to inner leaves.

PART TWO: SUMMER

Loomis J. Tebo, produce farmer, with melons, in front of Morrill Hall,
University of Vermont, about 1914. Photo from UVM Library.

EARLY SUMMER MUSINGS

I can't wait for the heat of summer. We shed our layers of cloth and feel the sun and light breeze on our skin. And it isn't long before the butterflies hover around the colorful world of the flower kingdom. Renewal comes in the act of turning the earth and sowing the first seeds.

Early summer arrives as lime-green leaves make their appearance on the trees and the woodland plants disappear. And so onward to the season of the sun and the perennial questions of when and what to plant, how to deal with unfriendly bugs, and of course, when and how to water, mulch, and weed.

PART TWO
SUMMER

CHAPTER 6

WHEN TO PLANT: PLANT HARDINESS ZONES

Early summer gardening officially begins after the last frosts, which occur from mid- to late-May, depending on your location or what's called your Plant Hardiness Zone (PHZ). PHZ refers to the early and late frost dates in your locality. Northern New England lies in Zones 4 and 5, with the colder pockets in Zone 3. The same could be said for northern New York and Pennsylvania and parts of southern Canada.

River valleys and lake regions in northern New England lie in Zone 5 because they are warmed by the water. The mountainous areas are in Zone 4 with some colder pockets in Zone 3— where growing of eggplants, peppers, and melons is a pretty risky affair, unless cold frames or greenhouses are used.

Gardeners can shelter plants from the prevailing winds with natural evergreen hedges and wide wooden plank fencing. Cold frames, unheated greenhouses, row covers, and mulch also protect plants and extend the growing season. Once the soil warms up, hay and leaf mulches help control weeds, maintain moisture, and hold the temperature in the earth. Black and red plastic mulches increase the soil temperature. These plant protection methods and materials are especially helpful in the colder plant hardiness zones.

Microclimates within zones, like south-facing hillsides, allow the sun to warm the earth compared to flat terrain or slopes facing north. The other advantage of slopes is that late frosts just roll off down into the valleys. Different soil types warm up earlier, like sandy and silty loams, as compared to the cooler clay soils.

In general, the farther north you go, the colder it is; however, there are exceptions. Large bodies of water such as Lake Champlain where I live increase the temperature of the area around the lake. Grape vineyards in southern Quebec below Montreal are also influenced by the lake. They are also affected by the heat of the city of Montreal flowing out into the countryside and held in check by the hills surrounding the vineyards. Toronto is warmed by Lake Ontario. Parts of Cape Cod are in Zone 7 because of the ocean and warm Gulf Stream currents. PHZ is an indicator of what and when to plant—even though I rely more on experience and good ole woodchuck common sense.

See Summer Appendix Guide 1&2 for Plant Hardiness Zone Information.

CHAPTER 7

RON'S OBSESSION WITH SUCCESSION

I plant cool-weather crops such as peas, spinach, onion sets, and potatoes in late April and early May. I do this in my community garden plots, which sit on rich, silty, river-bottom loam. But remember, most soil doesn't really warm up until the end of May. If the ground is still too wet and cold, some seeds may rot, especially in the heavier clay soils. Seeds planted in lighter silt and sandy soils have a better chance of germinating.

Gardeners need to be aware of one of the woodchuck principles: "If it's not one thing, it's another." Who knows what the weather will bring? Just wait a minute and see what you find—and then it may change again. May has us all on a roller coaster ride. That's why many gardeners who live in the higher elevations and those with heavy soils don't officially declare the summer gardening season open until Memorial Day, the last Monday in May.

The old farm saying, "A cold rain in May makes a barn full of hay," refers to the fact that wet, cool conditions help grass grow and

Two old-timers with wheel hoe and hoe.
Special Collections, Bailey/Howe Library, University of Vermont.

initiate an early summer hay crop. There is another saying just as appropriate, "Make hay while the sun shines."

Some gardeners sow corn and bean seeds in late May, place young plants like tomatoes, peppers, and eggplants into the earth, do a little weeding and mulching and then relax and drink some fruit punch or a brewski. Once their gardens are sown, they have completed their work for the summer—or so they think.

Planting, weeding, cultivating, mulching, feeding the soil, and harvesting are no easy tasks. Let's face it: Maintaining a garden is hard work. It's continuous and lasts throughout the season; at the blink of an eye, your garden can be overrun with weeds. There is no easy way to take the labor out of gardening. Even the boring, antiseptic, look-alike, Martha-Stewart, bark-mulched gardens of the suburbs you see on TV garden channels need maintenance. That said, it's time to head down to my garden and observe some rather peculiar behavior patterns.

Extremes prevail when it comes to garden work, and I am one of those people who can't help himself. I am obsessed with continual plantings of succession crops throughout the gardening season. It doesn't matter that I don't have much room in my four (30' by 30') community garden plots, I still have this propensity to keep sowing seeds and planting plants. Perhaps it's because I was once a commercial vegetable grower and became accustomed to repeated plantings ... or maybe it's because of certain child-rearing techniques ... or ... enough already! On to the garden and the first of many succession plantings.

After the April/May sowings of spinach, peas, potatoes, and onion sets, I jump into May by moving young plants from my cold frame into wide, raised beds. One bed is for lettuce and another for young broccoli, cabbage, and cauliflower plants, which are placed in 5-foot-wide and 30-foot-long garden beds. I then sow one long 25-foot row of cucumber and zucchini seeds in a 3-foot-wide bed and cover them with floating row covers for warmth and protection from flea and cucumber beetles.

From mid-May to early-June, I put in 70 tomato plants placed in seven 25-foot rows. Between the tomatoes, I transplant young lettuce plants, which I harvest just when the tomatoes are forming. (Tomato and lettuce are companion plants because the tomatoes shade the lettuce, which therefore grow better.) By then, the tomato plants are bushing out and need space to grow.

After the lettuce is harvested, I weed, stake, hill, and remove suckers from the tomatoes one last time, cultivate the soil around the plants, and put in some basil, another companion to the tomatoes. Basil, lettuce, and tomatoes go well together in a salad.

I plant my first crop of carrots and beets in early June, making sure to spread lots of compost on the rows. The long wide beds of early spring spinach are harvested in late June and early July and then replanted with beans.

After all the peas are harvested in July, I hoe down the vines, add compost, and rake all the grass, vines, and weeds out. I then reshape the garden bed and plant a second crop of cucumbers and zucchini. The yields are not as great as my earlier crop, but it's wonderful to have fresh cucumbers and zucchini in early September especially for pickling and freezing. Because the soil is so much warmer in midsummer, seeds germinate easily and plants grow quickly.

I plant corn and beans in mid-May, my second corn crop in mid-June, and beans again in July. When the second corn crop is about 2 feet high, I sow pole beans next to them, being careful not to disturb the roots of the corn. Sometimes it works and sometimes not; the beans can take over and pull down the corn plants. Much depends on timing, weather, and the strength of the corn stalks.

To have fresh vegetables all the way into November, I start fall crops in late June and early July: broccoli, cabbage, Chinese greens such as pok choi and tat soi, carrots, turnips, and beets. The heads of winter cabbage are much tighter than the spring crop and, if stored properly, last well into winter and spring. It's interesting to experiment with succession crops. Each season, you can try out a new combination.

My favorite early summer varieties: Cuthbertsen flowering sweet peas, Alderman telephone peas, Bloomsdale spinach, Early emerald acre cabbage, and Oregon super pod #2 flat Chinese peas.

My favorite hardy fall varieties are thick, dark orange Danvers carrots; large, round Lutz green leaf beets; Waltham broccoli #29 (Shumway Seeds), Gilfeather turnips; winter keeper cabbages like Ontario or Hybrid storage #4.

See Spring Appendix Guide 8 for a description of cold, hardy lettuce varieties such as Winter Density, Rougette du Mudi, and North Pole.

Cook's Garden Seeds has a list of winter greens along with flavorful descriptions. If you have a cold frame or unheated greenhouse, try some late fall and winter lettuce.

Potatoes

For early potatoes I plant the standard Red Norland. Two mid-fall types are Kennebecs, adaptable to varying soil conditions, and Katahdins, which take heavier clay soils. They can be stored over winter. The smaller Fingerlings are very popular these days. For

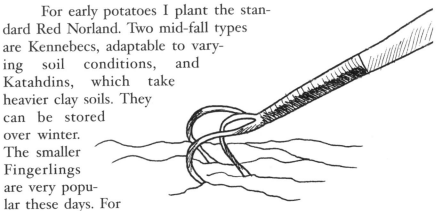

good winter keepers, I prefer Green Mountain and the Russet variety, Butte, which are good baking potatoes and very tasty because of their dry texture. Green Mountains are an heirloom susceptible to fungus diseases but are well worth growing in the home garden. The Maine Fedco catalog has a comprehensive description of potato varieties. Irish Eyes in Washington State also has a good section of potatoes. In the Fall section, learn how to save enough potatoes to plant as seed the following season.

Onions

In the last few years, I have noticed more rotting than usual with onions grown from commercial onion sets, which I use for winter storage. I grow just enough to last the winter. In the future I plan to grow onions from onion seeds such as Yellow Copra seed, a good winter keeper from Johnny's Seeds of Maine. Start the onion seeds in early March in flats or pots and trim the tops once or twice so the bulbs gain in size.

See Winter Appendix Guides 1-8 for comprehensive lists of seed catalog addresses, phone numbers, and web sites.

THE HUMMING OF THE BEES

My compulsive behavior is far from over. In late July and August, I plant cover crops (or what some call green manures) like annual rye grass or buckwheat in garden beds where vegetables have been harvested and in the rows between plants. When the buckwheat reaches seed stage in late summer, honey bees go wild, and I enjoy sounds of beautiful hummings. If you ever want to have a oneness experience, sit down and listen to bees sucking up the nectar in a field of buckwheat, like a Buddhist "ahhh-hummm...." You'll never forget it.

You can leave the annual rye grass and buckwheat alone; these cover crops die off over the winter, forming a light brown thatch in spring. Or you can hoe down the buckwheat or annual rye grass, then prepare the soil for a new cover crop by planting winter rye over the entire garden in September. You don't have to spend as much time tilling and breaking down rye grass or buckwheat in spring, as compared to winter rye, which is hardy enough to sustain the winter cold. Winter rye takes longer to decompose in the spring and if not tilled in early, it can take off in its growth and be a hindrance to spring planting.

More information on Green Manures is in the Autumn section in Chapter 17, Woodchuck Autumn Chores.

CROP ROTATIONS AND WEEDS

Crop rotation is the practice of sowing and cultivating different crops in the same area of your garden over time; it helps eliminate the weed population. When gardeners think of crop rotation, they are referring to the use of green manures and cover crops. But you can also rotate vegetables from year to year in your garden plot. For the best results, these vegetable crops should be from different families, because each family has its own nutrient needs and usually does not share diseases or attract the same insects as the others. For example, don't plant melons where you grew cucumbers, and don't plant cabbages in the same part of your garden every year or the root maggot might appear. Tomatoes, however, love to be planted in the same place—unless they become infected with a fungus. Make changes in planting and harvest times to avoid pest cycles that damage your crops. For example, planting potatoes in early spring won't limit the number of potato beetles in your garden, but the plants will get a head start.

Some gardeners use a tried and true method for dealing with weeds. They double the size of their garden, plant half in vegetables and half in a green manure rotation crop like white or yellow clover (legumes) and grasses. They leave the green manure crop in for two to three years and then till it in, plant the vegetables in the green manure space, and sow a cover crop where the vegetables once grew. This practice rejuvenates the soil with organic matter and lessens weeds in the new plot. In olden times, farmers and gardeners simply allowed some of the land to lie fallow.

Diversity

After reading about my obsessive planting habits, you may need to retire from the vegetable patch for a nap. Not everyone gardens as I do. After growing vegetables and fruit for over 35 years, I have developed a unique style, as do all seasoned gardeners.

Diversity is a buzz word these days; differences bring richness and depth to our lives as well as to gardening. There is variety among those who plant seeds and care for plants. That's why I'm going to stereotype gardeners into the four Greek archetypes of Air, Earth, Fire, and Water.

CHAPTER 8

THE GARDEN ARCHETYPES: AIR, EARTH, FIRE, WATER

There are all kinds of gardeners out there, some who never stop planting like me and others who just like to hang out in their garden, swaying gently with the breeze. Some gardeners plant gently off their front stoops or love to watch geraniums bloom on a sunny windowsill in winter.

There are the butterfly types who flit about, the earth diggers, the nonstoppers who are full of fire, and finally the quiet water gardeners who love to meditate and ponder the life cycles in nature and life. Let's delve into these garden archetypes and discover our real nature. Be prepared to meet your temperament, all the while remember none of us fits totally into one temperament. Some carry around two. And then there are the rainbow types who seem to have a little bit of each.

AIR: MOVER-MULCHER-STRESSOR

Deborah Stuart lives in Wentworth, New Hampshire, in the foothills of the White Mountains. As Deborah puts it, "I am basically a nonweeder type who loves to mulch and move my container plants from one place to another for color and aesthetics. Even when I am down on my knees, which is rare, I am looking more for arrangements of height and color than any interest in the natural phenomenon. I can't wait to move my plants about. I am also a mulcher and have started garden beds literally on sod by mulching with newspaper, pine needles, and horse bedding. In this way, I can divide perennials and replant with little work.

"Finally, I love to stress plants. Once I scared an old estate rose bush into blooming. It was one of those beautiful pale pink ones, but it was so scraggly I cut it back so severely I thought it would die, but it came back to be a beautiful rose."

Deborah went on to say, "If you take a flowering houseplant that hasn't been flowering and drop it and then repot the plant, it will bloom because it thinks it's going to die. The activity forces the plant to flower. I call this the woodchuck's post-traumatic stress syndrome. In general, plants do better when they are a little ruffled—just like the rest of us."

EARTH: THE WEEDER-DIGGER TYPES

While Deborah is hurriedly moving plants about and mulching, her friend Mel is on her knees, digging in the earth and pulling out weeds. Weeding is therapy for her because she hates mulching. Sometimes, she just lies on her back in the garden and squirms down amongst the plants and bugs. To Mel, the bug level is what's interesting. She likes being down there with the worms and beetles.

I also love to be close to the earth, to get my pants dirty and to wipe the sweat off my brow, but I don't like to get stuck in the mud like my old friend, Dick Barnes of Saxton's River, Vermont. I call Dick the Ultimate Dirt Farmer. He used to be a dairy farmer, but he was injured in an ice slide and is now a wheelchair user. That doesn't deter him from growing an entire acre of vegetables and berries. One day, I saw Dick out in his field hoeing carrots, and I noticed he was having trouble maneuvering his wheelchair through the wet earth. I told him it was difficult enough to be moving about the way he did, but didn't he think it would be better to put some air in those rubber tires.

FIRE: THE OBSESSED ONES

You may have guessed by now that I am one of those fire types with some earth mixed in. Remember how my compulsive gardening behavior never seems to stop? I can't wait to plant seeds and work the soil and keep on planting. I always start earlier than most gardeners by planting eggplant and pepper seeds in late February. The fire is still within me, and just starting seeds to seedlings indoors is not enough. In early March, I cover the cold frame in front of my home with a long sheet of clear plastic to warm the soil. By mid-to-late March, depending on the snow, I have removed the plastic, dug the soil, raked and smoothed it over, and planted early greens like spinach and lettuce. Come early fall, I keep planting seeds in the cold frame.

WATER:
THE LAID-BACK VARIETY

The water type is best illustrated by telling you a story about a neighbor of mine. When I look out my front door toward Lake Champlain, the first person I see across the common green is Marilyn Maddison standing in her garden. She always seems to be meditating more than working.

When I asked her why she just stands there, she replied, "I just love standing in my garden...and then there is my fear the seeds won't grow. When I first started, I was sure they would sprout and thrive for other people but not for me. Perhaps it was because I didn't plant them correctly or because I had a dark side. I didn't realize seeds and plants would do fine without me, and that my job is just to help them along.

"That first year, I needed a lot of help from my gardening friends. I had to run over to your house before I made any moves in the garden and that was kind of embarrassing. I didn't believe I knew anything, and I didn't want to make any mistakes. I didn't want to ask, but there I was. I was always worrying about what I was doing and when and how I was doing it. I even lost a lot of sleep over it.

"Sometimes, I would find myself standing in the garden and staring at the ground. Actually, I did that a lot. I don't know what it means, but it seems to be some kind of primal thing. It was as if I was trying to enter into something that was not conscious, trying to be one with the earth except I was self-conscious and wondered if people might be watching me."

Finally, I asked what had changed and how she was able to "go through the looking glass" to the other side? She replied, "I think I needed to get my hands dirty and my feet wet. Once I began to plant seeds in the earth, I witnessed the amazing power of the seed and how each seed has the potential to grow into a plant. After a year of gardening, I am doing much better. I am more comfortable and connected, less obsessive and neurotic. I put loving care into planting each seed and plant. Gardening has added a whole new dimension to my life. I find I can spend hours doing it. All in all, it's as if I have been transplanted."

Marilyn Maddison is in her third year of gardening next to her lovely cottage home overlooking Lake Champlain. She still asks me questions now and then and every so often I see her standing in her garden pondering the earth.

By now, you must have named your archetype and perhaps your neighbor's, children's, friend's, and lover's. I don't know which type you fit in, but be whomever you want and have any kind of garden you wish.

CHAPTER 9

THE GOOD, THE BAD, AND THE BUGGY

When summer arrives, all sorts of tiny, not-so-friendly critters discover the vegetable plants in your garden. And then there are the good bugs, beneficial insects like ladybugs that consume pests or bad bugs like Japanese beetles. Did I forget the plant diseases like powdery mildew? They love to spread their fungus spores over cucumber and summer squash leaves and roses. What can you do to stop these naughty creatures and blights in your garden?

Some natural organic controls, such as beneficial insects, bacteria, and parasites, prey on destructive pests. Botanical controls (derived from naturally occurring plant forms) kill insects and are easy on the environment. And then there are homemade remedies like baking soda, castor oil, and garlic.

Vermont garden writer and radio commentator Ruth Page told me the best thing to do is mix up your vegetable, herb, and flower plants in the garden. In other words, don't plant everything in rows. In that way, the bad buggers will get confused. Instead of going along the row from one plant to the next eating up all the leaves of the beans, they will become disoriented by the marigolds or sage plants next to the beans.

Ellen Sandbeck of Duluth, Minnesota, has done some pretty disgusting things with the creepy critters that love to eat her plants—all in the name of nontoxic gardening. She lures slugs into pits of dough, sprays aphids with vinegar, and even drops rose weevils into a blender to make a bug juice spray. Yet Sandbeck finds herself using few of the bug-battling techniques in her garden as insects aren't in much evidence. She says it's because she adds lots of organic matter in the form of worms and their castings to the soil.

Ellen Sandbeck believes as I do that healthy soil produces healthy plants that can withstand some attacks from pests. An organic, pesticide-free soil is also rich with animal life, including predatory species that eat the undesirables.

Sandbeck has written a book *Slug Bread and Beheaded Thistles: Amusing and Useful Techniques for Nontoxic Housekeeping and Gardening*, republished by Random House in 2000.

THE WOODCHUCK PEST-SPOTTER'S GUIDE TO SUCCESS

Your first act upon entering the garden should be to inspect the enemy's territory once or twice a week. It's not necessary to examine every plant; check by sampling a plant now and then. Identify your enemy by using some woodchuck spy methods such as a glass jar, a magnifying glass, and a good insect guide like *Rodale's Color Guide to Insect Pests* (Rodale Press). Your local University Agricultural Extension office can also provide information. Finally, take notes on your findings.

Biological Controls

Once you have identified the critter or fungus, decide on appropriate action. Age-old gardening practices include trapping, companion planting, and applying homemade formulas like table salt for cabbage worms or beer for slugs. Another slug repellent comes right from the breakfast table: leftover milk. Mix with equal part water and pour into pie plates. Bury these in the soil to the rim. When slugs come to drink, they fall in and drown. You can lay down old planks on garden paths. Gather them up in the morning and you'll find lots of slugs under the wood. For powdery mildew, mix up 3 tablespoons baking soda, 1 tablespoon Murphy's Oil Soap in 1 gallon of water and spray the roses every seven to ten days.

Some gardeners introduce beneficial insects like ladybugs or green lacewings into their home garden. I have never brought them to my garden because good insects are naturally attracted to healthy gardens. However, successful greenhouse growers introduce beneficial bugs into the closed environment because they do not naturally have access. *See Summer Appendix Guide 7, for more on Biological Controls in the Greenhouse.*

Howard Annable checking plants for bugs.
Photo by Jim Flint at the Starr Farm Community Garden, Burlington, Vermont.

BENEFICIAL INSECTS

Beneficial insects feed on destructive bugs: ladybugs eat aphids; green lacewings prey on a wide variety of undesirable insects; and praying mantises eat just about anything they can catch. Critters from bats to toads are also exemplary bug-zappers. Ladybugs and other beneficial insects are attracted to nectar sources like Queen Anne's lace, lamb's-quarters, and goldenrod. These plants can also reduce

6 3

pests. Aphids are sometimes attracted to lamb's-quarters, or flea beetles to mustard weeds rather than your garden vegetables. So it's good to leave some of these so-called weeds in and around your garden. Besides, lamb's-quarters are delicious to eat when the plants are 3 to 4 inches high. They have a nutlike flavor. Yellow sticky paper traps also attract aphids and other harmful insects.

Natural Insecticides: Neem and Bt

Neem, a natural insecticide, is derived from a common plant grown in India called *Azadirachta indica*. It arrests the development of various insect pests like the white fly in your home and greenhouse. Years ago, I was part of a peace delegation that went to a barrio (neighborhood) in Managua, Nicaragua. We planted young neem seedlings for use as shade trees (they grow rapido) and as an insecticide for the white fly.

After three to four years, the neem tree matures to form fruits and seeds. The seeds are crushed and the juice extracted to create a natural insecticide. Neem oil treats the common rose fungus disease black spot.

Bacillus thuringiensis (Bt) is a bacterium that occurs naturally in soil. Its different strains work for insect control; *kurstaki*, also known as Dipel, controls a number of worms and caterpillar larvae. These include tent caterpillars, green cabbage worms, tomato hornworms, and gypsy moth larvae. Dipel has been used for years on cabbages, cauliflower, and broccoli; it works quite well.

When you see those white butterflies dancing around the cabbages in midsummer, it's a sure sign they'll soon be laying eggs. The eggs hatch into green worms that begin munching on cabbage, broccoli, and cauliflower leaves. As soon as you observe the white butterflies, pick the green worms off by hand or start spraying Dipel.

A microbial fungicide, *gliocladium virens*, is a beneficial fungus found in minute amounts in soils. It is used to control root rot and damping off. Its trade name is SoilGard.

The biggest pest problem in my garden is potato bugs. I use another Bt strain, San Diego, to control them, but it doesn't work as well as Dipel does on cabbages. When I notice the potato bugs mating on the potato leaves, I crush them along with the yellow egg clusters on the underside of the leaves. Just crawl between the potato rows and lift the leaves with your hands. The eggs are easy to identify but it's tough to destroy all of them. Once the eggs go through their next metamorphosis into the larvae stage, that's when the real problems begin; they love to digest leaves and buds down to nothing.

These orange larvae are quite noticeable on the outside of the leaves. As soon as you see them, spray Bt San Diego all over the plants. If it rains, the Bt spray washes off so you need to spray again.

A last resort is to use a rotenone-pyrethrin solution to kill the adult potato beetles, eggs, and larvae. It's therapeutic to apply a liquid spray of nettle juice or seaweed solution to heal the damaged potato leaves. If you continue to have serious problems with potato bugs, you may need to plant them far away from your garden or drop out of the potato business for a year or two. If you are a home gardener with ten potato plants, you need not be squeamish; simply pick the eggs, beetles, and larvae by hand about twice a week. Place the potato beetles in a glass jar full of water or squeeze them between your fingers. Watch out: The juice may squirt you in the face.

RON'S FAVORITE PESTS

Like all gardeners, I have my favorite pests and ways to speed up their demise. The top five on my bug chart are potato bugs and green cabbage worms (mentioned above), flea beetles, striped and spotted cucumber beetles, and finally without undue warning, the cutworm.

Flea Beetle

The first to cause problems in the spring garden is the flea beetle, which makes tiny holes in the young plants especially those with a mustard odor like cabbage, broccoli, cauliflower, Chinese cabbage, and Brussels sprouts. You can use a rotenone spray or diatomaceous earth, which I prefer because it's nontoxic. It comes from the fossilized shells of tiny water-dwelling organisms, called diatoms. When ground, they have sharp edges that break the outer protective layer of the insect and desiccate them on contact or internally on ingestion.

Of course, the main line of defense is to have healthy, strong plants that can withstand the onslaughts of the flea beetles. I think the best defense is to use floating row covers. *See more on row covers in Spring, Chapter 4, Late Spring Gardening. Also, check out Spring Appendix Guide 7.*

Striped and Spotted Cucumber Beetles

Flying cucumber beetles can cause early damage to any young cucumber, melon, or squash plant. The striped ones lay eggs in the soil

65

as well as attack the flower blossoms and leaves. The larvae then feed on the roots. Spotted beetles like to chew on the leaves. Once the plants take off in their growth, flying yellow-and black-striped insects do little damage. One woodchuck trick is to pick them off early in the morning when the dew is on the plant because once it warms up, they love to fly off quickly and it's hard to catch them.

You can also cover young plants with row covers; however, once summer has officially arrived and blossoms appear on the plants, it's important to remove the row covers for pollination. You can always hand pollinate the squash-cucumber-pumpkin family by placing the male flower into the female flower and shaking your hand. If you don't know how to distinguish the male and female parts from one another, ask a friend or sex counselor.

If the beetles get out of hand, use a rotenone-pyrethrin spray. I prefer not to use this solution unless absolutely necessary because it is a strong poison. Make sure to read the directions on the bottle. Good observation is critical to grow plants organically. I don't recommend using any poisons—including organic ones—if your plants are only suffering minimal damage. They will recover.

Cutworms

Some gardeners find cutworms troublesome, especially on new plots of freshly turned soil. Some years they seem to be everywhere. An organic product called Grub-Away Nematodes can be effective on cutworms, those plump brown to light green worms that feed at the base of the stem of plants. You can also go out on night patrol with a flashlight to the scene of the crime, unless they have finished off the stem and moved on to other plants.

A woodchuck method of controlling cutworms is to encircle plants with a 3-inch-wide barrier of cardboard anchored 1 inch deep in the soil. This keeps cutworms from chewing into the stem of the plant. Frozen juice containers serve this purpose well (with both ends removed) as do discarded cardboard toilet paper rolls and paper towel rolls. Place the rolls or containers over the young plant and press them into the ground. A light sprinkling of cornmeal, which cutworms are unable to digest, around problem areas will also kill them.

A WORD OF CAUTION

Some organic products are poisons that must be handled carefully. Two examples are rotenone, derived from the root of the derris plant and other tropical legumes; and pyrethrin, which comes from the flowers of certain chrysanthemums. Another product, called Soap-Shield Fungicidal Soap, contains copper, which you must be careful in handling, especially around food and children. Soap-Shield treats black spot on roses and other fungal diseases. There is an ongoing debate within the organic movement on some of these controls, especially the use of copper compounds in fungus diseases. Bt and neem are perfectly safe.

One of the more dynamic ways of controlling insect pests is being experimented with by gardeners of the biodynamic persuasion. A powder/pepper spray is made out of dried potato bugs and sprayed when the sun is in Aquarius (the water bearer) to Cancer (the crab). Some gardeners have found the spray keeps potato bugs away from plants. It's too early to tell about the validity or reliability of this method of deterrence. More studies are needed.

See more on biodynamics in Summer Appendix Guide 8 and on Companion Planting and The Cosmic Influences in Chapter 10, **Let the Force Be With You.**

For more on biological controls, see the Summer Appendix Guides 3-7. Summer Appendix Guide 3 is called Silent Spring Revisited; it includes information on the dangers of pesticides and their increased use in the U.S. An alternative method called Integrated Pest Management (IPM) is described in #4. #5 lists organic control products and suppliers and an address for a Guide to Common Insect Pests and Diseases and how to treat them organically. #6 includes More Tried and True Woodchuck Tips for Insect Control and Down-Home Non-Toxic Insect Sprays. #7 covers biological controls in the greenhouse.

WHO ARE THE BIGGEST PESTS IN THE GARDEN?

An infamous woodchuck pest spotter, whose name I'll keep anonymous, asked me if I knew the biggest pest in the garden. I thought for a moment and before I had a chance to answer, he interrupted with, "It's you, you are the problem." He's right. People do more damage to their gardens than any bug or fungus-among-us ever could. The worm diggers tromp through my community garden plot every spring digging for night crawlers.

I don't want to forget the other gardeners who don't take care of their potato bugs and Japanese beetles. The result is that their insects fly over to my garden. For example, you can inject milky spores into the soil to control Japanese beetles; it works unless you live in a particularly cold pocket. But if your neighbor has roses just like you and they don't control the buggers with milky spores, it won't be long before you'll have your neighbor's problems.

Besides the use of milky spores and good old-fashioned hand-picking, try spraying beneficial nematodes around the plants the Japanese beetles love best; after all, that's where the beetle larvae will likely emerge.

And then comes midsummer when the hardened snatchers of the vegetable patch begin their annual pilgrimage to my garden and the other 135 community garden plots. Tomatoes, corn, carrots, and cucumbers are easy pickins for these garden thieves. Did I forget the garden "love" types who don't weed their garden plots? They just wanna commune with nature.

Enough already, I'll stop with the complaining.

Having dealt with the tiny buggers—and our own species—I want to mention a couple of woodchuck deterrents for those larger animal types like deer, raccoons, and real woodchucks.

My good friend, Ken Pick of Putney, Vermont, uses pie plates, strung up and flapping in the wind to deter deer. He also places 5-gallon buckets with rotten eggs in the bottom around his garden. He experiments with soaps such as Irish Spring hanging from the wire fence and I've heard he plays classical music from Vermont Public Radio in the early morning hours. I wonder how rock n' roll would work....

Years ago, I used to tether my dog in the corn patch throughout the night to keep the raccoons out of my garden. Bonzo was none too happy with this task, but I left the radio on through the night to keep him entertained. I wasn't sure which one made the difference, but I guess it was Bonzo.

KEN'S WOODCHUCK FORMULA

Woodchucks are one of the toughest critters to control. Ken Pick hooks up a low-lying electric fence about 4 to 6 inches off the ground. This is placed next to the main garden fence. Make sure to cut the grass around the electrified wire or it will short out the current.

Another method is to dig in heavy-duty chicken wire mesh fencing about two feet deep in the earth under the main garden fence. The remainder of the mesh fencing (3 to 4 feet) should be attached above the ground to the main garden fence. This has worked for some folks who almost gave up gardening. If you can find the woodchuck holes, fill them up with rocks and soil, and this may keep them out of your garden, but I guess they'll be back for a visit.

When I had a small farm in southern Vermont, I used to go over to the soapstone quarry in Proctor to buy 50-pound bags of talc (ground soapstone). I would dump it into the woodchuck holes. I believe it worked because the chucks would digest the talc and it would do them in. Of course, you can always use a friendly Havahart trap and relocate them far from your garden, or try one of the new electronic vibrational devices that supposedly deter woodchucks from the garden path.

Moles: Besides spraying castor oil to deter moles, a new mole contraption is shaped like a windmill. When it turns in the wind, it sets up a vibration that disturbs moles and moves them out of range of the sounds. These devices work. You will probably need more than one depending on the size of your garden. Fortunately, they are inexpensive.

Write to: Rabun Products Inc., P.O. Box 8, Tiger, Georgia 30576 for information and purchase of mole traps. 706-782-4224

HEALTHY SOIL MEANS HEALTHY PLANTS

The best deterrent for harmful pests is to build up the soil with compost and organic soil amendments like rock phosphate, greensand, dug potassium, and lime. Cover crops (green manures) like winter rye, annual rye, white and yellow clover, alfalfa, and grasses help stabilize the organic matter in the soil. Seaweed and fish emulsion solutions provide a boost to plants during the growing season. You can also mix up your own garden teas.

RON'S GARDEN TEA

Take fresh cut grass, weeds, and nettles. Stuff them all in a barrel, and fill it with water. Let it sit for a week and then pour or spray on your garden plants. I have seen a row of carrots turn from light to dark green in a couple of days after using nettle juice.

When it comes down to it, healthy soil means healthy plants, which translates into less insect damage. Insects don't attack healthy plants the way they do weak ones. Cleanliness and sanitation constitute the first step in preventing harmful insects and disease. Clean gardens have fewer problems with pests. A vigorous fall cleanup is one of the best ways to interrupt the life cycles of over-wintering pests.

After your last harvest, remove all plant residue from the garden and till the soil to dislodge eggs, larvae, and pupae from below the surface so birds can eat them or they perish from exposure to the elements. Other simple deterrents to preventing disease are growing varieties suitable to your area, selecting hardy plants, identifying pests and learning their life cycles, removing dead and diseased plants, and rotating crops.

I don't want to end without mentioning Ruth Stoudt's famous mulch garden. For years she poured beer in shallow bowls and placed them in the earth up to the lip of the bowl. The slugs found the beer irresistible, regardless of the brand. It sent them to their inebriated deaths. Now I know where the commercial "This Bud's For You," came from.

CONFESSION

I spent a lot of time telling you about garden insects and disease control because I am a detective at heart. I love to find creatures munching on my plants. However, to be honest, for the past 35 years,

I've experienced few problems except for potato bugs and flea beetles. A couple of years, a high amount of rainfall brought the fungus among us, but I only lost part of my crop. Like most organic home gardeners, I have been immune from the ravages of most plant diseases. This is not the case in large conventional commercial farms where the same plants are grown year after year, and harmful chemicals and pesticides are applied. This is called a monoculture. Compare this to the typical home garden or the small organic farm where a variety of flowers, herbs, vegetables, and fruits grow. I call this a diversiculture.

On small farms, raising animals and growing grains are added to the equation. The organic approach incorporates all of the above plus crop rotations, composting, and the addition of animal manures, soil amendments, and biological controls. Some organic farms and gardens also use the biodynamic methods of companion planting and planting by the stars and moon.

CHAPTER 10

LET THE FORCE BE WITH YOU

In the spring of 1969, I apprenticed under Erling Anderson at Hill & Dale Farm in Putney, Vermont. The farm included an organic apple orchard, beef cattle (polled Herefords), and organic vegetables. Erling was raised in Sweden and trained in Germany as a biodynamic gardener. He stressed the importance of balance in the vegetable patch. Erling told me it is better to grow 15 tomatoes per plant than 30 because the quality of the fruit is diminished the more the plant is stressed.

His goal was not to grow the largest cabbage but rather one with medium size, sweetness, and good storage capacity. The same held true for striving to produce the earliest tomatoes. Rarely do they have much taste, and look at all the energy you use to grow those early fruits.

When Erling was asked about companion planting, he would become rather Socratic and ask, "Well, what goes well together on your dinner plate? Use common sense," he would say. "If it tastes good together, it's a good companion, like beans and potatoes; and tomatoes, celery, basil, and onions."

A Brief History of Companion Planting

The following information provides a historical background to companion planting and where it fits into the mix.

When J.I. Rodale of organic gardening fame brought the teachings of the late Sir Albert Howard to this country some 50 years ago, he helped initiate the organic gardening movement in America. (J.I. Rodale's real name was J.I. Cohen; he changed to Rodale because of the anti-Semitism of the time.) Sir Albert Howard worked at the Haughley experiment in India for 40 years, developing principles inherent to organic gardening, especially the practice of composting. However, one concept was left out of the organic menu: plant symbiosis, or the ability of certain plants to help each other by their mere presence.

The concept of companion planting came out of the biodynamic movement from agricultural lectures given in 1924 by Rudolf Steiner in East Germany. Steiner was influenced by the famous German philosopher Goethe, whose original works on ecology said, "Nothing happens in nature that is not related to the whole." Ehrenfried E. Pfeiffer developed many of the principles of biodynamics in the U.S. in the 1940s and helped spur the organic movement along with J.I. Rodale.

COMPANION PLANTING

Companion planting is the planting together of crops that enhance one another's growth and protect each other from pests. In this sense, plants are like people in that they want variety. We all like some people more than others—and some we prefer never to see in the same room. None of our friends are the same and how boring it would be if they were.

Plants growing together interact within the relatively small space of a garden or field; for instance, one tall-growing species gives shade, thus temporarily helping or suppressing another species. One species may benefit the other because it forms a deep root system, thus loosening the ground, or because it enriches the soil with nutrients.

Plants excrete tiny quantities of perfumes from the pollen of their flowers, from the essential oils of the leaves, and from their roots. All this can affect plants growing nearby. One plant suppresses a soil disease harmful to the other; marigolds excrete substances from their roots that kill nematodes. Flowers and herbs have a repelling fragrance that can mask the odor of the crop plant, thus confusing pests. Examples: Chives protect lettuce from aphids; rosemary deters the Mexican bean beetle; and carrots and leeks planted together prevent attacks by the carrot fly.

Some plants protect others by luring pests away: Orange nasturtiums lure aphids away from cabbage, broccoli, and cauliflower plants (the brassicas). Marijuana deters the cabbage moth from the brassicas. I have noticed for years that growing potatoes and beans in adjacent rows makes not only a real difference in the health of the plants but also in fewer potato bugs.

Aboriginal Companions

The first settlers found native Americans planting corn, squash, and beans together. The squash benefits from the shade given by the corn, and the corn benefits from the protection of the squash vines; raccoons are said to dislike treading through squash vines. Both corn and squash profit from the beans, which enrich the soil by restoring nitrogen.

One plant's excretions, odors, and insect-repelling or -attracting qualities may directly influence the growth of other plants. They may alter the population of microorganisms that live around the roots, leaves, stems, and blossoms.

BIODYNAMICS

Two methods in biodynamics attempt to answer whether you can differentiate a living soil from deadened soil, a healthy seed from a seed bred from weakness. These two methods are sensitive crystallization and chromatography. Both methods can also be used to determine whether plant species are good or poor companions to each other in the garden.

You can actually see sensitive crystallization at work, as Helen and John Phibrick discovered in their Massachusetts garden. They said, "The most exciting thing happened during the night, and we saw it at 7:30 a.m. On the glass of the cold frame, the frost had made designs, and we could actually tell from the shape of the designs which plants were below the panes. The frost patterns in the first frame over the thyme plants were fine and feathery, suggestive of the thyme leaves. The next patterns over the pansies had larger leaves with a soldier-like shape. The other frames containing lettuce showed large, smooth geometric arcs with no fine leaves."

FROST PATTERNS ON THE BAKERY WINDOW

When E.E. Pfeiffer was a young man in Germany, he noticed as he passed a bakery window that frost patterns from different loaves of bread varied on the glass. I noticed this same phenomenon when I lived in an old drafty farmhouse in southern Vermont. Different herbs next to the cold windows created unique and varied frost patterns. Each herb had its own crystallized signature, like an aura, except in this case it could be seen by anyone. As soon as the sun hit the windows, the frost patterns vanished. Some people call this phenomenon the physical manifestation of the etheric or life force—others call it "voodoo agriculture."

E.E. Pfeiffer, from his experiences as a youth with help from Rudolf Steiner, formulated the sensitive crystallization process. He developed crystal pictures comparing grains grown with organic fer-

SENSITIVE CRYSTALLIZATION

Plant extracts are added to a copper chloride solution, which crystallizes on a glass plate. Typical patterns have been established for many plant species.

SENSITIVE CRYSTALLIZATION OF OATS USING ORGANIC FERTILIZER

SENSITIVE CRYSTALLIZATION OF OATS USING CHEMICAL FERTILIZER

tilizer and mineral fertilizer, and also pictures from the sap of plants. He discovered that plants that formed harmonious crystal patterns when placed side by side also did well as companion plants. Example: corn and beans.

Sensitive crystallization works when a copper chloride solution crystallizes on a glass plate and the tiny crystals form an irregular, chaotic pattern. If extracts from plant materials are added to the crystallizing salt, then a coordinated pattern is produced. Typical patterns have been established for many plant species.

A strong, healthy, vigorous plant will produce beautiful, harmonious and clearly formed crystal arrangements. The patterns of a weak, sickly plant will be uneven and unharmonious.

Let's look at another example of how the sensitive crystallization method can be used by comparing oats grown with organic fertilizer and oats grown using mineral/chemical fertilizer. (See the picture on page 74.) The organic oat crystals reflect regular patterns with strong bundles and broad angles of branches, whereas the chemically grown oats show unharmonious patterns with split bundles.

Dr. Pfeiffer also developed a second method of determining quality called, circular paper chromatography or the chromatogram. Companion planting lends itself to this qualitative method of analysis. The chromatogram pictures below show how cucumbers and beans are good companions as compared to beans and fennel, which don't go together. One can see harmony in the picture of the cucumbers and beans. The bean pattern is retained and the cucumber pattern somehow blossoms out, confirming the observation that beans help the growth of cucumbers. The picture of beans and fennel shows that the finer characteristics of the bean are lost and the undulating pattern is diminished. (See page 76 for pictures.)

The second example is a series on apples and potatoes, which are not good companions. This can be shown when apples and potatoes are stored in the same root cellar. The apples lose their flavor, as do the potatoes. In the chromatogram picture combining the apple and potato, the finer characteristics of each are lost and we have only a kind of empty, flat, dead inner zone. It takes time to develop a series of chromatogram pictures and learn how to analyze and interpret the results.

The procedure for creating a chromatogram of plant material is as follows: Take 5 grams of the plant and place it in a flask of 50ml of 1% sodium hydroxide. Place this solution in a porcelain dish. Lay a

CHROMATOGRAMS AND COMPANION PLANTING

Filter paper treated with a silver nitrate solution is laid on top of a dish with a wick dipped into a solution of sodium hydroxide and plant material. After the paper dries, a picture forms. Photographs from *Biodynamics Magazine*.

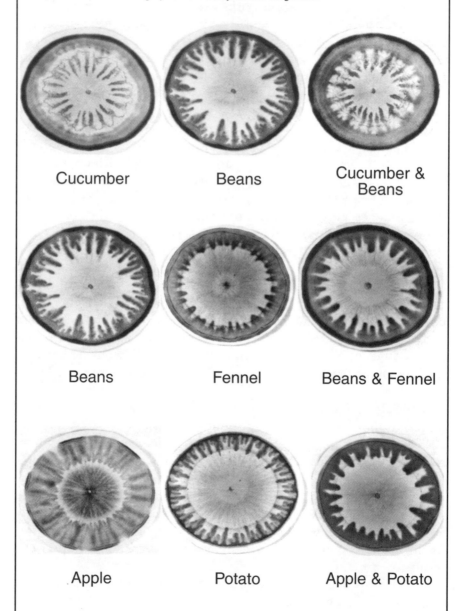

Cucumber

Beans

Cucumber & Beans

Beans

Fennel

Beans & Fennel

Apple

Potato

Apple & Potato

disc of filter paper that has been treated with silver nitrate over the top of the dish with a wick. The solution will be drawn up into the paper. After it drys, a picture forms.

Many standard, chemical quantitative methods are not sufficient to evaluate the quality of soils, compost and plants. Methods like sensitive crystallization and the chromatogram tell us something about the health of soils and compost and the relationships of plants. These methods don't take the place of standard chemical tests but are used to complement them.

THE COSMIC INFLUENCES

Cosmic forces can be understood by picturing a plant sitting between sun and earth, opening itself to the power of both entities. Have you ever walked to a high meadow at dusk in summer, laid down in the grass, looked up, and experienced the vastness of the sky. It's as if the earth is flat and a large bowl covers us with color, clouds, stars, and planets.

Wolf Storls in his book *Culture and Horticulture* writes, "There is a whole field of science that has only begun to explore the relation of plant growth to the rhythms of sun, moon, and other planets as they follow their course through the heavens. Ancient cultures knew of these connections and performed their agricultural tasks in concert with cosmic events. Our modern consciousness no longer knows the meaning of these events and is left with lone skepticism. To assume that what comes to pass in the wide expanses of the cosmic world that surrounds the earth has little or no effect on the life of the earth is a view that describes the cosmic elements of the stars and planets as dead matter held together by mechanical forces."

In the *Agriculture Course*, Rudolf Steiner pointed to the influences of the starry world on plant growth when he said, "Human life is almost totally emancipated from the cosmos. It is less so for animals, and the plants are to a great extent still embedded in and dependent on what is occurring in their earthly surroundings. That is why it is impossible to understand plant life without taking into account that everything on earth is actually only a reflection of what is taking place in the cosmos."

So what is out there and where do we go from here? Let's start with the simplest of relationships, the flower clocks, and move on to more intricate phenomena in nature's relationship to the cosmos.

7 7

Flower Clocks

The most obvious rhythm is the daily movement of the sun, which profoundly affects all life, including one-celled organisms. It includes the daily opening and closing of flower petals, and the movement of leaves in some plants, such as the bean, into nightly vertical sleep positions and horizontal day positions. These daily rhythms were so accurate that, in the 18th and 19th centuries, flower clocks were planted in gardens; there it became possible to tell time by the opening and closing of the petals. Morning glories open in the morning, passion flowers open at noon, bindweed closes at 4:00 p.m., and evening primrose opens at 6:00 p.m.

The Four-fold Plant

Each plant can be characterized by its root, leaf-stem, flower, and fruit-seed. As gardeners, we try to encourage the root growth of carrots, beets, and potatoes; the leaf growth of lettuce and spinach; the blossoms of our favorite flowering plants; and the fruit and seeds of such crops as wheat, corn, tomatoes, beans, and squash.

The four parts of the plant correspond to the four elements in nature known as earth, water, air and fire. It's not hard to connect the root of a plant to the earth; the green vegetable parts to the flow of moisture; the colorful flower opening to the light (the airy element); and finally fruit ripening by the warmth of the sun (the fire element).

Traditional wisdom has recognized the four elements can be found in the twelve constellations of the zodiac. Three constellations are associated with each element: Taurus, Virgo, and Capricorn with earth; Cancer, Scorpio, and Pisces with water; Gemini, Libra, and Aquarius with air; and Aries, Leo, and Sagittarius with fire. The moon passing before constellations enables the particular elemental forces to work more strongly in the plant.

Erling Anderson, the master gardener I worked under, didn't plant seeds astrologically as he wasn't gifted in that realm but certain days he would know instinctively what and when to plant. He couldn't really explain his actions, but I was aware he knew that root crops did better when the moon was in its waning or contracting stages, and that leaf crops were helped when the moon was waxing or expanding.

One garden practice that may surprise you is to go out in the evening to observe the stars. A star guide and a friendly star enthusiast are useful assistants. Begin to identify the constellations and their path through the night. Some of the easier ones are the Big Dipper and Orion. By performing agricultural practices such as seed sowing, transplanting, cultivating, weeding, and harvesting at times when the appropriate element is working strongly in the cosmos, you can enhance the size, form, flavor, and storage quality of your garden crops. It takes years of observation and patience to appreciate and comprehend planting rhythms.

Three Biodynamic Experiments with Cosmic Rhythms

Maria Thun worked in Germany for 28 years, experimenting with the timing of seed sowing, cultivation, and harvesting according to cosmic rhythms. She performed experiments with radish seeds by sowing equal amounts of the seeds daily into small perennial plots, noting the sign in which the moon was found. Radishes sown in the "earth sign" showed good root development, those sown in the "water sign" showed abundant leaf development, those sown in "air" and "fire" signs tended to bolt and seed well.

L. Kolisko carried out 15 years of experiments in the 1940s and 1950s with wheat, barley, and oats. A large number of seeds were sown during different phases of the moon with variables such as soil type, water, and fertilizer held constant. Measurements of the weight, length of roots, and leaves showed maximum growth always occurred in the waxing, the expansive stage of the second quarter of the moon. Another series of tests showed sprouting is best done two days before the full moon.

As early as the 1940s, J. Schultz established a relationship between the spiral leaf arrangements of plants and the rhythms of the moon, the sun, and the planets. How does this work? The force of the sun pulls vegetation upward, giving the vertical tendency. Just as the planets move in patterns around the sun, so do the buds, leaves, and flowers move around the vertical stem of the plant, mirroring the mathematical relationships that hold sway in planetary movements. For example, if you draw the path of Venus, it looks like the star revealed by cutting an apple in half. (The apple is part of the rose family, which has five petals in a five-pointed star.) If you view a flower diagram of a tulip, it is similar to the path of Mercury.

The archetypal patterns are even found in tree rings, wind and ocean currents, spirals and vortices of whirling galaxies, rings of Saturn, parallel lines of oyster shells, and spiral placement of leaves and buds around a stem. There are indications these organic forms are in symphony with planetary orbits, lunar phases, and other cosmic occurrences. People of the past, most of whom were peasants and gardeners, never doubted the influences of forces emanating from the cosmos. Today, we are just beginning to appreciate how plants, animals, and human beings live in relation to the rhythmical fluctuating fields of the earth and the cosmos. We are not alone.

Biodynamic methods form the basis for companion planting and cosmic influences. *See Summer Appendix Guide 8 for more information on biodynamics. Included is Stella Natura, the Kimberton Hills Agricultural Calendar. It provides practical advice for gardeners working with cosmic rhythms.*

CONCLUSION

The mutual influence of plants on one another belongs to a sphere of biological and dynamic behavior called companion plants. The German chamomile for example can be both good and harmful. If there is an occasional chamomile plant growing in a field of wheat, there is a positive effect; however, if it is grown thickly amongst the wheat, it inhibits growth. More research needs to be done in this sphere of dynamic horticulture.

State agricultural universities, funded in many cases by large agribusinesses and the federal government, have not seen companion planting or, for that matter, the whole field of organic farming, as a research priority. The same can be said for the practice of planting by the stars and the moon. Much of the agricultural research money today is spent on genetic engineering, the gene splicing of different plant species.

It's all fine and dandy to use companion planting and plant by the moon and stars, but there are other day-to-day practical matters to contend with like mulching, weeding, and watering. Let's get back to the summer garden and ask the ultimate question, "To Mulch or Not to Mulch?"

CHAPTER 11

TO MULCH OR NOT TO MULCH

The question "to mulch or not to mulch" can't be found in any Shakespearian drama; the best answer can only come from woodchuck gardeners who tell you it depends on the weather, soil conditions, and temperament of the gardener. Mulch is a layer of material made of old hay, straw (stalks of grain after threshing), leaves, or newspapers placed on the soil surface to conserve moisture, hold down weeds, and improve soil fertility. Some tillers of the earth take a total-dirt mentality; they want nothing to do with mulch. They would rather play in the soil like kids in a sandbox, and that's fine.

Other gardeners just love to mulch like my friend Deborah Stuart of Wentworth, New Hampshire, who would not be able to live without hay, grass, pine needle mulch, and horse manure bedding. Deborah's favorite mulch is newspapers, the gardener's best friend. They are now deemed environmentally safe because of the nontoxic soy dyes used in the printing process. Deborah is a "mulch collector," always looking out for grass or a pine needle stash. She has rakes, baskets, and black plastic bags ever-present in her arsenal of collection paraphernalia in the trunk of her car. Deborah told me, "I can be driving down the road and see a pile of grass or pine needles, quickly jump out, and lickety-split, procure them without notice. I used to rake pine needles off the macadam road near my home and place them in a wheelbarrow. People would drive down the road and see me raking needles, and I am sure they thought I was nuts. Today, I am given bags of pine needles by a campground, and I am in heaven."

The Alternative Attack

Deborah Stuart has learned that instead of using the attack-and-kill-the-weeds-and-grass-at-any-cost attitude, she simply smothers her perennial beds with newspapers and then adds pine needles or a grass mulch. This past year she included horse manure bedding in her mulches; the bedding adds humus and nutrients to the soil as it breaks down. She told me, "One way I occasionally use newspaper is on the borders of beds being invaded by clover or grass. I dig a little trench, and tuck some newspaper down in the trench, round it up into a border, and add some pine needles. It interrupts the growth of weeds, grass, and clover. If I plant a bush or a flowering crab out in the field, I smother newspaper around the perimeter of the tree, and it keeps down the growth of grass."

THE FINER POINTS

Mulching serves a number of purposes, not the least of which is weed control. A thick mulch saves moisture in the soil in the summer and holds soil temperatures steady. Earthworms are drawn especially to leaf mulches. Cover your fall garden beds with leaves. This will protect the soil from the elements and add nutrients in the form of worm castings. You will also be able to plant earlier in the spring. Hay and straw mulches cool the soil slightly in the summer while others, like black plastic, warm it up. A new red plastic mulch supposedly works 20% better for plant growth than black plastic. However, I prefer to use natural mulches that will stay in the earth not the landfill. Well-decomposed organic mulches, whether they come from sawdust, wood shavings, leaves, hay, straw, or other plant material, provide nutrients and improve the physical condition of the soil.

Mulches also protect plants from winter injury. Cover plants like strawberries and perennials loosely with dry mulch in late October.

Hay and straw mulch can be applied anytime, even though it's best to lay them down in the garden in mid-June because you want the soil to warm up first. Placing mulch in your garden in May when the soil is cool is not advisable.

The Ultimate Woodchuck Mulch Recipe

Take a 6 by 8 foot area on your lawn or back forty where grass sod is in full sun. Add many layers of wet newspapers with complete abandon. Top off with grass clippings, leaves, and whatever mulches you have, including kitchen wastes. Keep adding on mulch throughout the summer. Let sit until next spring, where it will break down over winter, and whadahyagot but a small garden site. You can dig it up in spring and create a perennial bed or throw on some old composted manure and plant pumpkins and squash, or start a strawberry patch.

What you have done is create a low maintenance compost-

Mulching experiment with newspaper and hay mulch.
Photo by Robert King at his garden in Putney, Vermont.

mulch pile that will break down and provide a place to grow vegetables and fruits, flowers or herbs. It will last for years.

WEEDING AND MULCH

Before putting down mulch, get rid of the weeds and saturate the soil with water. Remember, many hay mulches contain lots of weed seeds so try to find one free of them. Rots o' ruck. Ask the farmer or store you purchase the mulch from about how free the mulch is from weed seeds. Straw mulches are generally much cleaner than hay mulches, but they are more expensive.

When using hay or straw mulches, put down 6 inches at the very least and ideally more. If you use less, the weeds will begin to push through, so it's critical to keep enough mulch material over the soil and to continue adding when necessary. Transplants may be placed through a hay mulch, by pushing back the mulch. Holes can be made in a black plastic mulch. You can also lay down hay mulch after the plants have grown to a reasonable size, but with black plastic, it should be laid down first unless you are placing the plants between two plastic strips.

CHAPTER 12

THE THREE Ws: WEEDING, WHACKING, AND WATERING

ELBOW GREASE

Before going much further, I need to state unequivocally to the world that I spend more time weeding than any other garden activity and that goes for planting, mulching, cultivating, and harvesting. My main implements are my hands and arms along with the use of a long-handled sharp hoe, a hand cultivator with tines (fingers), and a wheel cultivator with scoops.

THE WAR OF WEEDS

As a gardener, you'll never win the war of weeds even though you may win a couple of battles. Your first line of defense is to identify the wild warriors. The most prodigious weeds in my garden are amaranth (pigweed), lamb's-quarters, gallant soldier (galinsoga), witch and crab grass, purslane, ragweed, bindweed, and chickweed. Each one shows its face at different times, with lamb's-quarters leading off in the first and chickweed taking its place in the seventh inning stretch, or August in my garden. Just when you think you've done a good job of weeding, chickweed takes over.

WEED WHACKERS

If it rains as it did continuously in the summer of 2000, weeds may run rampant and take over your garden. One woodchuck trick is to use a gas-powered or electric weed whacker to cut down all the weeds between the plants and in the rows. Just be careful not to cut all the vegetables down too. After whacking weeds, cover them with newspapers and old hay.

THE FOUR KEYS

The four keys to weeding are timing, hard work, mulching, and letting go. Hoeing them in as soon as they appear is critical. It's best to mulch after weeding, but this should only be done after the soil warms in early summer, so you may need to weed twice before mulching. Finally, make sure the weeds don't go to seed. And remember, you'll never get all the weeds unless you are one of those compulsive types who refuses any semblance of wildness in their garden or in their life for that matter. Each to their own. If the weeds overwhelm you, be good to yourself by tilling up the soil and replanting, or use a weed whacker.

If you are part of a community garden, you're in for a real challenge because some gardeners just don't seem to understand the importance of controlling weeds. Their mischief will provide you with weeds for years to come. I knew one community gardening chap who wanted to see how tall his weeds would grow. He wasn't given an invitation the following year.

Now that I have knocked weeds down, I would like to lift them up by mentioning a fascinating book entitled *Weeds and What They Tell* by E.E. Pfeiffer, Biodynamic Press. Pfeiffer tells us weeds play an important role in nature. They resist conditions cultivated plants cannot, such as drought, acidity of soil, lack of humus, and mineral deficiencies. Weeds want to tell a story if we would only listen. There are three major weed groups: The first comprises weeds living on acid soils, like sorrels, docks, and horsetails; the second group indicates crust formations and hardpans in soil like field mustard, chamomiles, and quack grass. The third group follows human steps like lamb's-quarters, chickweed, and pigweed.

Each group tells us something about the soil conditions and what we need to do to rejuvenate our gardens. For example, the acid-soil-loving groups indicate when changes begin in our soil. The acidity in soil increases with lack of air, standing water in the surface layer, cultivating too wet a soil, excess acid fertilizers, erosion, and lack of humus.

A good weed identification book is *Weeds of the Northeast* by Uva, Neal and DiTomaso. Cornell University Press.

CARROTS

Since vegetable plants grow at different rates, it's easier to weed potatoes, corn, and beans than carrots; this root crop is notorious for its slow growth. That's why some gardeners mix a few radish seeds in with carrot seeds. The radishes grow more quickly than the carrots so you see the line of radishes before the carrots, which emerge soon after. This allows you to weed along the row more easily. I know a chap who plants sage seeds in his carrot rows. As he thins the carrots, little sage plants emerge, which he gives to friends.

THE ONION PATCH

For reasons I cannot explain, the weeds in my onion patch always seem to get out of control even though I weed them thoroughly. By the time the weeds take over in July, the onions have already formed large enough bulbs so I can harvest them in August. As I pull out the onions, I also pull out the weeds and lay them down as a mulch. Believe it or not, it works every year as long as the onion plants get a head start.

SHEET WEED MULCH

As I mentioned earlier, I combine weeding and mulching by using the "sheet weed mulch" method. After pulling up the weeds and old plants like the lettuce going to seed in midsummer, I lay the weeds down over the garden bed right where I pulled them out. I find this method easier than carting them off to the compost pile. I turn the mulch over in about two weeks, mixing it with a little dirt, let it sit another week, and rake the plant residues that have not broken down into a pile, which I will later use as mulch material. Then I replant the garden bed with a late crop of beans or cucumbers. Juices in the weeds mixed in with the dirt provide nourishment for this crop. It is helpful to add some compost and make sure the bed is watered thoroughly before planting.

A new product called Original Wow sold by Gardens Alive suppresses the growth of weeds. Wow is a byproduct of corn syrup production that eliminates weeds just after they germinate. It controls crab grass, lamb's-quarters, dandelion, purslane, and other weeds up to 90%—according to Gardens Alive.

Read their catalog for more information: Gardens Alive, 5100 Schenley Place, Lawrenceburg, IN 47025; (812) 537-5108; *www.gardensalive.com*. Other garden companies carry similar products, such as Gardener's Supply.

WATERING AND MULCH

During the dry part of summer, I place a hose underneath the mulch and let the water run until the earth is totally saturated. This works especially well where rows of mulched vegetables, like tomatoes with deep furrows, run between the rows. I hill the soil up at the end of the rows to create a dam. This method holds the water in the furrows and uses much less water because the mulch keeps the moisture in the soil. I call this The California Woodchuck Watering Method. You can also use a soaker hose with small holes in it. This allows water to move slowly out from the holes of the hose. Both work well and use less aqua than overhead-sprinkling systems.

MORE WOODCHUCK WATERING TIPS

A Quick Watering Test

Dig a 1-foot hole in the earth, fill with water, cover with soil, and wait a couple of days. Check it out for moistness by the way it feels. This method tells you something about the water holding capacity of your soil. If the earth stays moist for a week, then you probably need to water once a week in the summer. If not, you need to water more often. It all depends on the soil, amount of rainfall, and whether you use mulch.

Soils

Clay soils hold water better than sandy soils, and silt is somewhere in between. However, a clay soil saturated with too much water will not allow plant roots to breathe. Plants will just sit there, not grow, and eventually yellow, and possibly die unless the soil is aerated. Loam is a combination of clay, sand, and silt. You can have a loamy sand, a silty loam, a light clay loam or.... Experienced gardeners know how much to water having worked with their soils year after year. They can tell by looking at the plants or feeling the earth. I find it's best to scratch the surface, and go deeper if necessary, to see how far the dryness has penetrated. Soils where seeds are just planted need moisture, as do young seedlings. Once the plants have taken off in their growth cycle, it's not necessary to water, as long as moisture is deep in the earth. Plant roots reach down into the soil to find moisture.

Watering Devices

Many devices are used for watering: overhead sprinklers, soaker hoses, hoses with nozzles and wand sprayer attachments, plastic tubing with sprayers that stay in the ground, and underground tubing with holes in it. This is called drip irrigation. Garden catalogs sell many types of watering equipment. Study them.

Watering and Watering

When watering, saturate the earth thoroughly rather than just covering the top inch or two. Sometimes, if the soil is extremely dry and you water only the top of the soil, the plant roots will reach up toward the moisture. This stresses the plant. The key is to find a balance between over-and under-watering.

Because I am part of the 143-plot Tommy Thompson Community Garden, I have had the opportunity to watch people water their gardens in various ways. Some love to use a sprinkler hose at midday when the sun is beating down on the earth. Others turn on the spigot and spray their vegetables after a heavy downpour. It's obvious: "They know not what they do." At times I try to explain the best times to water are in the early morning and late evening. I tell them when the earth is saturated with water, the fine feeder roots of the plants are perfectly happy. But, you know, those water-hose lovers still want to hang out at the garden around midday or after a rainstorm and deluge the earth and plants with the silver-white liquid. Go figure.

BALANCE IN THE TOMATO PATCH

Garden tomato plants develop blights when a lot of moisture fills the air. One woodchuck trick is not to water the leaves of the tomato plants but to do it at ground level. Some commercial growers use hoop type greenhouses along with black plastic and drip irrigation. These materials provide plants protection from the cold and keep moisture off their leaves.

As a home gardener, I believe it makes sense to have balance in the vegetable patch and not to go to extremes with technology unless you are trying to make a living from farming and even then, it's a matter of values. So water the soil around your tomato plants and even if you lose some to fungus, you will still have plenty for the kitchen table and the canning shelves.

Sunflower.
Photo by Jamie Mittendorf, Tommy Thompson Community Garden.

CHAPTER 13

FLOWERS

Now that midsummer has arrived in all its glory, life forces in the plant kingdom are going through dramatic changes. Flowers are opening fully to the sun and breathing out their essence in color, scent, and pollen. Midsummer is a turning point in the year. It's just opposite midwinter. The sun has reached the highest point in its progression in the sky, and the power of the light, having come to the climax, begins to decrease. Just as the sun starts to turn back to the earth at midwinter, so it turns away at midsummer. This is when great summer bonfires are lit to celebrate the sun, as in the St. John's Festival on the summer solstice. For many people, St. John's Day is associated with fairies and flowers, as immortalized by Shakespeare in *A Midsummer Night's Dream:*

A MIDSUMMER NIGHT'S DREAM

Through this house give glimmering light
By the dead and drowsy fire:
Every elf and fairy sprite,
Hop as light as bird from brier;

And this ditty, after me
Sing, and dance it trippingly.
First rehearse this song by rote:
To each word a warbling note,
Hand in hand, with fairy grace,
Will we sing, and bless this place.

Midsummer is when flowers and fairies are at their peak. What could be more magical than the spirit of these elemental beings? Let's learn about flowers by visiting Diana Doll at Stray Cat Farm where she has grown blooms and blossoms for 13 years.

STRAY CAT FARM

In the late fall of 1987, Diana Doll, or Didi as she's called, went out into the woods in northern Vermont with friends to collect balsam boughs, cones, and berries to make Christmas wreaths. She enjoyed the experience so much that in the spring of 1988 she decided to purchase some flower seeds and start a dried flower business. She made wreaths for three years in a neighbor's barn. That's where the name Stray Cat Farm came from: She was forever taking in stray cats that turned up in the barn where she was drying flowers. That's also when she branched out into the fresh-cut flower world.

Diana Doll.
Photograph by Ron Krupp.

ANNUAL CUT FLOWERS

Annual flower plants arc started in plug trays in a greenhouse adjacent to her quarter-acre plot. Plug trays are like tiny cells, 1/4-inch wide. Seeds for fresh-cut flowers are planted in April and May. Once they form small plants, they can be placed into larger plugs or kept at their current size and then transferred into her (zone 5) garden between May 15 and May 30.

Remember: If you start plants too early, they may become root bound and unhealthy, so it's important to know about starting dates. You can find this information in good seed catalogs. Stokes Seeds has close to 100 varieties of cut flower seeds. P.O. Box 548, Buffalo, NY 14240; (800) 396-9238; *www.stokesseeds.com*.

Planting young annual plants into the earth in mid-May is chancy because the soil may be cold and wet. One way around this is to cover the plants with row covers in case of frosts. Of course, that's a lot of work. Commercial growers will take chances placing plugs out in mid-May, whereas the home gardener should simply wait till the end of the month. Didi plans to lengthen the growing season by increasing greenhouse production in an unheated greenhouse where she would grow cold-weather cut flowers.

FRESH-CUT FLOWERS FOR THE HOME-STYLE COTTAGE GARDEN

Didi tells us you can grow a wide variety of fresh-cut flowers in your garden. When planning, grow varieties of cut flowers, some tall, some short with different shades of color.

- **LAVATERA** (mallow): rose pink, white (both annual and perennial)
- **ZINNIA:** many colors
- **COSMOS:** pink, red, crimson, white
- **CLEOME** (spider flower): rose pink, pale pink, white
- **SUNFLOWERS:** smaller, shorter varieties
- **SNAPDRAGONS:** many colors; must start early, cold hardy
- **BLUE SALVIA:** good for home garden; not viable for commercial production. Color blue balances out the pinks, reds, and yellows.

More on Snaps

Snapdragons are one of the loveliest annual cut flowers. This woodchuck gardener grows his own snaps. I start seeds in March and put the plants out in late May. Even though they take a long time to grow, I love the dark green foliage and amazing profusion of color when the snaps flower in August and continue to bloom until a number of hard frosts burn them off in late fall. It's inspiring to have color extend the growing season.

See Summer Appendix Guide 9 for a great book on raising cut flowers. See Spring Appendix Guide 4 for a comprehensive list of Annual Flower Seed Starting dates.

DRIED FLOWERS

Didi tells me dried flowers are the sisters to the cut flower world. The key to drying flowers is to pick them early in their maturity; if you wait, they may "blow out," meaning they continue to develop by losing their blossoms and then going to seed. Pick them when they are perfect but not when they are too perfect. In other words, pick them on the first day or soon after they fully open. The art of when to pick dried flowers can be found in books but ultimately must be learned in the school of life.

Drying Herbs and Flowers the Old-Fashioned Way

This woodchuck gardener starts early by cutting pink chive flowers. Cut the stems in late May and early June just when they are in full color. Then tie the bunches with twine, hang them from a beam, and let them dry. The color will last for at least two years. I also cut and hang herbs for my famous tea called Bonzo Punch mentioned in the Autumn part entitled "Putting the Garden By." I tried drying roses this summer, but the colors grew pale because I picked them too late; I should have harvested them before the rose petals fully opened.

According to Didi, if you aspire to grow dried flowers commercially, understand they take up lots of space when hanging and drying. Ideally, you need a well-ventilated barn with a lofty second story that is dry and dark. The darker the space, the better they keep their colors. For the home gardener, you can dry them in the darker areas of your home. By the way, dried flowers are pretty fuss-free when it comes to growing them. Most of the flowers Didi grows are annuals except for the yellow-gold tansy and achillea, which are perennials.

Pick the flowers in late morning, after the dew has dried and when the flowers are close to being fully open. Hang them in a place that is not too crowded, where there is good air movement. Some flowers that dry well are strawflowers, nigella, statice, globe amaranths, celosia, oregano, and ornamental grasses. They do fine on their own as long as it's a reasonably dry area like a shaded back porch, or in a dark attic with good air flow.

Didi's Dried Flower Favorites for the Home Gardener:
- **BLUE SALVIA:** delicate, navy blue florets.
- **GLOBE AMARANTH:** strong colors: purple, red, pinks, like little round globes that hold their colors well.
- **STATICE:** strong blues and purples, pinks, yellow, peach, and white.

Pretty but hard to grow in colder climates. If rained on just when it's about to mature, the delicate flower petals are ruined. If you know it's going to rain, cut all the flowers that are ready or close to ready because if you wait they might be lost. Some gardeners grow statice in a greenhouse just to keep the rain off.

- **TANSY:** yellow, gold. They grow wild along railroad tracks. They are a New England native wildflower and grow easily in your garden.
- **NIGELLA:** Navy blue, pink, or white. Takes a long time to germinate, so it needs to be started by April 1. Nigella balloons beige with maroon stripes. The seed pod is what you actually harvest and dry.
- **LARKSPUR:** Navy and light blue, white, and all shades of pink. Sow late March because they take a couple of weeks just to emerge, and a month to grow to the size where they can be planted in the garden. Plant them with sweet peas when it's cool.
- **STRAWFLOWERS:** Come in many colors, easy to grow and dry, lots of flowers per plant, pick when just a couple of rows of petals open.

SAVING DRIED SEEDS

Diana Doll advises the home gardener not to plant all the seeds in a packet since many contain 100 or more. Just plant a few seeds and save the rest. You can also save the seeds of certain plants, the easiest ones being nigella, poppies, sunflowers, celosia, marigolds, and salvia. Because most seeds have been hybridized, a lot of plants don't come back true to form, especially sunflowers. Didi grows a smaller variety of sunflowers, not the large striped, bird-seed type. Even then, there is a lot of variation year to year.

Other seed tips

It's best to use more than one seed company and to read different catalogs for germination times, temperatures, etc. Didi's favorites are: Cook's Garden, Burpee's, Stokes, Johnny's, Pinetree, Parks, and Thompson and Morgan. Stokes Seed Company of Buffalo, New York, has excellent information in their catalogs and is very helpful when you call because you can speak to a horticulturist. *Find the addresses, phone numbers, and web sites for these catalogs in Winter Appendix Guide 2.*

FLOWERS THROWN TO THE WIND

Many "fast-food" annual flower seeds don't have to be started indoors. You can simply throw them to the wind in early summer;

they are easy to plant and don't take a lot of soil preparation. In fact, some seeds such as the common marigold and nasturtium are very tolerant in their soil requirements.

A close friend of mine Karen Caldwell told me you can sow amaranth seed and annual poppy, cosmos, and other flower seeds directly into your garden in early summer. No need to buy a six-pack of cosmos. You can do the same with asters like the early blooming compact varieties. One of Karen's favorite annuals is alyssum, especially the old-fashioned variety called Carpet of Snow. This dainty white ground cover stays cold-hardy until November. A similar variety, Pastel Carpet, comes in shades of violet, pink, rose, and white.

Another favorite of Karen's is the versatile amaranth (lamb's-quarters) with its striking foliage, flowers, and grains. Different varieties of amaranth serve various purposes. Some produce leaves that can be eaten like spinach and don't bolt, that is, they don't go to seed. Others are used to grow grain. Amaranth originated in South America and is making a comeback as a grain, especially in Asia and organic food circles in the U.S. One reason is that amaranth has more protein than wheat.

Amaranth flower seed can be purchased from Fedco Seeds in Waterville, Maine (04903). Two flower heirlooms, Amaranth Gigantica and Elephant Head, develop tall, deep red, almost purple blooms used for decorative purposes.

Karen's third favorite is the annual poppy. These Asiatic plants can be started outside. Direct-sow the tall, orange opium poppy in early May, and it will sometimes flower by the Fourth of July. Make sure to thin out any annuals you start outside. Continue to sow annual flower seeds in June and have continuous blooms with a variety of colors throughout the growing season. There is something rejuvenating about watching little green seedlings shoot up soon after you throw them to the wind at the end of May and later.

Up to now, I have written about annuals. It's high time to visit my two other favorite woodchuck plants, the daylily and the geranium. They're tough, hardy, and long-lasting. My other favorite flowering plant, the rose, is featured in the Autumn section of the book.

"Lest us not forget" the iris, named after the goddess of the rainbow. It is one of the loveliest perennials on the face of the earth. Tall, German-bearded irises are probably the most common in gardens, but many other varieties also do well. What could be more beautiful than a dark, purple-blue bearded iris, even though I am also fond of the Siberian and Japanese types with their smooth petals and thin, grasslike leaves. Midsummer is a good time to plant new iris rhizomes or to divide established clumps of bearded irises. Plant them by the end of August so they'll have time to get established before winter.

THE DAYLILY
The History of Olallie Farm
Chris Darrow of Olallie Daylily Farm in South Newfane, Vermont is thankful his grandfather chose to experiment with many different daylily varieties. This is how it all began:

Chris's grandfather George MacMillon Darrow and the famous former Vermont Senator and Governor George Aiken started the Putney Nursery in 1916. Years after his grandfather died, Chris found some stationery that said, "Darrow-Aiken Nursery, Purveyors of Fine Jams and Berries."

George Darrow went on to become a plant breeder of berries for the United States Department of Agriculture (USDA) in Maryland. He traveled all over the country collecting new varieties of berries. Once when he was out on the West Coast, he came across the name Olallie, a Native Indian word meaning, "place where you find berries." When he retired, he bred over 300 varieties of daylilies. About a year before his passing, he asked Chris and his family to come down to Maryland to take a sample of each daylily and that's how Olallie Daylily Farm began in South Newfane, Vermont.

MAIL ORDER AND BARE ROOT
According to Chris, daylilies are easy-to-grow, hardy plants. He said, "As a mail-order business, I want to send them in the best possible condition. I dig the plants up, shake off most of the soil from the roots, dip them in water, and wrap them in paper. I don't use any special wrapping paper or chemicals. I send them all over the country from June till September, bare root in the mail."

You can divide daylilies anytime during the growing season, though fall and spring are the best times for transplanting. Dividing them in spring may delay the flowering; dividing them in early fall gives them plenty of time to become established before their next bloom cycle. It's best to wait until the plants have finished flowering before dividing, but you don't have to wait until the foliage turns brown. Use a garden fork or shovel to dig up the entire clump, then shake off the soil. Use a spade to slice the clump into smaller sections, then plant the divisions wherever you want.

You can plant them almost anywhere, even in partial shade. They can be planted in moist areas around ponds and streams; however, they don't do well in areas that hold water after every rain because they don't like soggy roots.

Daylilies don't have rhizomes or tubers but a strong bulbous root system. The narrow green foliage, arching and upright, is attractive before bloom and the perfect disguise for fading spring bulbs. You can get started with daylilies by ordering them from a mail-order nursery like Olallie or bum a bunch from friends with overcrowding clumps in need of thinning.

If you decide to buy daylilies, look for plants with two or three fans (clusters of foliage), and if plants are already blooming, choose ones with lots of flower buds. Finally, check out the condition of the roots. The bigger and heavier the roots, the faster the plant will take off.

Keep Coming Back, It Works

One classic woodchuck story tells how Joe throws some orange daylilies over the bank near the stream. When the spring freshet comes, the daylilies float downstream to Sally's place where they grow with abandon. Eventually Sally and Joe meet and a relationship begins.

Chris Darrow knows quite well how daylilies thrive at Olallie farm. They just keep coming back. Try throwing some over the bank to see what happens or just plant some in your garden or around your home.

Queens For a Day

Daylilies last forever as compared with the shorter life span of many perennials. They adapt to almost all plant hardiness zones, with the flowers ranging in size from miniature 3-inch-diameter blooms to 8 inches. These versatile sun-lovers are easy to grow and bloom for up to six weeks, depending on sunlight and the variety. In fact, they are called daylilies because each flower only blooms for a day. That's why woodchuck gardeners say daylilies are "queens for a day." It's best to leave them alone when it comes to picking the flowers; if you cut the stems for the flowers, you lose most of the blooms. One clump of daylilies has on average ten buds per stem, which can therefore produce many blooms from one plant. So when you cut the stems, you won't "get no more blooms for your honey"—or kitchen table.

For information on Olallie Farm, books on daylilies, and a list of early, mid-season, and late bloomers, *see Summer Appendix Guide 11-12*. There is also information on their origins, varieties, colors, heights, and time of blooms.

PELARGONIUM

My other favorite woodchuck plant is the geranium. It's been said hardy geraniums are known and loved by more people than any other flowering plant in the world, though rose lovers would challenge this assumption. I have also heard geraniums are harder to disturb than any other plant. Whatever your passion or fancy, geraniums, known in botanical circles as pelargonium, are a most popular and hardy plant.

The Trek West

They were introduced to England in the early 1600s from southern Africa. Almost two centuries later, the famous American botanist, John Bartram, received some pelargonium seeds from a colleague overseas. He planted them, and they became a favorite in the colonies, always associated with home and hospitality. When the settlers headed across the country, geraniums went with them. In fact, they were one of the few plants that survived the difficult trek out West.

One of the things you hear about settlers in this country and the British Isles is that geraniums were the plants every woman had on her windowsill and in window boxes. One reason is they are so hardy. You can take them out of their pots, hang them from the beams in a damp cool cellar, let them get a little dried out, and they will not die. I have taken geraniums that looked like Godzilla had beaten them, cut them back, repotted the withered plant in a light potting mix with lots of vermiculite and a little compost, watered heavily, sung sweet spring songs, and Voilà! they have grown back into nice bushy plants.

NO PRIDE AND TAKING IT HOME TO ROOT

My good woodchuck friend and gardener Deborah Stuart of Wentworth, New Hampshire, also loves geraniums. She is disturbed because the number of varieties of geraniums is diminishing. Deborah told me, "If I see a geranium I like in someone's house, I have no pride. I will just ask politely for a cutting and stick it in a plastic bag with a tad of water and bring it on home to root. I first slice it below a node at an angle, dip it in a little rooting compound, and stick the cutting in some germinating mix, and it invariably takes root." Deborah has a friend—whose name she won't mention—who, if she sees a lovely large bushy geranium plant and there is no one around, will break off a small cutting and "take it on home to root." She does the same with roses because they are also easy to root.

You can also take a cutting from a geranium plant and place it in just water and it will root, though placing it in potting soil works best. An ideal time to take a cutting is at the beginning of the growing season when the plant will quickly put on new growth. Most home gardeners buy geraniums as budding or flowering pot-grown plants ready for the garden. But they can also be grown from cuttings or seeds.

COLORS AND PROPAGATION

There are some beautiful colors of geraniums: whites, pinks, reds, and purples. My favorite is a purple-red I found at a flower shop in Richmond, Vermont. Once you learn you can root plants from cuttings, you are more willing to pay $4 to $5 for a special-looking geranium plant because you know you can take cuttings, propagate them, and give the young plants to friends. Your original geranium stays with you a long time.

Deborah Stuart and her sister each bought a slightly expensive geranium at Logees in Danielson, Connecticut, which is the granddaddy of the unusual plant world. The nursery has been around for over a hundred years. Deborah says, "If you ever want to have fun, go to Logees. You will want everything they sell, and some of the plants are in little $3 to $5 dollar size pots. They also have larger pots so you can see how they look when they grow up. They had the most amazing range of geraniums, and I got one where each floret looked like a tiny closed rose bud in a lovely deep red."

Make sure to bring in your potted geraniums come fall. They will do fine sitting next to a south-facing window. *See Summer Appendix Guide 13 for some geranium favorites.*

During the winter months, Deborah places most of her geraniums in a back room that is cool and full of light but not in direct sun. Come spring, they bloom like crazy. She waters them every couple of weeks; however, they don't like to be soaking wet. If they dry out, they will form brown leaves, but you can just prune them back, pour in some water, and soon they put out new leaves. After the flowers begin to wither, just pinch the tips throughout the growing season; snip them off and in that way the flower buds will open sooner rather than later.

EYE CATCHERS

No matter where you go, there are pelargonium lovers. Some gardeners use geraniums in their yards for borders. Most just simply love them for their vivid colors, long-lasting blossoms, and green-lobed leaves. Others are attracted because they thrive in window boxes. Many species have distinct leaf shapes and markings. Some leaves are scented, such as lemon and peppermint, and are used in potpourri, perfumes, and flavor jellies. Left as they are, we can take in their wonderful perfumes during the long winter months in northern New England.

In California, geraniums grow up to five feet tall, resembling shrubs, and can grow outdoors year-round with little attention. Geraniums are like the old dependable VW Bugs that never seemed to die unless you went on a long trip. They don't form close relationships with the fuchsias, the cadillacs of the gardening world. They are true woodchuck plants. Try out a couple of pelargoniums. You'll never be the same.

The best flower garden and design magazine I know of is called, *Fine Gardening*. The Taunton Press Inc., PO Box 5506, Newtown, CT 06470 (203) 426-8171. *www.finegardening.com. See Winter Appendix Guide 15 for a complete list of garden magazines.*

CHAPTER 14

THEME GARDENS

In times past, most people were happy just to have a garden. The wealthy experimented with specialty theme gardens, but today in our age of choice, that's all changed. Who knows what type of garden will show up in your yard: a moon, hummingbird, butterfly, Victorian, Zen or could it be a winter garden?

According to the Bible, there was a garden when it all began, but we fell from paradise by eating the apple in the Garden of Eden.

Robert King stakes his tomatoes with political posters.

Perhaps we've all been trying to make up for lost time ever since. Let's roam the countryside to see what turns up. And give a prize to the winner in The Theme Garden Contest.

ROBERT KING'S GARDEN

There is a season in every state when the political candidates litter the pristine countryside with their signs and placards. If their unwillingness to clean up after themselves bothers you as it does me, here's a recycling solution from my gardening friend Robert King of Putney, Vermont: He salvages the political posters and stakes of the various candidates. He has found, for example, that in New Hampshire during the presidential primaries, former candidate Bob Dole had the strongest stakes for his tomato plants, due to his roots in an agricultural state. Steve Forbes of flat-tax fame had the weakest.

Robert not only collects stakes for his tomato plants, he also has a theme garden called, "The Saints Garden Gone to Rest." There you can find scattered remnants of Saint Fiacre, the patron saint of gardening; Saint Joseph; The Holy Mother; and Saint Frances. Buddhas cast in concrete are interspersed with crows, some beakless and others without tails; angels with wings amiss; lions; turtles; and frogs.

THE JUNKYARD GARDEN

If you were to wander through the hinterlands, you might also observe some other unique theme gardens. One day while traveling to New Hampshire, I met a gentleman who grew squash and pumpkins in the seats of old rusty cars in his junkyard garden. The profusion of vines spewed forth through the open windows out onto the junkyard floor. The advantage of this theme garden was you could buy pumpkins, radiators, and tires all at one location, one-stop shopping at its finest.

THE NO RULES GARDEN

The next contestants in the theme garden contest don't follow any rules. They do exactly as they wish and don't worry about the right look or whether the tall plants go in the back with shorter varieties in front. They don't fret about which plants need shade or sun or their Latin names. And they don't care if others see their gardens even though the weeds sometimes outgrow the flowers.

Which garden do you think deserves to win the theme garden contest? I think all of them reflect the character of their creators, but I'm not the judge. In the final count, everyone wins. Contestants receive a pink plastic flamingo to decorate their garden. The moral is that whatever type, shape, or size garden you have, yours is special and unique. Diversity is a buzz word these days and for good reason; differences bring richness and depth to most everything— including gardening.

THE WOODCHUCK GARDEN

Oops, I almost forgot to tell you about an honest-to-God, woodchuck garden. If you go out in the country to an old Vermont homestead, there's a traditional rectangular garden with long rows of peas, potatoes, tomatoes, squash, corn, and beans, and definitely a rhubarb and asparagus patch. The local farmer dumped heaps of old cow and horse manure on the quarter-acre plot. Flowers like petunias and pansies flourish in garden beds next to the house. Lilac bushes abound, as do sweet-smelling white peonies, tawny orange daylilies and geraniums that sit in pots on the front porch.

P.S.: Woodchuck gardeners get quite a chuckle at the Yuppie garden catalogs chocked full of expensive bird baths, teak benches, and politically correct daylilies. Where are those practical items and tools that don't cost an arm and leg, like a well-made hoe? People spend far too much on having the right paraphernalia. Today, the correct look is in. Perhaps the old woodchuck saying, "Give us this day our daily illusion," is apropos.

MERRYSPRING

If you want to experience the best in theme gardens, take a summer trip along the beautiful coast of Maine to Merryspring Park just south of Camden. I visited Katherine Does at Merryspring in the summer of 1997. Her herb beds, designed about 15 years ago, are shaped like two fish chasing each other's tails in the archetypal symbol of Pisces. The gardens include the Dyeing, Culinary, Gray and Silver, Fragrant, Medicinal, Decorative, Bee, Flowering, Medieval, Children's, and Shakespeare beds. It's hard to see the shape of the fish unless you are a hummingbird hovering over the flowers and nectar below.

Each bed has a theme. For example, the Dyeing Bed includes monkshood, the yellow tansy, and the elecampane, which provides blue dye from its roots. Bloodroot produces a strong orange hue on fabric. The medicinal garden is especially interesting with the renewed interest in herbal remedies such as St.-John'-wort for nerves and depression. The medieval garden has many plants once used for religious and spiritual purposes. In those days, people lived closer to nature and the spirit world. They had deeper connections to the plant kingdom with such plants as the alliums (onions) and narcissus, which they believed were directly connected to the constellations. Plants were used as food, medicine, and as links to the spiritual world. Some might consider such practices akin to magic; others would find this work healing and meaningful. More and more people are rediscovering the potent life force and healing energies of the plant kingdom.

Merryspring Horticulture Nature Park

P.O. Box 893, Camden, Maine 04843 (207) 236-2239.

Merryspring is a 66-acre park started in 1973 by Camden's noted horticulturist Mary Ellen Ross. It became a place of cultivated gardens and a preserve for Maine's native flowers, shrubs, and trees. As the park grew, specific gardens of hardy ornamental plants, not necessarily native, were established.

If you want to read a well-illustrated, comprehensive book on theme gardens, I recommend *Theme Gardens* by Barbara Damrosch, Workman Publishing, 1982.

SUMMER FADES

Soon the bright petals of the blossoms fade and fall to the earth, replaced by fruits and seeds. Corn turns from green to shades of yellow and brown. The leaves of the trees also change from the muted green of late summer to touches of red, a sign of early autumn to come. Recall how in spring they were adorned in all the endless shades of greens and yellows? Nature is always going through a metamorphosis—just like us.

Before summer ends and fall officially christens us with her frosts, please keep watering in the dog days of August, the driest time of the summer season. This can make all the difference in extending the growing season into late September and October.

Remember, I planted a second crop of cucumbers and summer squash in mid-July and covered them with mulch. In August, I watered heavily under the mulch and by the end of the month had fresh cucumbers for pickling and more summer squash for freezing. I also grew a late crop of lettuce, beets, carrots, turnips, broccoli, and Chinese greens. They all needed watering in August and September, unless there was adequate rainfall.

When the cool fall days arrive, I cover the cucumber and squash plants with row covers to extend the growing season a couple of weeks. Eventually, summer ends not with whimper but with a snap of frost. Then comes Indian Summer with its lovely warm days and cold nights. If your tender plants survive the first hard frosts, they last longer into the autumn. The hardier plants can be harvested as late as mid-November. On to autumn.

CHAPTER 15

SUMMER APPENDIX GUIDE

Summer Appendix Guide Number One

PLANT HARDINESS ZONE INFORMATION

New Vermont Hardiness Map, Publication # OH 43
CTR/Publications, Agricultural Engineering Bldg.
University of Vermont, Burlington, Vermont 05405

This is the nationwide standard USDA Plant Hardiness Zone Map. The 11 distinct Zones in the United States are based on their extreme low winter temperatures:

USDA Plant Hardiness Zone Map of the U.S.
Send $6.50 to: Superintendent of Documents
P.O. Box 371954, Pittsburgh, PA 15250

Summer Appendix Guide Number Two

SWEET AND SOUR CHERRIES AND PEACHES

Gardeners need to be careful when reading seed catalogs that denote plant hardiness zones. Some catalogs will state that sweet cherries can be grown in Vermont in Zone 5, which in most cases is not true. There are a couple of exceptions. Nick Cowles of Shelburne Orchards (Zone 5) near Lake Champlain does grow sweet cherry trees, but he doesn't sell the fruits commercially because they don't produce large amounts of fruit. The warmth of the nearby lake warms the orchard. The home gardener can grow sweet cherries in Zone 5 if they are protected from the wind and have plenty of sun.

Sour cherries can be grown in Zone 5. I worked at a sour cherry orchard in Putney, Vermont, in the early 1970s. Check with other home gardeners to find out how they have done with sweet and sour cherries. You may have a to place netting over the cherries if the birds start to eat them.

Miller Orchards in Dummerston, Vermont, is located on the hills above the Connecticut River Valley. They grow organic apples and peaches. The peach trees produce fruit about every other year depending on the weather. The peach orchard (Zone 5) has a southern exposure and is protected from the wind. Most gardeners cannot grow peaches in Vermont, but if you have the right varieties and your plant hardiness zone is agreeable along with other good conditions like soil type, plenty of sunlight, protection from the wind, and southern slope, you might do okay. The question of whether it's worth it is up to you.

Gardeners need to know that Plant Hardiness Zone Maps are very generalized. In many cases they only act as an indicator of what you can and cannot grow in your locality. For example, when you look up the Champlain Valley where I live, most Plant Hardiness Zone Maps show Zone 4, when in fact many parts of the valley are in Zone 5. One of the woodchuck principles is, "It depends."

Summer Appendix Guide Number Three

SILENT SPRING REVISITED

Do you remember Rachel Carson's monumental work of 26 years ago? It was called *Silent Spring* and described how large numbers of birds including ospreys, American eagles, peregrine falcons, and bluebirds were dying at alarming rates. This was the result of the pesticide DDT, which caused the eggshells to become so thin they cracked under their mother's weight. *Silent Spring* needs to be revisited as human deaths directly attributable to pesticides number 250,000/ year worldwide by conservative estimates and poisonings exceed 3 million.

Pesticide use in the U.S. has increased and chemicals less well known than the infamous DDT have been linked to cancer. For example, widespread controversy surrounds the herbicide atrazine and its connection to cancer. Atrazine is a weed killer sprayed on corn fields harvested to feed dairy cows. We simply don't know what atrazine and other chemical pesticides are doing to our soils, waters, other creatures, and ourselves.

Other pesticides are not allowed in this country because of their dangerous effects—even though they are manufactured in the U.S. and then exported to Latin America. These chemicals are sprayed on flowers, fruits, and vegetables—which are then imported to the U.S. and end up on your kitchen table.

Did you know that 80% of the flowers you buy in the winter from florists come from Latin America? How many of these are sprayed with harmful chemicals? The national news media came out with shocking information in the winter of 1999 telling parents to be careful about feeding children too many fruits and vegetables grown with pesticides. Their message was clear: Peel certain fruits and vegetables. Buy canned fruits that have no skin on them. Buy organic.

I'm not in favor of sending garden pests back to the stone age with poisons like malathion, lindane, captan, or sevin. I've been using biological controls for over 30 years as an organic farmer and gardener, and for the most part have not had any major pest or fungus problems. There was one occasion when I was going to lose a field of potatoes and I decided to spray the insecticide sevin on the plants to control the potato bugs and larvae. In that case, I didn't sell the potatoes as organic. The potato crop was not located in the same vicinity as the other vegetable crops. I could not afford to lose the potato crop. We don't live in a perfect world. C'est vrai, bien sur.

Summer Appendix Guide Number Four

INTEGRATED PEST MANAGEMENT (IPM)

The newest commercial system for controlling pests is known as Integrated Pest Management (IPM), where pest populations are monitored. Chemicals are applied only when necessary to prevent serious damage to the crop. With IPM, more attention is paid to factors like soil fertility, cropping systems, and weather. IPM is used in many apple orchards in Vermont.

The first step in IPM is to identify the insect pests and figure out how to control them, but only if the population goes beyond a tolerable level. If this happens, mechanical and nontoxic methods of control are used. Chemical pesticides are then targeted to the specific pest if the crop will be lost, and even then pests are monitored as well as the amount of chemicals used. IPM stands somewhere between conventional and organic gardening and farming.

Summer Appendix Guide Number Five

THE GOOD, BAD, AND THE BUGGY: ORGANIC SUPPLIERS

- *Peaceful Valley Farm Supply*, P.O. Box 2209, Grass Valley, California 95945 (888) 784-1722 *www.groworganic.com*. Peaceful Valley Farm Supply catalog carries lots of information on natural pest management including:
  Pest monitoring tools, beneficial insects
  Pheromone traps and lures, sticky traps
  Biological insecticides, fungicides, and nematicides
  Botanical insecticides: pyrethrum, rotenone
  Soaps and mineral-based insecticides
  Oil products for pest management, fungicides
  Animal barriers, repellants, and traps

  Peaceful Valley also carries growing and propagating supplies, watering and irrigation supplies, season extenders, natural weed controls, open-pollinated organic seeds, tools, and equipment.

- *Fedco*, P.O. Box 520, Waterville, ME 04903; (207) 873-7333 *www.fedcoseeds.com*. A good selection of organic controls and supplies.

- *Garden's Alive,* 5100 Schenley Place, Lawrenceburg, IN 47025; (812) 537-8650. *www.gardensalive.com*. The Gardens Alive catalog has an extensive list of organic controls as well as a section called *A Guide to Common Insect Pests and How To Treat Them Organically.*

- *Gardener's Supply Company*, 128 Intervale Avenue, Burlington, Vermont; (800) 863-1700 *www.gardeners.com*. Gardener's Supply carries some information in its catalog on natural pest controls along with earth-friendly products. Reading and studying these catalogs will provide you with a fuller understanding of biological controls and the life cycles of insects. And it's a good winter activity.

Summer Appendix Guide Number Six

TRIED AND TRUE WOODCHUCK TIPS FOR INSECT CONTROL

SQUASH: If you see your summer squash dying, check around the base of the stem of the plant for squash borers. Take a knife and dig them out of the flesh and push the soil back around the plant.

TOMATOES: Large green-yellow tomato horn worms can be picked off by hand.

BEETS AND SPINACH: If the leaves of these greens are being damaged by leaf miner, simply pick them off or use floating row covers early in the season to discourage leaf miners.

CARROTS: These root crops love coffee grounds. Sprinkle over plantings to discourage root maggot.

POTATO FAMILY: Dust dry wheat bran on eggplants, potatoes, and tomatoes, all members of the nightshade family. Apply the bran early in the morning. The potato beetles will eat the bran, drink dew to quench their thirst, and as the bran expands from the water, they burst. Bran and cornmeal sprinkled around the plants also help control cutworms.

Ron's Down-home Nontoxic Insect Sprays:

Mix 1 tablespoon biodegradable liquid soap like Dr. Bronner's with 1 tablespoon vegetable oil and 1 quart water. This down-home recipe controls aphids, red spider mites, and mealy bugs. Add cayenne pepper and stale beer to the mix. Or add cayenne and garlic powder to old flour and spread on your plants. Or use the woodchuck method of blasting insects off foliage with a strong jet of water from a hose. It works for a bit and then the insects return.

Summer Appendix Guide Number Seven

BIOLOGICAL CONTROLS IN THE GREENHOUSE: SUNGARDENS

When Norma Maege started Sungardens in 1997, she was philosophically committed to using biological controls in the greenhouse. This differs from most operations, which use pesticides and fungicides as well as growth regulators.

Norma said, "I wanted to minimize health risks in the greenhouse to workers and customers. My goal was to use the new greenhouse to prove you can control pest populations without using harmful chemicals." The most serious greenhouse pests are white fly, aphids, and gnats as well as fungus problems such as powdery mildew. Norma Maege has introduced a number of natural predators, such as parasitic wasps that lay their eggs in the white fly larvae, wasps that eat aphids, and mites that eat gnat larvae.

These predators have helped a great deal in controlling the pest populations in the greenhouse; however, the white fly continues to be a problem. The predatory wasps are not active enough at the cooler temperatures, and it's hard to maintain an effective population. Nontoxic chemicals are needed to supplement the natural predators; one of these is neem oil, which helps eliminate the larval stages of gnats and the white fly.

Powdery mildew can be avoided by keeping the greenhouse clean of debris by removing all the unhealthy plants. Provide good air circulation and remove any water puddles. You can also use sulfur powder or copper compounds to help control fungal problems.

Norma has learned that how to control fungus and bugs using organic methods, providing appropriate lighting and utilizing good watering techniques. You don't want to over or under water because this stresses the plants.

Summer Appendix Guide Number Eight

BIODYNAMICS

Biodynamic gardening and farming is referred to throughout the book. Biodynamics (BD) began in Koberwitz, Germany, in 1924 with a series of lectures by Rudolf Steiner. Biodynamics is the oldest alternative agricultural movement in the world. It began in the U.S. in 1938 and was centered in Kimberton, Pennsylvania, and Spring Valley and Chester, New York. You can receive biodynamic literature, the biodynamic preparations, the bimonthly biodynamic magazine as well as a list of annual pamphlets and books through the Biodynamic Association. Two of E.E. Pfeiffer's books, *The Pfeiffer Garden Book* and *Weeds and What They Tell,* are included in the list.

The Biodynamic Farming and Gardening Association

25844 Butler Road
Junction City, OR 97488
(541) 998-0105

The ***Biodynamic Resource Guide*** covers most of this information. Call toll free (888) 516-7797 for a copy. Also included are The Kimberton Hills Biodynamic Agricultural Calendar, 1999, called Stella Natura. It provides practical advice for gardeners and farmers working with plants and cosmic rhythms. This is a 40-page booklet that folds out into a 12" x 18" wall calendar giving daily and monthly charts that explain what and when to plant according to the planetary rhythms.

Biodynamic/Organic Agricultural Training Course

FOUR YEARS: First two years focus on the practical care of animals and plants. The next phase includes farm internships and the study and practice of farm management, economics, and marketing.

Write to: Emerson College, Forest Row, Sussex, England RH185JX *www.emerson.org.uk;* e-mail: *mail@emerson.org.uk*

MORE BIODYNAMIC SOURCES

For biodynamic herbal/animal preparations, write to:

The Josephine Porter Institute, Box 620
Woolwine, VA 24185
(540) 930-2463

Biodynamic Seed Exchange and Sowing Circle
Amy Bohn
433 Williams Creek Road
Oakville, WA 98568.
(260) 273-8702
e-mail: *amybohn@olywa.net*

Biodynamic practical training programs, workshops, and seminars for gardeners, teachers, and students:

The Pfeiffer Center
260 Hungry Hollow Rd.
Chestnut Hill, NY 10977

(845) 352-5071 Ext.20.
E-mail: *info@pfeiffercenter.org*

Summer Appendix Guide Number Nine

CUT FLOWERS

The Flower Farmer: An Organic Grower's Guide to Raising and Selling Cut Flowers, is a good resource book for gardeners and small farmers. Chelsea Green Publishers, Post Mills, Vermont, 05058, (802) 295-6444.

The Flower Farmer is a comprehensive guide to growing and marketing cut flowers, giving specific instructions on the best time to harvest each flower, along with marketing suggestions. For example, one of the tricks to growing sunflowers organically is to cut them before insects have a chance to destroy their beauty. By cutting them when the petals have just opened and placing them in a bucket of water, the blooms remain vibrant.

Summer Appendix Guide Number Ten

OLALLIE FARM

For more information, write or call Chris Darrow, Olallie Farm, Box 1, HCR 63, South Newfane, VT 05351; (802) 348-6614.

Summer Appendix Guide Number Eleven

BOOKS

Daylilies, The Perfect Perennial by Lewis and Nancy Hill, an easy-to-use guide on daylilies by two Vermont farmers and authors. Storey Communications Inc. 1991.

Arlow Stout's classic daylily book of the 1930s is now in print for a second time. It's called *The Wild Species and Garden Clones, Both Old and New.*

American Hemerocallis Society
1454 Rebel Drive
Jackson, Mississippi 39211-6334
(601) 366-4362 web site: *www.daylilies.org/daylilies.html*

Summer Appendix Guide Number Twelve

DAYLILY ORIGINS, VARIETIES, AND COLORS

The original species of daylilies came from China, Korea, Japan, and the Amur region of Russia. Two species, the Vermont Orange Ditch Lily and the rarer fragrant Lemon Daylily, were probably introduced into the Americas over 200 years ago. Beginning around the turn of the last century, gardeners began crossing the various species. Arlow Stout was the first person in the U.S. to hybridize daylilies on a large scale. Considered by many to be the father of the American daylily, he published the first book on them in the 1930s. In the 1950s, the daylily society started, and in the past 40 years this plant of the Orient has taken off. You see them everywhere.

Daylilies come in fewer colors but more flavors than Ben and Jerry's ice cream. There are over 30,000 varieties of daylilies derived from 13-15 wild species.

Color, Height, and Time of Bloom

It's easy to breed daylilies because of the high success rate of pollination. Just remove pollen from the anther and daub some on the end of the pistil, found in the middle of the six anthers.

Various cultivars bloom from spring to autumn. By crossing the different species, a large range of colors have been produced: near white shades (no pure whites), some dull purples, pinks, orange, peach, yellow, and reds. There is also much genetic variation, like size, height of bloom, and time of bloom. Daylilies range in height anywhere from a foot to a lofty 6 feet.

Daylily Types

Daylilies don't go tropical or live at the North Pole, but they do grow everywhere else including parts of the Caribbean. There are three types: dormant, evergreen, and semi-evergreen. Dormant foliage dies in the winter in the north country while in the south, daylilies with "evergreen" foliage remain green and growing.

The dormant ones require a cold period during winter; evergreen varieties don't need that period of cold and will stay green all year in the south. Semi-evergreens seem to grow well everywhere, yet evergreen varieties generally do not survive northern winters. The largest area for breeding is in the southern states. Georgia has its own daylily zone while Vermont, New Hampshire, and Maine together compose one zone.

Summer Appendix Guide Number Thirteen

GERANIUM FAVORITES

THE MARTHA WASHINGTONS: also called fancy, show, royal, or pansy geraniums. These bloom in loose round clusters, and each flower can be 3 inches wide.

IVY GERANIUM: has a unique blossom. The star-like flowers bloom in small clusters on long glossy-leaved stalks. Best suited for hanging baskets or window boxes because of its trailing stems.

COMMON GERANIUM: also known as zonal, horseshoe, or fish geranium. Boasts long-lasting flowers and continuous blooms. Older varieties used to get tall and straggly, but new varieties stay compact and shorter.

AUTUMN

Alison Flint with pumpkin at Starr Farm Community Garden.
Photo by Jim Flint.

AN AUTUMN THOUGHT

From late August through September, the dry dog days of summer wane and the cool fall rains begin. For one brief period, there is a stirring here about as the grass gets greener and my dog's energy picks up along with mine. Some spiritual gardeners contend it's because meteoric iron descends from the heavens to bring strength and courage for the coming winter months. In truth, fine traces of metals do shower down from the cosmos in greater numbers in the fall.

Each season reflects what's happening in nature; we are not immune to these changes. From late spring through early summer to late fall, the plant kingdom springs forth, then wilts and withdraws from the perceptible world. New formative forces arise within the seed as it prepares for winter. Autumn is a time of great activity, both above and below the earth. The gnomes are working overtime pushing the carrots up through the earth, and we are digging the orange roots—and checking out the pantry, freezer, and root cellar to see how much food we have put by for the long winter months.

PART THREE: AUTUMN

The haze on the horizon
the infinite tender sky
the bright red glint on the cornfield
And the wild geese flying by.

All over upland and lowland
the chain of the Golden Rod
Some people call it Autumn
some people call it God.

Author UnKnown

PART THREE
AUTUMN

CHAPTER 16

PUTTING THE GARDEN BY

Gardening isn't just putting seeds in the earth, weeding, watering, and weeding some more. Sure, it's great to have a large bowl of summer greens, tomatoes, and cucumbers, or some fresh sweet corn on the cob, but what about the rest of the year? I have never quite figured out why some gardeners give up along the garden path. After all, why prepare the soil, plant the seeds, weed, mulch, and weed some more, if you don't use it to the fullest? Sure it takes a lot of hard work and then some to grow food, and quite a bit of skill to take the bounty of the harvest and transform it into a hot bowl of homemade soup on a snowy winter's night, but the rewards are worth it. Selecting your home-grown carrots and potatoes, adding them to the homemade canning jars full of tomatoes, cooking it slowly over the stove, and finally sipping the hot soup warms both limbs and soul.

When I think about putting the garden by, I remember Guy Kelsey from Putney, Vermont, who used to say, "Let's count crops on September 15th and see what you have on your canning shelves and in your root cellar. That's more important than having the first tomato in mid-July, which doesn't have much taste anyway." Guy had an ample store of wise farm and garden pronouncements. He farmed and gardened for 50 years and knew how well plants grew when the soil warmed up in early summer. Guy would plant seeds and young plants after Memorial Day and sure enough, they always caught up. By September 15th, he and Gula, his wife, had as many tomatoes, potatoes, and winter squash as any gardener who planted early in the season. Guy used to travel to the grocery store in Brattleboro where he bought canned mackerel because that was the one thing he couldn't grow or raise. When he saw all that stuff he grew at Faraway Farm in his freezer, on his canning shelves, and in the root cellar, he would say how rich he was.

RON'S KITCHEN

Late August through September is one of my busiest times of the year. That's when the canner steams up the kitchen, and the bounty of the harvest is prepared for storage in the freezer and pantry. Actually, I start putting the garden by much earlier. In June and July, I freeze spinach and peas, and can the first beans with fresh dill and vinegar. In late August and early September, I freeze corn, can tomatoes, pull up onions, dig potatoes, and harvest winter squash. I dig carrots, beets, and turnips in my community garden plot in October.

BONZO PUNCH

And then there are the herbs I dry for teas. What could be better than a hot cup of my famous herb tea mix and a homemade blueberry muffin on a cold winter's morn. The tea is called Bonzo Punch, named after my Polish setter of 18 years. Let me tell you about its ingredients and then move on to jams and muffins and Canning with Kim on the next page.

Do you remember the days when someone would ask for a cup of tea and you would place a bag of Lipton in a cup of boiled water. Life was real simple then. Now it's a task just to list all the herbal teas like Red Zinger, Lemon Mist, or Almond Sunset. I follow one of the woodchuck principles of keeping it simple by offering friends my own brew of mint, lemon balm, wild berry leaves, comfrey, and a touch of sage.

During summer and early fall I collect herbs, then string and dry them on the beams in my home. Sometimes the mix changes, like in 1999 when I added St.-John's-Wort, which I find grows in poor sandy soils along roadways, abandoned industrial sites, and fields.

Only now it's been overpicked, and some people pull up the whole plant rather than snipping off the top leaves and flowers. Tip: During cool fall mornings, make a thermos full of herb, black, or green tea. It will last all day and keep the chill off.

Woodchuck Jams

I love to make strawberry and raspberry jam. First I cook the fruit down on the stove in a little water and honey. Then I bake it for a while to take out the moisture, then cool the jam and freeze it in small yogurt containers. It's easy. When I want some jam, I thaw the frozen containers and spread the jam on toast. I also freeze blueberries for blueberry muffins. I almost forgot rhubarb, the first fruit of the gardening season. Remember, rhubarb gets too tough to pick after the summer solstice on June 21st, which is also close to St. John's day on June 24th. That's when the days begin to shorten.

Canning With Kim

When I have a question about canning, I call my good friend Kim Potter who started canning and freezing when she had her first garden in 1972. Kim has taught food preparation and health for 13 years at middle schools and high schools. Her canning bible is the *Ball Blue Book* of 1972, which tells everything you need to know about canning and freezing. It sold for 50 cents at the time.

Kim learned many secrets to cooking from local Vermont farm wives who were more than willing to share their years of wisdom. For example, vegetables that grow below the ground like carrots and beets need to be placed in cold water and then brought to a boil. For all the other vegetables, it's best to first bring the water to a boil and then place them in the pot. This method holds true regardless of whether the next step is canning, freezing, or preparing a meal.

I hope you have a good fall canning and freezing vegetables and making relish and pickles. It won't be long before the frosts begin to harden the ground and I'll be canning applesauce. That's when I know autumn has arrived for sure.

Autumn Appendix Guide 1 has more of Kim Potter's Tips on Canning. See Autumn Appendix Guide 2 for McKenzie's Bread and Butter Pickles.

HOW ABOUT THEM APPLES

If I had to choose one fruit to take along in my spaceship to Mars, I would pick the apple. It's hard to fathom the autumn season without apples or the delicious desserts from the world's most popular fruit. After all, they don't leave a slippery peel behind like bananas, and unlike oranges, they don't make your fingers sticky. You can't get fat eating apples and just look at all the varied and tasty foods apples provide like cider and sauce, pies and cakes. And what could be better than the sweet, tart taste of an early Mac (MacIntosh) taken right from a tree in late September? Anyone for applesauce, applesauce cake, apple pies, apple crisp, apple butter, or dried apples?

See Autumn Appendix Guide 3-6 for a list of the various types of apples you can use for different desserts, recipes for Apple Crisp, Apple Cake, Mary's Apple Butter and Dried Apples. The History of Apples is in Appendix Guide 7. Also see Chapter 19: How About Some Apple Cider?

RON'S TRADITIONAL APPLESAUCE

One of my favorite excursions on a crisp autumn day is to locate an old abandoned apple orchard with wild apples or travel to an orchard where you can pick up the less expensive drops. Back at home, I wash and quarter the fruit and put them in a large pot adding just a bit of water. After cooking them down, I use my potato masher to mash the soft apples into what else but—of course—a mash. I then run the mash through my hand-cranked Foley food mill that I've had for twenty years.

I don't add any of that yuppie stuff like bananas, onions, or peppers, but I do sweeten the sauce with maple syrup and sometimes add a little lemon juice to give it a zing, or cinnamon for a touch of spice. Just like most woodchuck applesauce makers, I believe it is best canned rather than frozen even though I have been cheating the last couple of years and simply freezing it. Applesauce is great with cereal for breakfast, or with yogurt or ice cream for dessert. By the way, applesauce goes great with homemade potato pancakes or latkes. It cuts the grease and adds tartness.

APPLE PIE: One of the tricks is to add freshly grated orange peel. I learned this from my good friend Antonia Messuri of Burlington, Vermont who found it in the *Moosewood Book of Desserts*. Helen Pyke of Bakersfield, Vermont, told me that if you use 1/2 cup of lard to 2 cups of flour, you will make a mighty good crust. Just chop it in with a pastry blender and roll out the dough between waxed paper. When using whole wheat flour, use less lard.

Well folks, you're probably wondering if we're ever going to get out of the kitchen and into the garden. There's so much to do besides putting the garden by. It's time to get on with the fall gardening tasks.

CHAPTER 17

WOODCHUCK AUTUMN CHORES

In the north, autumn's work never seems to end until you're done and then there is more to do. I often hear woodchuck gardeners commiserate with, "If it's not one thing, it's another." To ease this truth, follow the rhythms of this season; pause and allow the autumnal colors and light to surround you—and then get to work. For some, it's sad putting the garden to rest, but for others it's a blessing. After all, they won't have to weed anymore or moan to the perennial lament, "Oh, my aching back."

Begin by rummaging for some old blankets to cover your favorite flowers before the frosty nights freeze them. The lovely multicolored snapdragons do quite well in autumn, even with a number of frosts. You can collect the best green tomatoes, bring them inside, place in an open box, and cover or wrap the tomatoes with newspapers. Check them every week and collect the ripe ones. Or just use the green ones to make green tomato relish.

Plant some fall bulbs, remembering that mice and squirrels love the taste of tulip bulbs and crocuses more than daffodils. Like most of their relatives in the amaryllis family, daffodils contain a toxin that kills any squirrel dumb enough to keep eating. Other amaryllis relatives like snowdrops and snowflakes do just fine. Their small white flowers may not be as dramatic as crocuses, but planted thickly, even a few square feet make a beautiful statement and the squirrels won't eat them. Bluebells and grape hyacinths, members of the lily family, also deter rodents.

If it's raining, go organize the tool shed and clean, sharpen, and oil your tool heads and handles. If you are a member of a community garden, volunteer for fall work. Once all the work is complete—which it never is-it's an ideal time to plant a green manure crop in your garden.

GREEN MANURES, COVER AND PERENNIAL CROPS

Green manures are plants that provide organic matter to the soil; their fine roots also improve its structure. These crops also shade out weeds and aerate the soil with their long, fine roots. The foliage acts as a canopy and directly blocks the wind and rain from eroding the soil. Finally, green manures interrupt the life cycles of insect pests and discourage plant diseases.

The term green manures refers to annual plants that are turned under within one gardening season. They are also called cover crops. Some examples of summer cover crops are buckwheat and annual rye grass. They germinate quickly and are inexpensive to purchase. Cover crops such as winter rye are planted in the fall to cover the earth and protect it from the elements. Others are planted in the summer. Fall cover crops are tilled into the earth in the spring.

Perennial forage crops are left to grow in the soil for more than one season. They are planted as part of a three- to four-year crop rotation on many farms and large gardens. For example, a market gardener might plant vegetables in a field for three years and then sow in a crop of clover and grass for the same length of time. This system allows the soil to rest and rebuild itself. The longer a crop is in the ground, the greater the mass of roots produced, thus increasing the organic matter in the soil.

Organic Matter Content

Though organic matter makes up generally less than 5% of the soil, it's critical to maintaining soil life. Keeping organic matter at the correct levels helps the soil foster a healthy microbial environment for plant roots, provides it with the ability to hold water like a sponge, conducts oxygen, and releases nutrients to the plants.

Legumes such as clover, vetch, and alfalfa provide short-term benefits to the soil in terms of nitrogen as compared to the grasses (wheat, oats, rye grass, winter rye), which provide more organic matter to the soil because of their extensive root systems. A combination of grasses, legumes, and composted manures are vital to maintaining the organic content in the soil, which in turn is critical for healthy soil.

Animal manures are especially important in feeding the microorganisms in the soil; they provide nutrients for the fine feeder roots of the plants. Planting the same crops for many years in a row like cow corn is harmful to the soil. It's called a monoculture. When people add the use of harmful chemical fertilizers and pesticides, they are creating a recipe for the destruction of the very life of the soil. I am referring here to the microorganisms and fungi that provide the basis for organic matter content. That's why green manures, cover crops, perennial forage crops, and animal manures are so vital to preserving the organic matter: They feed the bacteria and micro-life and help them to thrive.

THE HOME GARDENER

An ideal scenario is to have a garden large enough for the rotation of food crops and perennial cover crops. However, it's difficult to rotate crops in many small home gardens because there just isn't enough room. The best strategy is to use lots of fresh grass clippings or hay mulches along with compost with some animal manure mixed in.

Winter rye is a perennial fall cover crop because it survives the cold months. Two summer annual cover crops are buckwheat and rye grass. They can be sown after a food crop has been harvested. Organic soil amendments such as phosphate rock and greensand (potassium) may be needed as well as lime to maintain the pH in the soil. It's a good idea to have a soil test every five years. Of course, if all your plants are healthy and strong, there is no need. A soil test will measure pH (soil acidity or sweetness), phosphorus, and potassium. More extensive tests measure nitrates and organic matter. These tests can be performed by your local agricultural extension service.

Woods End Lab in Maine can test the quality of your compost along with the quality of your soil: P.O. Box 297, Mt. Vernon, Maine 04352; (207) 293-2488; *info@woodsend.org* .

See Autumn Appendix Guide 11 for more information on green manures and cover crops.

See Chapter 20, Black Gold, for information on manure and composting..

An informative book on green manures, cover crops, forage crops, organic matter, and organic soil amendments is the New Encyclopedia of Organic Gardening, *Rodale Press. See address under books in the Winter Appendix Guide.*

Winter rye is an ideal green manure crop for northern New England because it is hardy and the seed is inexpensive. It's best to plant winter rye in early September, but it can be planted later. Spread the rye seed by hand and rake it in lightly. It grows so well that by late March and early April or later, it will be necessary to dig or till it in. Winter rye does not have a deep root system, so it's easy to turn it over. However, don't wait too long because it grows rapidly in the spring. It takes about two to three weeks to break down in the soil, depending on its growth. Then, it's okay to plant early crops like peas and spinach.

CREATING A NEW
GARDEN BED FROM SOD

In autumn, begin creating new garden beds by turning the sod over with a heavy-duty fork, breaking it up with a spade, and adding compost. It won't decompose completely but will save you time in the spring when nothing is harder than breaking down sod. If the grass and roots don't properly decompose, you will be pulling up sod all spring and summer, so start early. You can also deal with sod by using the Ultimate Woodchuck Sod Recipe as described in the summer chapter, To Mulch or not to Mulch. This method of placing huge amounts of mulch (newspaper, leaves, old hay) on the sod and letting it sit for about two years is simple. It works and where are you going anyway?

PERENNIALS WITH A VERMONT DEADHEAD

I don't know whether Catherine Vost follows the music of The Grateful Dead, but she is a full-fledged Vermont "deadhead" when it comes to fall gardening. Deadheading means cutting off the stalks and tops of plants. This is a good practice because many insects like to burrow down in the stalks and find a warm place to rest from the cold.

According to Catherine, you have choices when it comes to perennials: Simply cover your perennials with a warm blanket of spent leaves, do some weeding and start dividing the perennials, or do some of both. You might ask, "What should I do with those colorful annuals like marigolds and begonias?" For most gardeners, it's just not practical to bring annuals inside, so I suggest you pull them out, throw 'em in the compost pile, or follow the advice prescribed below.

BRINGING THE ANNUALS INDOORS

Much can be rescued from the garden in fall. When other outdoor garden chores are done, there is a small window of opportunity in the North to save seeds and take cuttings for a second harvest. The cuttings will grow slowly over the winter and can be placed out again in the spring. Depending on where you live, it may not be too late to rescue many plants that have not been killed by a hard frost. Annual flowers that are slow to germinate or bring to full bloom in the spring get a head start if cuttings are grown over the winter.

TIPS ON PERENNIALS FROM CATHERINE

If you cut off the tops of plants, you can save the seeds. The plants, like us, prepare for winter. By deadheading, you allow the plant to focus its energy on root production during October and November. It's also a good time to add bonemeal and compost to bulbs and to weak plants that were subject to pests and disease during the growing season.

If you found during the summer that certain areas of your garden stayed wet, you may want to move the perennials to another area because the ground will go through a freezing-thawing phase, and this might kill them.

Most people think of spring as the time to divide perennials, but fall is also a fine time. It has the added benefit of getting more flowers in the summer from fall divisions. For example, dividing daylilies gives them time to develop new roots, leaves, and ultimately flower stalks the next season. September is by far the best month to divide perennials, including peonies. Newly divided perennials need at least four weeks of growing time before the hard frosts arrive.

Peonies are a little different than most perennials. Like Siberian irises, they rarely require dividing, but if you want to move or break a mature plant into several small ones, the work is best done in early fall.

Make sure the plants have died down until they look somewhat ragged before digging and separating them. Use a knife to divide and cut the roots in sections that have at least three prominent buds (eyes).

Don't put down mulches too early over the new perennials; wait until the ground begins to freeze up in November because the mice like to find a home underneath the mulch, and they will eat your plants. Let the mice secure another place to nest for the winter.

Those plants that had serious mildew problems like phlox and bee balm need to be cut back. Take the diseased leaves and stalks and burn them or place them in the compost pile.

Finally, find all your garden notes and record what changes you want to make for next spring. If you're like me, you'll forget a lot of what you learned from the previous season if you don't get it down right away.

MUM'S THE WORD...OR IS IT?

Most gardeners buy mums for decorative purposes in the fall and then discard them. This is in part because chrysanthemums (mums) purchased in stores are not cold hardy. Go to a professional nursery to buy mums. You might be surprised to learn there is a way to keep them over the winter and into next year.

Deborah Stuart, my woodchuck friend from Wentworth, New Hampshire, says, "I have white mums that have been in permanent perennial beds for ten years. I mulch them heavily with pine needles in late fall or use a new method of shredding leaves from a blower-shredder. The whites tend to winter outside most easily. The pinks, purples, and more unusual colors don't do as well, and those are the colors most people love. I winter over these other colors in the cellar."

Deborah goes on to advise, "When you buy mums fully bloomed from a grocery or garden store, they have been forced into bloom in a hot greenhouse environment and are root bound. I have not had much luck wintering these over; however, if you take them down to the basement, clip the tops off and keep them in a dark place with a little dampness in the soil, come spring there will be a million green shoots down in those roots and they will survive.

"Take the whole clump, separate it, and start many mum plants in a nursery plant bed or put them in the borders."

The good news is: Perennial, field-grown mums have a better chance of surviving the winter than the ones grown in a greenhouse. Try them and see. They look a little on the wild side compared to the annual mums you buy at garden centers in the fall. You can also start perennial mums from seed.

FALL GREENS, BELIEVE IT OR NOT

Margaret Daniel, (*see Spring chapter, The Good Witch on the Hill*) continues to collect wild greens well into the fall. As long as there aren't any killer frosts, wild greens survive and thrive in the cool, wet conditions of autumn. The dandelion comes back in the fall as well as mustard greens, plantain, and chickweed. The wild greens sometimes have a bitter quality that can be lessened with cold water and fine chopping. Besides, a little bitter in foods is good for you.

I start lettuce, radish, and spinach seeds in August in the cold frames. These cool-weather plants keep growing if I cover the frame with glass on cold nights. I can extend the season until late October and sometimes till Thanksgiving depending on the weather. In the main garden, long rows of pok choi (Chinese mustard), Chinese cabbage, chard, kale, fall cabbage, cauliflower, brussels sprout, and broccoli last until the end of October and into November.

See Spring Appendix Guide 8 for a description of fall and winter greens.

CHAPTER 18

FALL GARDEN TASKS CONTINUED
SEED SAVING IN NORTHERN CLIMATES

Fall is when seed formation is at its greatest, so if you save open-pollinated seeds, this is the time to act. I know one resourceful woman who collects seeds from the healthiest flowers she can find in a cemetery. The home gardener can save a large number of vegetable, flower, and herb seeds even though the north country is not the ideal region for commercial seed growing; this is because it rains in late August and September, the best seed gathering time of the year. Fungus diseases can thrive. Arid climates are preferable like the drier parts of California.

The home gardener has the advantage of time and flexibility. I have found my home-grown open-pollinated seeds to be hardy and vigorous accompanied by high germination rates. They have adapted to the soil and climatic conditions in my garden. The two best overall guides to seed saving are both published by Chelsea Green Publishers:

Seed to Seed by Suzanne Ashworth. This offers crop-by-crop instruction for the seed saver.

Breed Your Own Vegetable Varieties by Carol Deppe.

A good layman's guide to understanding seed saving and plant genetics. If you want to save heirloom seeds, read *Heirloom Vegetables: A Home Gardener's Guide to Finding and Growing Vegetables From the Past* by Sue Sticklind (Fireside Books). *See Spring Appendix Guide 1 for a complete list of seed books.*

Hybrid seeds should not be saved because you never know what you're going to get. They are the products of the crossing of two genetically different parent plants as compared to open-pollinated seeds, that maintain their original characteristics.

Farmers and gardeners have cross-pollinated seeds for centuries in an attempt to produce sweeter corn with more, larger kernels, tomatoes with greater disease tolerance, and new flower colors with higher bud counts. This has been done using open-pollinated and hybrid methods. Hybridization takes much less time to produce seeds. This is where it has an advantage over open-pollination. Both methods have a place in the world of gardening.

The first seed breeders in the Americas were in South America. These First Nation Tribes bred corn, white and sweet potatoes, peppers, tomatoes, amaranth, sunflowers, and more.

Let me tell you how to save open-pollinated seeds for peas, beans, tomatoes, corn, potatoes, and flowers. This information was supplied by Tom Stearns of High Mowing Organic Seed Farm in Wolcott, Vermont.

PEAS

Pea varieties can be grown next to each other and rarely show any crossing. Make sure all peas grown from seed are trellised because the drying seed can be easily damaged by moisture if the vines lie on the ground. Let the pods grow large until they dry out and become papery. Pick the pods, place them in a dry location, and shell the peas when you have time. Pea seeds store well for three years under cool, dry conditions.

BEANS

Beans, like peas, do not readily cross with one another. Ten feet should be sufficient between varieties. Space the plants more than usual to help with drying. Like peas, the pods should be papery and dry when they are ready to harvest. Beans store well for four years under dry, cool conditions.

TOMATOES

Tomatoes, being mostly self-pollinating, generally don't need to be separated more than a few feet to maintain purity. Pick the tomato when it is as ripe as possible, cut it open, and squeeze the seeds and juice into a jar. Add a little water, mix, then set the jar in a warm place and allow it to ferment for 3 to 6 days. The seeds will separate from the pulp and shed their gelatinous coating. Rinse the seeds and set them out where they will dry quickly. When fully dry, store in a dry, cool place. Tomato seeds remain viable for four to ten years if stored properly.

CORN

It's tricky to save seed corn because it cross-pollinates, so isolation and hand pollination are necessary; one quarter of a mile is recommended between varieties. Grow a population of at least 200 plants or the seed you save will have lost some of its genetic variability. Save seeds by allowing the ears to remain on the stalk until the whole plant is dry. Once harvested, some additional drying is necessary before the ears can be easily shelled. Seed corn can remain viable for five to ten years under cool, dark storage conditions.

FLOWERS

Every flower is different, but many follow a similar pattern of seed growth. The individual flower becomes a cluster of seeds or seedpods. Leave these on the plant until they are dry. It's then best to gather and store them in a dry location, even though some additional drying may be necessary. Flower seeds remain viable for different lengths of time. Consult a seed book for more information.

BIENNIALS

Root vegetables like carrots and beets and members of the cabbage family don't develop seeds until their second year. To grow carrots from seed, store the carrot roots after the first year, then replant them during the second year so the tops are just above the ground. During this second cycle, they will go to seed.

DRAINING THE GENETIC RESERVOIR

During pioneer times, there weren't any garden catalogs to peruse on a cold winter's night. Heirloom seeds were passed on from one generation to the next. All seeds in those days were open-pollinated, heirloom varieties. Today, most are hybrids.

One real concern in our time is the loss of plant diversity and seed varieties. Only in the last hundred years have thousands of plants and seeds become rare. Many are on the verge of extinction. Once they are gone, their special characteristics such as flavor, vigor, and medicinal value will be lost forever. Sure, hybrids are strong producers and look good on the grocery shelf. The cucumbers are straight, but wouldn't it be interesting to present to your table an Early Short Prickly, a West Indian Gherkin, or a Long Green Turkey cuke? Or how about an Early Blood turnip, a Vermont cranberry bean, or a Connecticut field pumpkin?

Heirloom varieties represent choice and diversity in our gardening practices. Some we know from the descriptions in early farmers' journals. The Jewett bean, known as "the fastest bean in New Hampshire" has been lost forever.

Heirloom gardeners who include a rare bean variety in their gardens or care for an ancient apple tree are participating in a worldwide effort to preserve plant resources. Nearly all domesticated plants can be traced to the wild species from which they descended. One example illustrates the importance: A plant explorer in Iran spotted an unusual onion in the market of Kashan. He sent samples to American plant breeders, who discovered that the tight neck of the Kashan onion frustrated the onion thrip, a major pest for onion growers.

Tips for planting and saving seeds including heirloom varieties:

- Never plant all the seeds of a rare variety.
- Dry your seeds in a low moisture environment.
- Try out a couple of new heirloom seeds at a time.
- Store all your seeds in a well-sealed container. Glass works best.
- Label all seeds with dates and other pertinent information.
- Keep the containers in a cool, dark, dry location.

See Winter Appendix Guide 8 for a list of heirloom seed-saving companies. Included is a description of Seed Savers Exchange (SSE), a non-profit organization that saves seeds from extinction. 3076 North Winn Rd. Decorah, IA 52101; (319) 382-5990; www.seedsavers.org. SSE has over 8,000 members and a commercial seed catalog.

FALL VEGETABLES

Onions and Spuds

Lay onions and spuds out in the hot summer sun for 3 to 4 days to dry and cure. Then place in paper bags, bushel baskets, or cardboard boxes, whatever is at hand, and store them in a cool dry place. If the weather turns cold, cover them up. Onions are tricky to dry so they may need more time for curing. Make sure to check them out after a month to see if any rot has appeared. One rotten onion or potato can ruin a whole bag, box, or bushel. Don't clean the potatoes or onions off. I make sure to save about 40 pounds of five different varieties of seed potatoes; I don't replant the infected or diseased ones. Label the baskets you store the potatoes in or you will do what I have done and forget which ones are which.

Winter Squash

I harvest winter squash (my favorites: butternut, buttercup, acorn, Hubbard, delicata) and pumpkins from mid-to-late September, before an early hard frost can damage them. I make sure they have time to cure in the sun for a couple of days. If I don't bring them inside right away, I pile up the squash in a hill and cover them with hay or a tarp for protection. Before bringing in winter squash, potatoes, and onions for storage, check for any rotten fruit. Some gardeners dip the winter squash in a weak solution of chlorine bleach and water to kill any diseased parts.

Root Crops

Leave carrots, onions, beets, and turnips in the ground until late October or early November. Parsnips can be kept in the earth over winter as long as they are covered with mulch. Mark them with stakes so you know where to find the whitish, light brown roots on a spring day when snow still lies on the ground. The sugars become stronger through the long winter months. There is nothing like the taste of a sweet parsnip in early April. Leave a couple of parsnips in the earth and watch them grow into a giant umbellifera-like plant. Umbel plants are part of the carrot family, which are characterized by a cluster of flowers whose stalks arise from a single point on a stem. Ask your gardening friends to identify the plant and collect the seeds for next year's parsnips.

June and Frank Way with wheelbarrow full of Hubbard squash.
Photo by Jim Flint at Starr Farm Community Garden.

Storage

If you don't have a root cellar, store carrots, beets, and turnips by placing them in plastic bags in the icebox. They will last a few months. Potatoes, onions, and winter squash can be kept in a dry spot in a cool upstairs room. You can also place root crops in a box of dampened sand in the coldest part of your basement. However, if there is a furnace in the cellar, it will most likely be too warm and dry for the root crops. Some gardeners build a separate, unheated room in the cellar to store vegetables like carrots, potatoes, and beets.

In warmer climates, gardeners dig holes in the ground, line them with hay, place the vegetables in the holes, and cover them with hay. This system might work in a very mild winter, but where the ground freezes three or four feet down, you better make other plans.

I heard about one gardener who lives in a cold pocket; he decided to experiment by not digging up his carrots and potatoes. He left them in the ground and covered the area with a foot and a half of mulch hay. Then he dug them up as he needed them. This system may work if there is a good covering of snow, but I suspect if the winter had little snow, the roots and tubers would freeze. I prefer a root cellar where I don't have to go out and dig up carrots under two feet of snow. Each to his own.

"It all depends" is one of the woodchuck principles. I remember one mild winter in the 1970s when my late cabbage got covered with a heavy snow in November. The snow never left and kept coming down all winter. Come spring, the cabbage hadn't frozen, and it tasted sweet and delicious. Go figure.

Many old farmhouses had earthen floors; they were cool and damp in the winter, ideal for storing root crops, potatoes, and apples. Sometimes, a small stream ran through the cellar floor, which provided a cooler for milk, cheese, and other food and drink. Rural folk traditionally stored food in their home cellars or in outside root cellars. This changed when urban food production began after the Great Depression of the 1930s, along with central heating and refrigeration.

You can still find root cellars in the hinterlands. Why don't we visit one on Putney Mountain in southern Vermont. The past helps to connect us to the present and, who knows, maybe one day in the future, root cellars will be back in vogue.

THE UNDERGROUND GARDEN

Elliot Coleman, in his book *Four-Season Harvest,* says, "I think of my root cellar as a secret underground garden into which I spirit away many of my crops when winter threatens." Many woodchuck gardeners used to have root cellars; I am afraid it is becoming a lost art.

My good friend Robert King, who lives on Putney Mountain, built a root cellar in the 1970s on the hillside just south of his home. Easy access came from the gravel road, where he could drive his truck right up to the door. The site was protected from the north wind and snow drifts. The door opened to the east, not the south where it would have received too much sun. Robert used the Scott Nearing, simple stone construction method. First, pour concrete footings and then, using movable wooden frames, fill them with cement and rocks and let them dry. Then move the frames above the first poured section and start again. It's simple and practical woodchuck technology.

Externally, the root cellar is 7 feet wide and 13 feet long, which translates to 5 feet wide and 11 feet long inside. Robert built a framed, flat tar roof and used orange foam board to give the structure additional insulation, then filled in the sides with soil. Before you enter the root cellar, there is a mud room that provides an air-lock space between the outside and the cellar. This was why the structure was so long and why Robert could enter the root cellar with ease in the winter. Two half-doors swung in, then the main insulated door with two barrel bolts kept it shut. For ventilation, a four-inch aluminum pipe went through the top of the cellar. The pipe had a damper, just like those used with a wood stove. If it was too moist, the damper was opened all the way.

Timing is critical when using a root cellar because the temperature has to be cool enough to protect the vegetables. You don't want carrots ripening in September when the cellar is still too warm. The key is to grow crops that ripen late in the season when the cellar has begun to cool down. The way to do this is to start opening up the doors in the evening and closing them in the morning. A rhythm of lowering the temperature starts in October and November. On a cold November day, a decision must be made to harvest the root crops and fill up the root cellar, which now is the correct temperature.

Robert, his wife Linda, and their two children, Posey and Katharine, went through about eight bushels of potatoes and carrots and two bushels of turnips and beets. Cabbage is tricky to store because the cellar has to be at the correct moisture level. Store cabbage closest to the mud floor where there is more moisture. And make sure to leave the main root on the cabbage hanging up.

The right root varieties are also critical. For example, Robert grew the Lutz Winter Keeper, a variety of beets, and Burpee's Short and Sweet hardy carrots. He couldn't grow the longer, thicker winter keepers like my two favorites, Nantes or Danvers carrots, because his soil had too much clay. Carrots have difficulty penetrating heavy clay.

The root crops were stored in plastic milk crates found at the Putney dump. During the coldest times in winter, when there were seven days of sub-zero temperatures, a candle was lit in the mud room that kept the thermometer at 33 in the root cellar. If it had been colder, you know what would have happened.

One final note for all you cosmic gardeners out there. During the 12 holy nights right after Christmas, Robert placed his garden seeds in sealed containers in a box of compost in the root cellar. According to biodynamic gardening, burying seeds during the holy nights imbues them with cosmic life-giving forces. After the holy nights, the seeds were moved to the garden shed. Keep in mind, in nature, seeds live in the earth, and just look how well they do in the spring—especially those weed seeds in your garden. Most of the seeds the public purchases stay up on the fifth floor of a seed storage building all winter.

Maybe we can all meet this winter in Robert's Underground Kingdom. It would be a great place to see the many bins of potatoes, carrots, beets, turnips, and cabbage, and perhaps sip some sweet apple cider. Us Woodchucks call it, "Sie-dah." It makes me thirsty just thinking about it.

In November, Robert King made his last batches of apple cider. He would fill glass gallon containers to within 1/4 inch of the top and cap them. The sweet cider was unpasteurized. By then the temperature in the cellar was down around 35 degrees and the cider kept all winter. Apples are not stored in the cellar because they give off gases that affect the root crops, but Robert did store a 5-gallon wooden apple barrel of vinegar.

CHAPTER 19

HOW ABOUT SOME APPLE CIDER

THE ART OF CIDER MAKING ON PUTNEY MOUNTAIN

I worked with Robert King at Hill and Dale Farm in Putney, Vermont, in the late 1960s. Every fall, we made real apple cider—not the kind you reach for on your market shelves. I say "real" because we mixed a variety of apples like Northern Spy, MacIntosh, Cortland, Baldwin, Delicious, and wild apples, never using more than 25% of the wild ones because it would be too tangy. Besides the fact the apples were organic, the cider had both a sweet and tart taste as well as body and richness most cider is lacking today. Most supermarket pasteurized cider comes from MacIntosh apples, which is okay if you like the taste of apple juice but it just doesn't have the lift of "real" cider. Many small farms make their own cider and it's quite good.

See *Autumn Appendix Guide 10 for The Politics of Apple Cider and the new rules on pasteurization.*

OLD AND NEW APPLE MILLS

The old apple cider mill was a two-stage process: first grinding the apples by hand in a cast-iron hopper and teeth. After the fruit was crushed into the pomace or mash, it was pressed by a screw-type mechanism; the outside was made of wood and the screw or auger made of iron. People turned the crank by hand, which pressed the mash into cider. Animals were once used to power the crusher.

Modern electric presses are more efficient in the amount of juice pressed per gallon. The apples are washed and then go through a hopper where they are shredded by a metal roller with sharp blades. The resulting mash drops onto a heavy-duty cloth whose ends are folded between slated wooden or plastic racks. The mash is then pressed by a hydraulic piston and results in sweet cider.

THE LAST PRESSINGS

Robert King told me the last pressings of cider are the finest. For the best cider, pump the hydraulic press down a little harder but not too hard. Just like the old Maxwell House commercial: "Good to the Last Drop." Robert's last pressings took place in November. Cider stored in the glass jugs in his root cellar lasted until Easter.

When the sun begins to climb higher in the sky at Easter, the root cellar warms up and the cider turns into vinegar. You can also store cider in a refrigerator in glass jugs or freeze it in plastic containers, making sure again to leave a little space at the top. Because apples can be stored more easily than in the past, the cider of today is not stored for any length of time but pressed close to the time you buy it.

Not that long ago, many Vermont farms made cider in late fall, storing it in large wooden kegs, with an air lock to allow the cider to ferment into hard cider. Much of the time, the hard cider was siphoned off into ceramic jugs, the kind you see at antique shops.

Cider in those days was pretty much all hard, and when it turned, again, you had vinegar, which had many uses on Vermont farms. For example, during haying season, a good drink to cool off with was "Haymakers' Switchel," a combination of apple cider vinegar, honey, and water. Maple syrup could be substituted for honey. Many

Apple picker.
Special Collections, Bailey/Howe Library, University of Vermont.

people today make a daily drink of vinegar and water that they believe improves their health.

Robert King washes his hair with apple cider vinegar and water. Others use vinegar and water to clean vegetables such as my friend Johnny Cunavelis of Burlington, Vermont. There is even a small political group in Vermont called the Vinegar Party. Dr. DeForest Clinton Jarvis of Barre, Vermont, wrote a book in 1958 entitled, *Vermont Folk Medicine,* in which he extolled the wonders and virtues of apple cider vinegar. The book is a Vermont woodchuck classic. I highly recommend it. By the way, did you know a tablespoon of vinegar in boiling water keeps blue potatoes blue while they are cooking?

In the 1800s, cider was a fermented drink of apples from one-half to eight percent alcohol. Today, few farms make cider that has been fermented, another name for hard cider. You can pick up a six-pack of Woodchuck Cider, an alcoholic beverage, at your local supermarket.

It won't be long before the last honkers will have passed overhead and the cider we made has turned hard and settled in the oak barrel in the cellar. Now we can nestle down for a while before getting on with the other autumn chores. Bottoms up and have a good rest. After your snooze, it will be time to go out and check your roses. By the way, did you know apples are a member of the rose family? So why not share a few words about this sister of the apple and how to grow hardy roses.

A ROSE IS A ROSE IS A ROSE AND MOM

You might wonder why I choose to write about roses, the "Queen of Flowers" in the fall of the year. In the spring, I wrote about the woodland plants. In summer, the lilies and geraniums were mentioned, and now that we are into autumn, I want to feature another favorite woodchuck plant, the rose, and how to protect it from winter's wrath in northern New England.

But the main reason I want to write about the rose is personal. My mother's name was Rosalie. She was born on September 18th, 1915, and passed on December 5, 1999. I wish she could see all the roses in my front yard, from the hardy rugosas to a few climbers, to a wild variety of hardy pink shrub rose.

A neighbor, Judy Newman, found the wild pink rose in Huntington, Vermont, a variety no one seems to know the name of. Next year, I want to plant a lovely yellow hybrid tea rose called Peace for my mother. It was recommended by Lula Ducas of Burlington, a long-time rose grower. Roses were my mother's favorite flowers, as

ROSES

Best and dearest flower that grows,
perfect both to see and smell,
words can never, never tell,
half the beauty of a rose.
Nothing about the rose is beautiful except itself.
- Cecile Mary Barker, 1923.

they are for many people.

In 1998, a "Diana, Princess of Wales" rose was developed by the rose producer Jackson and Perkins, (800) 292-4769, *www.jacksonandperkins.com*. The new rose, in hues of light white and pink, had the approval of the princess's estate. "Diana" was officially unveiled during a ceremony at the British embassy in Washington, D.C., in the summer of 1998.

THE ROSACEOUS FAMILY

The rose family comprises herbs, shrubs, and trees. Some shrubs are roses and blackberries, a few herbs are strawberry, meadowsweet, and bloodwort. Apples and American Mountain Ash or Rowan are examples of trees of the rose family. If you cut an apple in half, you see a five-pointed star, the signature of five permeating the entire rose family in the petals and leaves as well as the fruit.

The shrub rose lives in the central plant realm between the tree and the herb. Let us observe the plant and its laws of formation. On the one hand, plants gravitate toward the earth by way of their roots; on the other hand, plants conquer gravitational forces by the growth processes that lead to flower and fruit. Blossoms present us with sugar-like substances, and roots accumulate something of a salt substance with bitterness and tartness.

The apple fruit culture is at one extreme with its strong sugars, and the roots of bloodwort herb contain 20% tannic acid. As for the rose, it sits in the middle with a balance of sugar and tannic acid. *See Autumn Appendix Guides 12-14 on the rose family: from the Cultural History of the Rose to information on how to create rosary beads from rose petals.*

WINTER ROSE PROTECTION IN COLD CLIMATES

Fall in northern New England is when most roses go into dormancy or sleep, so it's appropriate to learn which roses grow in the north country. Charlie Nardozzi is a rose expert who used to work for the National Gardening Association in South Burlington, Vermont. Charlie recommends choosing a reputable, local nursery that carries winter-hardy roses such as the shrub roses Bonica and Fairy. The better rose-growing companies like Jackson and Perkins replace any rose that dies, but who wants to go to the trouble of planting a rose that succumbs to the elements? Modern roses like hybrid teas, floribundas, and the climbers are not winter hardy in northern New England; however, they can survive here with special care and attention. Of course, you can simply purchase roses in the spring and just grow them as annuals.

Winter Rose Protection

Woodchuck rose growers don't worry about the hardy ones because they do fine on their own; however, if you insist on growing roses that aren't as hardy, listen to what Lula Ducas and Deborah Stuart say about the roses that need six months of winter protection.

Tidbits from Lula

According to Lula Ducas, an old-time rose grower from Burlington, Vermont, it's critical to check the hardiness zone of the rose variety you purchase. This information tells you whether the rose needs winter protection. Stop fertilizing roses during early August to hinder any new tender growth from forming. Also, leave any major pruning work till spring.

In November, Lula strips all the leaves from the canes. She lays down the long canes of the climbers and covers them with soil in late November or early December, depending on the weather. Her preference is not to put the rose leaves in the compost pile because some might be diseased with black spot, the most serious rose fungus disease. Some of Lula's favorite climbers are New Dawn, Viking Queen, and William Baffen as well as Blaise, a red climber. The newer Blaise variety is hardy.

Her favorite tea rose is called Peace Rose. This lovely yellow rose needs to be cared for rather carefully as it is not as hardy as some. Her favorite shrubs are Bonica-pink and Morden rose, blush and red. Lola buys her roses from a local greenhouse or from Pickering's, which she says has a great catalog. (See address below.)

Advice from Deborah Stuart

Deborah Stuart of Wentworth, New Hampshire, offers us a number of unconventional methods for protecting roses during the long winter months. She grows some of the larger roses like the David Austins in heavy-duty paper pots. In late fall, they are laid over on their sides in Deborah's funky old plastic, three-sided greenhouse connected to the garden shed.

Deborah simply covers the roses with shredded leaves and any old blankets she happens to have around. She uses shredded leaves because she doesn't have a lot of extra soil hanging around. Shredded leaves can be created by using the reverse gear on a leaf blower.

Deborah covers the roses she left out in the garden with shredded leaves, drapes them with Remay (floating row covers), and finally, with large plastic garbage bags filled with holes. The pretty, everblooming, miniature roses, like Raindrop, a soft lavender, and Center Gold, are left in their pots and brought inside for the winter. If they begin to look pathetic, she cuts them back as long as there is some life left in them. Her miniature roses spend the winter in Deborah's cool back room on a sunny window. She keeps them watered and lets them rest but not go dormant. In early April, she feeds them and, by late April, they're covered with buds and bloom continuously.

Some roses, such as Fancy Lady's, an heirloom patio type, are brought in and left on the cellar stairs to go dormant. In this case, Deborah allows the ground to freeze before bringing them in; she wants the cellar to be cool and for the rose to shut down (go into dormancy). Finally, Deborah places some roses under grow lights in the cellar beneath a water mat. Come early spring, they bloom like crazy. *Autumn Appendix Guide 14 has more information on Winter Rose Protection.*

THE HARDY EXPLORER SERIES

Charlie Nardozzi told me you can't go wrong with the rugosas or the old-fashioned varieties from Europe that have been around for a couple of hundred years like the Apothecary Rose or the Great Maiden Blush. And then there is the very hardy Explorer series developed by the Canadians in Ontario. The series is named after explorers such as John Cabot, William Baffen, and Henry Kelsey. Their bush and climber roses are very hardy, everblooming, and have the look of wild roses.

ROSE CATALOGS AND NURSERIES

Stone's Throw Nursery
East Craftsbury, VT 05826
(802) 586-2805
(Carries the Explorer series.)

Pickering Nursery
670 Kingston Rd.
Pickering, Ontario LIV186
. (416) 839-2111
(Very hardy roses)

Lowe's Own Root Roses
6 Sheffield Road
Nashua, NH 03062
(603) 888-2214

The Rosarie
Waldboro, ME 04572-0919
(207) 832-6330
(Grows practical roses
for hard places.)

Jackson and Perkins
Medford, Oregon
(800) 872-7673
www.jacksonandperkins.com
(They offer a small
pamphlet *Home Gardener's
Guide to Roses.*)

Well folks, after making cider and taking care of your roses, there may still be time to spread some compost in your garden, that is, if the ground hasn't already frozen. This doesn't usually happen until mid-November, depending on your location. Woodchuck gardeners of the organic bent like myself consider compost the "soul food" of the soil.

CHAPTER 20

BLACK GOLD

Compost or what some enthusiasts call *black gold,* is the heavyweight champ of the organic gardening world. Compost is becoming rather "in" these days as natural food and organic gardening and farming are making a resurgence throughout the United States. Healthy food without the use of harmful chemical fertilizers, pesticides, and genetically modified seeds is a priority for many families. This is fostered in part by the increased rates of cancer.

Ironically, most farms and gardens used nothing but organic methods as late as the 1930s. That's about the time nitrate fertilizer, (chilean of nitrate), was dug from the rich bat caves of Chili where the soil is sandy, dry, and easy to mine. Soon after, the Haber-Bosch method was developed to create nitrogen artificially.

Animal manure and compost were inseparable in those days, and rotted manure was the main source of fertilizer on small New England hill farms. Mucking out animal stalls was as much a part of life as milking. It was a hard but necessary task. Farmers knew animal manures and other vegetable matter were more beneficial to the soil after going through a process of breakdown and stabilization.

Animal manures add beneficial organisms, disease resistance, and organic matter to the compost pile. Some commercial compost operations no longer use animal manures in their mix of organic ingredients. This significantly lowers the value of the compost. The soil needs composted animal manures. Studies show animal manure is critical to creating the right balance of bacteria, fungus, and microorganisms in the pile. Today, you can drive through the rich farmlands of Ohio where miles of soybeans and corn are grown and not see a single cow. This was not the case 50 years ago. To view a farming landscape without animals is not only sad; animals and their manure are essential to a healthy soil.

The art and science of composting began over 5,000 years ago in China where compost is still the fertilizer of choice even though chemical fertilizers were introduced in the 1950s. When you consider China is home to one quarter of the world's population on 7% of the earth's cultivated land, there must be something special about compost.

THE NATURE OF SOIL

To understand why compost is so critical, we need to learn about the nature of soil. Soil in a healthy condition is a collection of crumbs made of a combination of sand, silt, clay plus minerals, fungi, and other decaying matter—and the bodies (both living and dead) of millions of microorganisms. These microscopic organisms give off sticky substances that hold the particles together into a cluster-like structure. Roots of plants move through a honeycomb of passageways made possible by this structure. Fine feeder roots meander through this maze of tunnels searching for nutrients, minerals, and moisture.

Chemical fertilizers and poisonous insecticides destroy the microorganisms, fungi, and bacteria and can change the very structure and life of the soil. This is where compost comes in; it provides the glue that binds the particles together and much more.

THE BENEFITS OF BLACK GOLD

Whether you make it at home or purchase compost from a reliable source, it is the key to a fertile soil, and good soil is the key to healthy fruits and vegetables. Black gold improves soil structure and aeration, increases its water-holding capacity, and adds beneficial microorganisms. These microbes break down organic matter and convert nutrients into a more available form for plants. Finally, compost infuses the soil with natural antibiotics.

COMPOST TIDBITS

You can use old compost as an inoculator just as you would with sourdough bread or yogurt. No need to buy those expensive compost starters. Go over to the compost pile you started last fall or spring. The compost that was piled so high has now shrunken down. The organic material on the top hasn't broken down too much, but the stuff halfway down and on the bottom is ready to place on your garden. Spread it generously on your fall garden and dig it in lightly. Save some of the older compost that sits at the bottom of the pile. Mix it with peat, vermiculite, and perlite for potting and germinating mixes in the early spring.

COMPOSTING MADE EASY

Did you know the average American throws away almost four pounds of garbage every day? One-third is kitchen waste that could be used in a compost heap. In other words, most people could have bins of compost cooking in their backyards. And when you can add in leaves, old mulch, animal manure, strips of newspapers, fresh green lawn clippings, weeds, your neighbor's vegetable wastes, wood ashes from the wood stove and more, there is enough potential for compost to heal the earth.

A compost pile can be started any season of the year. The basics are easy: Collect the organic matter, pile it up, and let it rot. All you need to do is to keep the microorganisms in the pile well supplied with proper proportions of food, air, and water and follow some sim-

BEFORE AND AFTER

BEFORE: (at top) Art Tatro and friend standing next to young compost pile.
AFTER: Pumpkin plants are growing out of the compost pile.
Photos by Jamie Mittendorf, Tommy Thompson Community Garden.

ple rules described below.

COMPOST MAKES GOOD SENSE

According to many woodchuck gardeners, composting is easy when you use your sense of sight, smell, touch, and taste.

• Use your eyes. Well-ripened compost is a black-brown crumbly

147

material, colored somewhere between chocolate and spice cake.

- Use your nose to smell when the sweet compost has completed its cycle.
- Use your hand to feel the wetness or dryness inside the pile. It should feel like a wet sponge that doesn't quite drip.
- If the heap is too hot, you can tell because your hand will burn. In this case, open up the pile and add some hay. It's good to turn the pile at least once. If you can't turn it, that's okay; turning it too much is a waste of time and effort and it upsets the natural process of decomposition.
- Finally there is the sense of taste. Once I had a friend who liked the taste of well-ripened compost. Hm! He said it was sweet to the palate, and he used taste to tell him when it was time to spread it on the garden. Each to his own.

WOODCHUCK'S QUICK FIX COMPOST ADVICE

- If the pile is too dry, water it.
- If there are too many leaves or old hay, i.e., too much carbon, it breaks down very slowly. Replenish it with nitrogen in the form of fresh green grass, weeds, kitchen scraps, and animal manures.
- If the pile gets too hot from too much nitrogen, cool it down by opening it up and adding some carbon materials like hay and leaves. You will smell ammonia (nitrogen gas) where too much fresh animal manure is present. Have you ever been overcome by the odor of chicken manure? What you smell is the ammonia (nitrogen gas).
- If the pile is too soggy, there is not enough oxygen; aerate the pile and add some dry materials.
- Add lime or wood ashes if the heap begins to smell like garbage. Don't throw in meat scraps unless you want skunks in your backyard—and the sound of screaming neighbors.

The key to successful composting is to have enough air and water, the right ingredients, and the correct carbon (straw, hay) to nitrogen (fresh grass clippings, animal manures) ratio. Fresh manure mixed with hay bedding from a barn is the ideal combination. This translates into about 12 to 15 parts carbon and one part nitrogen or a

12-15 to 1 ratio. Most home gardeners use whatever materials are available.

Backyard compost bins generally don't have enough nitrogen. That's why they just sit there and take longer to break down. My neighbors supply me with nitrogen in the form of fresh lawn clippings, and some even throw their vegetable scraps in my backyard compost bins.

WHERE TO PLACE AND HOW TO BUILD A COMPOST PILE

Compost piles can be free standing or they can be contained in a compost bin. If you have plenty of land, I suggest you place one pile next to the garden and one close to the house for kitchen wastes. At the community garden, we have three open compost heaps piled with weeds, old plants, and other organic materials through the season. Animal manure is added when we can find it. The piles are turned once a season. It takes about a year for the bottom half to decompose.

COMPOST BINS

Woodchuck gardeners can create enclosed compost bins from straw bales, cinder blocks, old snow fences, or wood pallets. You can also use an old garbage can with holes in the sides and one large hole on the bottom for the final product. Or you can purchase plastic compost bins at a garden store. Even plastic bags with holes are used for compost bins. The possibilities are endless. The ideal scenario is to have three bins built next to each other, the first holding fresh stuff, the second for compost in process, and the third for completed compost. Then you just keep rotating them. By the way, most composting is done in open piles, not bins. Go figure.

TURNING

Turning a compost pile is a debatable topic and is certainly not mandatory. If backyard gardeners build a proper pile, they don't have to turn it. I try to turn mine in the fall, but there are years when that's not possible. It may take a little longer to decompose but that's okay. Two of the woodchuck principles relating to compost piles are "you do what you can do" and "it depends." It's certainly easier to turn an open pile than one located in a bin.

Most commercial operations turn the pile at least twice, some as many as five times and more. It's clear raw compost will break down more readily the more it's turned, but will this result in a higher quality compost? It's debatable.

HOW TO START

Begin the process by placing old mulch at the bottom of the pile to soak up all the juices. Add any remains of an old compost pile. Clean up your garden and put all the weeds, stalks, and sod on the pile. Throw in leaves and old mulch, wood ashes, kitchen garbage, manure, and whatever else you have. If you have any well-ripened compost, use it as a starter. Most backyard compost needs to sit about a year to decompose properly once the pile is built. If you keep adding organic materials to the top of the pile, it only makes sense that the bottom half or more breaks down into compost and the top part needs more time to break down. Creating black gold takes patience and experience—like anything else in life.

HOW TO USE COMPOST AND LEAVES IN YOUR FALL GARDEN BED

One woodchuck trick is to place heaps of compost over your garden beds in the fall and then cover them with leaves. For some reason, earthworms seem to be attracted to leaves more than mulch hay and other organic materials. The worm literally pulls the leaf down by the stem into its home and has a meal. In the spring, you find worm castings—the richest compost in the world—spread throughout the beds. This results in warmer soil, easier tillage, and earlier planting, as compared to garden beds that haven't been covered with leaves or other types of mulch.

See more material on composting, leaves, the four stages of compost breakdown, and the role of microorganisms, beetles, worms, and other insects in the composting process in the Autumn Appendix Guide 15 and 16. Also included is information on biodynamic preparations as growth regulators in the compost pile.

A MODEL OF A CLOSED LOOP SYSTEM

Let's leave the backyard compost heap and learn how black gold is spreading its nutrients around Vermont. In the Intervale, a rich flood plain that lies along the Winooski River in Burlington, Vermont, the Intervale Compost Project processes leaves, yard waste,

Photo of Troy-Bilt rototiller tilling corn stalks in Robert King's garden.
Photo by Robert King.

horse and cow manure, sawdust, liquid wastes from Ben and Jerry's ice cream, and organic material like vegetable scraps from the local hospital, restaurant and food stores. Most of the compost is sold to home gardeners, nurseries, and landscaping businesses. A number of organic market gardens in the Intervale use the compost to grow vegetables, which are then sold back to the restaurants, food stores, and the hospital. Quite a cycle, eh?

In 1999, the Intervale received about 10,000 tons of waste and converted it into 5,000 tons of compost. It charged $25 per ton—compared to the fee at the landfill of $84 per ton. Just look at the ecological and economic advantages of converting waste into organic soil amendments. Composting projects such as the one in the Intervale are sprouting up throughout Vermont. It won't be long before black gold takes over the Green Mountains and then—you guessed it folks—New Hampshire and the world.

P.S. The Intervale Compost Project along with The Chittenden Solid Waste District has embarked on a pilot project to collect household food wastes for pickup in special bins to be taken to the compost yard in the Intervale. So far so good. Some folks are even hauling the smelly stuff down to the composting site on their own. 51% of the respondents in a 2000 survey were willing to separate food scraps and nonrecyclable paper into a separate container for pickup at no additional cost. Time will tell if the project succeeds.

CHAPTER 21

FINAL AUTUMN MURMURS

By late October, the tourists, or what we call "leaf-peepers," are gone. They love to come and take pictures ad infinitum of the lovely red, orange, and yellow maple leaves, and experience the hues and glows of autumn colors. They also tie up traffic.

By late October, the hard-and softwood leaves take on the look of washed out watercolors, sort of like grandma's tattered comforter. They eventually rest on the forest floor. Only the yellow needle-like leaves of the tamarack (larch) and the green needles of the firs and other conifers are left standing. A late cold October sun shining through them is a glory to behold. It almost makes the other gray, raw days seem bearable.

November is a quiet time, a period in between, a space where we wait for the snows to come. In the year 2000, we had three inches of snow on October 29, but that was early and only stayed for a day. The folks that live in the higher elevations and the Northeast Kingdom of Vermont always experience colder fall temperatures, earlier snows and longer winters than I do in the warmer Lake Champlain Valley.

November is the last time of the year to finish garden chores unless you are one of those nonstop gardeners who grow greens in their greenhouse all winter. My energy level begins to wane, but there are a couple more tasks to complete: I cover some of my raised beds with leaves so the earthworms can have a good meal, pick those sweet brussels sprouts, cut off some kale or chard, and dig beets and carrots.

Robert King's root cellar is full, my pantry is packed with canning jars full of summer's bounty, and the cold frame still has some fall greens waiting to be picked. The compost has been spread and dug into my garden. It's comforting to know the garden has been laid to rest. The honkers have now flown south, and, at last, there ain't no more weeding to do. Perhaps I'll sit in the easy chair next to the wood

152

stove and think back to early spring when the first seeds germinated and the young green plants grew in summer and finally produced their fruits in fall. There is much to be thankful for.

I know from years of experience that working in the fall garden is like insurance for the spring season. I temper this with the idea that even though the gardening season is complete, the end is just another beginning. Of course, some tasks do not get done, like the sumac patch that continued to grow and further its expansion. But that's okay. Sometimes we forget that the strong red hues of the sumac add glory to the symphony of autumn colors.

I make applesauce and start carving pumpkins and roasting the seeds on the wood stove for Halloween or what some call All Hallow Even. After the pumpkin festival is over, a great autumn festival unique to North America arrives. Thanksgiving is a special holiday in New England, for this is when the First Nation Tribes shared their gifts with the "newcomers."

CHAPTER 22

THE GIFTS OF THE FIRST NATION PEOPLE

When the early settlers arrived in the New World, they were dependent on Native populations. The first years of settlement were focused on survival; shelter was important but most vital was food production. The indigenous people kept the settlers alive by teaching them gardening and farming techniques. With the use of hand tools, they tilled and planted maize.

The methods the Native population employed were different from those used by the Europeans. For example, the land wasn't totally cleared of stumps and roots. Trees were killed by the girdling method. Most crops were planted in hills. Corn and beans were sometimes planted together, the stalks of corn serving as poles for the beans to climb. Fish were planted with corn as a source of nitrogen. Winter squash were planted among the beans and corn. The settlers also witnessed methods for storing food: Corn was dried on mats in the sun and then stored by placing the maize in holes in the ground lined with grass mats.

In New England, tillage was done entirely by hand. The staple food crops were supplemented by hunting and gathering. The river valleys were paradise for the Native populations because of an abundance of fish and game. The soil was fertile and at some sites agricultural tools, such as the stone hoe fashioned from sandstone, have been found.

Tribes in northern New England gathered sap from the sugar maple tree and boiled it in clay pots into maple syrup. Corn was ground in clay mortars; it grew in colors of red, blue, and cream, and the beans were flat and white. These two vegetables, mixed together, made a favorite dish called succotash. This is said to be an Algonquin word, but the mixture was also called bean-swaggin.

The gifts the Native population shared with the first English settlers saved their lives. Today we are only beginning to appreciate their other contributions: a respect for the earth and its inhabitants.

If you are interested in learning more about the gifts of the First Nation People, please read *Indian Givers: How the Indian of the Americas Transformed the World*, J. Weatherford, Fawcett Columbine Press.

Much Depends On Dinner: The Extraordinary History and Mythology, Allure and Obsessions, Perils and Taboos of an Ordinary Meal, M. Visser, Collier Books.

A BLESSING FOR
THE PLANT KINGDOM

Blessings on the blossom
Blessings on the Fruit
Blessings on the Leaf and Stem
Blessings on the Root

CHAPTER 23

AUTUMN APPENDIX GUIDE

Autumn Appendix Guide Number One

KIM POTTER'S BASIC CANNING TIPS

If you want to blanch vegetables for canning, make sure not to over cook them. Place them in boiling water for two to three minutes depending on the vegetable. The woodchuck rule of thumb is to cook vegetables some-what firm and crunchy—you know "El Dente" not "Over dunte." If you over cook vegetables, they get mushy and who wants soft vegetables? The Ball Blue Book and other canning books like *Putting Foods By*, tell you how long to cook vegetables for blanching as well as basic information about the water bath canner as compared to the pressure canner.

Make sure you start out with the freshest and best produce when canning and freezing. You don't want anything that is not top quality. If you are canning tomatoes, you need to first blanch them and then take the skins off.

When canning, clean off the edge of the lip and threads of the cap. This helps ensure a good seal. A tomato seed or some fibrous material may not let it seal properly. When a jar seals, the center of the lid should remain down when you push. No one wants to die of botulism, so make sure to check the seal.

You can use a water bath canner on tomatoes, which are a high acid vegetable. Corn and beans need a pressure canner. A pressure canner is used for low acid vegetables like corn, beets, beans, carrots. Kim never actually uses a pressure canner because she freezes all her corn, peas, and beans. Her mom had one blow on her even though people have used them for years with no problem. Just make sure the valve is not plugged or stuck.

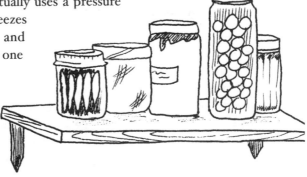

Autumn Appendix Guide Number Two

MCKENZIE'S FAMOUS
BREAD AND BUTTER PICKLES

When the cool days of fall come, I cover the cucumbers and squash plants with floating row covers, which extends the growing season another 2 to 3 weeks. This gives me one last chance to make a batch of McKenzie's Famous Bread and Butter Pickles.

McKenzie's Famous
Bread and Butter Pickles

6 quarts of pickling cukes, thinly sliced
  Use (12-18) 6-inch cucumbers,
  makes about 12 pints.
6 good sized onions, sliced
1-1/2 quarts white vinegar
1/2 cup whole mustard seed
1-1/2 cups pickling salt
4-1/2 cups sugar
1 tablespoon celery seed

Can also add some sweet red peppers. Put sliced cukes, onions, and peppers in stainless steel bowl; combine with 1-1/2 cups pickling salt. Let stand for 3 hours; drain but don't rinse. Combine celery seed, salt, sugar, vinegar, and mustard seed in pot and bring to boil. Add veggies and bring to boil over low-medium heat. Pack immediately in clean, hot 1-pint jars; leave half-inch for head room. Process in hot water bath (185 degrees F) for ten minutes. Remove jars, cooling upright. Give them 6-8 weeks for the flavor to develop before eating.

Autumn Appendix Guide Number Three

APPLE RECIPES:
APPLESAUCE CAKE AND CRISP

APPLESAUCE CAKE: Another of my favorite desserts is applesauce cake. I am one of those people who can't follow directions, but I'll give you a couple of the ingredients. My mother was one of those great bakers who also never followed directions because she said it was in her hands.

Applesauce Cake

2 cups of sifted flour
1 teaspoon baking soda
1/4 teaspoon salt
1 egg
some maple syrup
1-1/2 cups applesauce
Spices

Bake at 350 degrees. Taste the batter to see whether you need to add more spices like cinnamon, nutmeg, cloves, or sweetening. Bake for about 30-35 minutes and, voila!, you have The Woodchuck Applesauce Cake.

Apple Crisp

Topping:
1 cup all-purpose flour
1/3 cup light brown sugar
4 tablespoons
**   granulated sugar**
1 teaspoon cinnamon
1/3 cup unsalted butter

Filling:
7 apples
1 tablespoon
**   granulated sugar**
juice from half a lemon

Preheat oven to 375 degrees. In a large bowl, combine the butter and dry ingredients and work the softened butter in with your fingers until the texture resembles coarse sand. In a bowl, drizzle the lemon juice on the apples and sprinkle them with the sugar. Place the filling into a baking dish, and spoon the topping over the apples. Cover with foil and bake for twenty minutes until top is crisp and brown and apples are tender. Serves a family of five.

Autumn Appendix Guide Number Four

APPLE BUTTER

Mary Miller is a famous apple butter maker from Wolcott, Vermont. She begins with good apples like Northern Spy and cooks them down to applesauce. She then adds maple syrup, places the sauce in a roaster pan, and cooks it down at about 300 degrees until it just begins to caramelize. I can personally attest to its delicious and unique taste.

P.S. Northern Spy is one of the hardest apples on the earth. They take a lot longer to cook down than a MacIntosh but are well worth it. Just make sure to cut them into smaller pieces.

Autumn Appendix Guide Number Five

SUN-DRIED APPLES

What to do:
- Peel the apples and take the cores out.
- Slice the apples crossways into rings.
- Place the rings on an old sheet in the hot sun and cover them with cheesecloth to keep the bugs off.
- Turn the apples to the other side when the tops are dry. This should take several days. Cover them at night from moisture.
- Store the dried apple slices in glass jars.
- Apple rings can also be dried on a rack on the wood range.

Autumn Appendix Guide Number Six

APPLES IN THE KITCHEN

Applesauce: Apples suited for pies are usually good for sauce too, as are a few strongly flavorful types that are too watery or not firm enough for

158

pies. MacIntoshes make excellent sauce.

Pies, pancakes, muffins, and cakes: Look for assertive-tasting fruit that's not too watery. The apples should have some tartness. Examples: Granny Smith, Pippin, Rhode Island Greening, Ida Red, Jonathan, and Jonamac.

BAKED: Firm fruit that holds its shape makes the best baked apples. This includes Cortland, Northern Spy, and Rome Beauty.

OUT-OF-HAND: Most apples that are good for pies, applesauce, and baked apples are delicious raw too, with the exception of very tart or mealy types. Try Braeburn, Empire, Fuji, Honey Crisp, Gala, and Winter Banana.

APPLE BUTTER: Use drier apples that produce a thicker sauce.

Autumn Appendix Guide Number Seven

THE NATURE AND HISTORY OF APPLES

Apples are the rounded flesh of a red and yellow edible pome fruit of a tree (genus *Malus*) of the rose family. The exact place where they first appeared is not known but is believed to be between the Black and Caspian Seas. The ancient Greeks were growing several varieties of apples in the late 300s B.C. The Romans also grew and loved the fruit. Researchers even found the charred remains of apples at a Stone Age village in Switzerland. And let us not forget the Bible legend of Adam and Eve eating an apple in the Garden of Eden.

Early settlers to North America brought apple seeds and trees with them to the New World. Records from the Massachusetts Bay Company indicate apples were grown in New England as early as 1630. In 1796, John McIntosh of Ontario discovered a variety of apple enjoyed by people around the world today. Can you guess the name?

Americans have a favorite story about a pioneer apple farmer named John Chapman from Leominster, Massachusetts. Chapman, now known to many as Johnny Appleseed, became famous in the 1800s when he handed out apple seeds and trees to settlers in Ohio, Indiana, and Illinois. The apples were used to make cider, which fermented into the national drink, hard cider. Legend claims that Johnny Appleseed traveled barefoot, wearing old torn clothes and a tin pot for a hat. He is celebrated in American mythology as a symbol of the westward expansion.

When I came to Putney, Vermont, in 1966, I was fortunate to live near a number of apple and sour cherry orchards, one owned by the late Senator George Aiken. I worked at Hill and Dale Farm in the late 1960s where we raised organic beef, vegetables, and apples and made the sweetest apple cider on earth. The secret was to mix wild apples with different varieties like Northern Spy, MacIntosh, Baldwin, and Cortland. You don't taste cider like that anymore unless you find a small farm that mixes and presses its own apples. It's a vanishing art.

Autumn Appendix Guide Number Eight

WORLD APPLE PRODUCTION

Of all the fruit trees, apples are the most widely cultivated. Apple production around the world is about two billion bushels every year. The Soviet Union, prior to its breakup, led the world in apple production, followed by the United States, China, France, Germany, and Italy. Even warmer countries like Iraq and Mexico are able to grow apples in their cooler upland regions. I worked on a kibbutz in northern Israel in 1968 where apples were the main crop. We were so far north you could see Lebanon from the highest point and watch the snow fly now and then. You could also hear the sound of guns.

In the United States, the yearly apple crop totals about 235 million bushels, with a wholesale value of $1 billion. Washington State produces more apples than any other state. Unfortunately, the high yield of apples produced there is possible because of the extensive artificial irrigation that causes some environmental problems.

Vermont averages 1.1 million bushels as compared to a New England total of 5.5 million bushels. 80% of the Vermont apples are sold fresh, with the others being used for cider, applesauce, and wine. 70% of the apples are MacIntosh and 30% Red Delicious, Empire, and Cortland.

There are about 40 wholesale operations and 35 farm market and roadside stands throughout the Green Mountains. (Vermont Department of Agriculture Statistics)

Autumn Appendix Guide Number Nine

APPLE VARIETIES

Even though there are 7,000 varieties of domestic apples grown in the world, and about 2,500 in North America, the marketplace is dominated by the MacIntosh, Red Delicious, and Granny Smith. There is also Vermont Gold, Jonagold, Mutsu, Fuji, Macoun, and yes, the Braeburn, a New Zealand apple. Take a bold bite into something new.

Apples come in a variety of shapes, textures, and tastes. The color may be green, yellow, or various shades of red. Some yellow apples have brown spots, while some red ones have white spots like the Jonathan. The flesh of apples may be yellow, white, or cream colored. Each variety has a slightly different flavor, from sweet to tart to bitter. Textures vary from soft and mushy to firm and crunchy. Some apples, like Empire developed over in New York State, are sweet and crunchy when eaten fresh. Other firm varieties like Rome Beauty are best used for baking. Many species are the result of breeding different apples together like the Delicious with the Ralls Janet, which resulted in Fuji, Japan's most popular apple.

A LIST OF APPLE VARIETIES

BRAMLEY'S SEEDLING: a good cooking apple.

CALVILLE BLANC: a great winter apple, highest in vitamin C.

MANTET: the best early apple.

NORTHERN SPY: a late-bearing heirloom, often the oldest apple in the orchard. My favorite late fall fruit. A hardy winter keeper.

VERMONT GOLD: ripens at the end of September about a week after MacIntosh. This new Vermont variety, similar to a Golden Delicious, is just coming into its own.

Autumn Appendix Guide Number Ten

THE POLITICS OF APPLE CIDER

In the fall of 1997, the Vermont Health and Agriculture departments sent a letter to the state's schools warning them not to serve fresh cider or other unpasteurized juices to children. The letter warned of the dangers of E coli bacteria, which had contaminated unpasteurized fruit juice in the western United States. Some of the larger Vermont cider producers were forced to use an expensive process called flash pasteurization to kill any potential pathogens.

I have to confess I bought some of that flash-pasteurized cider, and it tasted somewhere between apple juice, water, and apple cider. I won't drink it again. It just doesn't taste like—you guessed it— "real" apple cider. By the way, there hasn't been a single documented case of E coli directly caused by apple cider in New England. Many small cider operations have closed because the cost of flash pasteurization is prohibitive.

Autumn Appendix Guide Number Eleven

COVER CROPS AND GARDEN CROP ROTATIONS

Most garden soils need to rest every three years because vegetables take a toll on the soil, especially corn and potatoes, which are heavy feeders.

Four Rotation Methods

- Rotate vegetables around the garden every year.
- Plant summer cover crops between the rows.
- Plant summer cover crops in garden areas after crops previously grown are harvested and removed.
- Plant a cover crop in the fall after the garden is tilled.

Rye grass, oats, buckwheat, and winter rye are cover crops that can be used for methods 2-4. Winter rye is the best cover crop for method 4.

The ideal scenario is to have a garden large enough so half of it can be planted in food crops and the other half in a legume (clover, alfalfa, vetch) and grass mix for 2-3 years. The legumes fix nitrogen in their root nodules, and the mass of roots from the grasses help keep the organic matter content of the soil. The final touch comes from adding composted manure to the legume-grass mix. This increases the micro-life in the soil.

Autumn Appendix Guide Number Twelve

A CULTURAL HISTORY OF THE ROSE

The rose was first mentioned in ancient Persian writings, and Persia (Iran) may be generally regarded as the origin of rose breeding. In old ancient Persian sun-mystery centers, rose and sandalwood were used as incense. Prayer beads were carved from sandalwood in the shape of rose blossoms. The Roman Catholic rosary beads are best known to us.

Rose History Continued

In ancient Persia, rose ointment was used for hygienic purposes. In Babylonia, the bodies of dead rulers were covered with rose petals. Hippocrates cherished the rose as did Pliny the Elder, who lists 32 remedies. During times of pestilence, sick rooms were fumigated with rose oil, juniper, and frankincense. Even today, following the traditions of the past, many remedies include rose oil, especially for skin conditions.

Rose petals were strewn on guests' beds by slaves during famous Roman feasts. In the Roman streets of ointment manufacturers, there were publications with instructions on how to adulterate rose oil with less precious oils. In Europe, the crusaders brought rose ointments and oil home to their castles. The Rosicrucians took the image of the rose bush winding the cross to be deeply significant for their meditations.

When writing of rose oil today, we think of Bulgaria, where factories produce the substance. The rose is also cultivated in Turkey, Morocco, and parts of southern France. In Pakistan, along the Jhelum river in the Punjab, roses grow in profusion. The region's Sanskrit meaning is "five river land." During the blooming season in spring, producers of rose water come from all parts of Pakistan to purchase rose flowers, which they later distill into rose water.

Rose products: high quality rose cream, oil, and soap for the skin. Weleda Products, 175 North Route 9W, Congers, N.Y. 10920; (800) 241-1030; *www.weleda.com.*

Autumn Appendix Guide Number Thirteen

ROSARY BEADS

A friend of mine from Bethel, Vermont, Margaret Daniel, told me the original rosary beads were made from rose petals ground up into a paste. The paste was shaped into beads, dried, strung with thread and, as the story goes, the fragrance lasted 100 years.

Rose Bead Necklace Instructions

Gather about one-third of a shopping bag of fresh, wild rose petals. They are the best for scent. You may use faded ones, but avoid brown petals. If you cannot find enough in one day, freeze your first or second picking in an airtight plastic bag. Put them through an old-time hand grinder. Store the paste in a pottery bowl. Repeat the grinding 2 to 3 times in a row for about eight days. Don't add water.

Keep at room temperature, covered with a kitchen towel. Each day the paste becomes thicker, and the color turns from pink to mahogany. When it reaches the consistency of a smooth clay-like mass, it is ready.

Take a little of the paste into the palm of your hand; with the other hand, form it into smooth round balls, a little smaller than a regular-sized marble. Stick a pin through the middle of each bead and pierce it onto a soft board a half-inch apart. You can use a piece of insulation board.

Depending on the length of the necklace, use 50-60 beads. It takes three to four weeks for them to dry depending on the weather. Remove the pins. Use a fine paper file to get the roughness off before hand-polishing each bead with a cloth. String them on a good silk or nylon thread found at a craft store. You can also use beads of malachite, rose quartz, and turquoise in between each or every other rose bead.

To retain the fragrance of the beads, store the necklace in a small wooden, airtight bowl. Two drops of real rose oil rubbed into the wooden bowl enhances the scent even more. The smell of roses will permeate your kitchen all summer.

Autumn Appendix Guide Number Fourteen

WINTER ROSE PROTECTION TIPS

For the not-so-hardy varieties: The action of freezing and thawing is what kills not-so-hardy rose plants. The stems and tiny root hairs can become damaged easily without proper protection.

Start in early November by stripping off the leaves from the lower parts of the canes; gradually remove all the foliage by late November. Tie the canes together to reduce wind damage if they are not cut back. In mid-November, add 3" to 4" of soil to miniatures and 8-10" to hybrid teas, grandifloras, and floribundas. Some gardeners bring in soil if there are a lot of diseased plants. Rose growers have different preferences; some prefer bark mulch or chopped leaves instead of soil because there is less chance of rotting in wet years.

Styrofoam insulation boxes are a good way to protect rose plants in mild and severe winters, but make sure to allow some ventilation. Rose cones work well if the winter is not too cold and there is good snow cover during sub-zero temperatures. Allow ventilation during warm days. As a cheap woodchuck substitute for rose cones, scrounge old styrofoam coolers at the dump or buy them on sale at the end of the season. Be sure to punch holes in them. An old time-tested protector has been burlap bags to wrap roses.

For the protection of climbing roses, place boards or cardboard over the entire plant after bending the canes over to fit under the coverings.

Own Root vs. Grafted Rose: An "own root" rose is more likely to survive than a "grafted rose," which is a rose where a grafted union is made to the parent root stock. Make sure the grafted union holds; a different color rose may arise in the spring. This effect comes from the parent root stock.

Lowe's Own Root Roses are of good quality: 6 Sheffield Road, Nashua, NH 03062; (603) 888-2214.

Each autumn, the temperature and amount of moisture varies as do the changes in the freezing and thawing of the soil. The art and science of protecting roses depends on how you deal with these factors and the methods you use to protect the plants. Roses need to be insulated from the cold as well as provided some air circulation.

A word of caution

When buying cheaper roses from the McSprawl Stores (Home Depot and the Wal- and K-Marts of the world), be aware they generally sell grafted roses of the hybrid tea variety, which are adapted to hardiness zones 5, 6, or 7. Vermont is in zones, 3, 4, and 5. These roses need winter protection. The plant union, the place where the graft forms, needs to be buried three to four inches deep for winter protection. This is called mounding. In the spring as the frosts lessen, you can begin to remove the dirt. If you do purchase roses from the McSprawls, it's best to choose them as soon as they arrive in the spring because they tend to dry out quickly and go into shock.

Autumn Appendix Guide Number Fifteen

COMPOST

The Four Stages of Breakdown:
Fire, Air, Water, and Earth

A fresh manure pile goes through a succession of four phases.

- **IN THE FIRST PHASE**, a kind of primal condition arises in which microorganisms proliferate in the breakdown of organic substances. The microorganisms create heat by decomposing the organic material.

- **THE SECOND PHASE**, in which quantities of microorganisms and fungi continue to increase, is characterized by an interchange in the air with oxygen respiration and the escape of carbon dioxide and ammonia gas.

- **IN THE THIRD PHASE**, the transformation of the substances takes place in the fluid medium in which proliferation slows down to an inner structuring of the solid element.

- **THE FOURTH AND FINAL PHASE** completes the structuring in the solid element.

The Roles of Bacteria, Actinomycetes
and Fungi in the Compost Pile

The compost pile supports a food chain with three main characters: bacteria, actinomycetes, and fungi—along with guest appearances by worms, slugs, mites, snails, ants, beetles, flies, centipedes, and more. Bacteria do most of the primary breakdown of the waste and generate heat. Then the fungi and actinomycetes get to work when the temperature begins to cool.

They are joined by white worms, round worms (nematodes), slugs, earthworms, mites, millipedes, and flies.

Later on, the waste encounters protozoa, flat worms, springtails, mold mites, and beetle mites. Chomping, chewing, munching, these critters finish off the physical breakdown of the waste. Finally, compost is almost ready except for the centipedes, ground and rove beetles, and the ants that continue to eat and aerate the pile.

What's fascinating is how different insects permeate the different stages of breakdown. In the first stage, they show little relationship to light with slight coloration, and their eyes are reduced or absent. As the pile goes through the four changes, the number of insects increases and they develop eyes and more coloration. When the heap changes in the fourth stage to humus-rich soil, worms begin to appear with few insects left. Eventually, the worms leave the pile in search of other food sources.

Autumn Appendix Guide Number Sixteen

BIODYNAMIC PREPARATIONS
AS GROWTH REGULATORS

The biodynamic preparations are growth regulators consisting of fermented materials made from plant and animal parts. They are applied as field sprays on the soil, manure, and compost piles. Some of the preparations consist of herbs to inoculate manure compost (made from yarrow, chamomile, stinging nettle, oak bark, dandelion, and valerian). Other field sprays are made from fermented cow manure (horn manure) and silica (horn silica).

The biodynamic preparations function in the following ways: Yarrow enables sulphur to draw in and organize the potassium activity. Chamomile enables sulfur to balance the potassium and calcium activities. Nettle regulates iron activity. Oak bark prevents plant diseases. Dandelion draws in silicic acid. Valerian regulates the phosphorous activity. When all these influences are working together, they achieve their prime purpose: stabilizing nitrogen.

Although used in small amounts, they have been shown to stimulate crop growth, especially in the early stages of development. They increase root growth by stimulating activity in the organic matter in the soil. This assumes the organic matter content is being maintained through crop rotations and the use of manures and composting.

For information on how to obtain and make your own biodynamic preparations, see the Summer Appendix Guide under biodynamics.

Autumn Appendix Guide Number Seventeen

LEAF ME ALONE

Leaves are the most abundant and easily accessible material for the compost pile. One of gardening's enduring misconceptions is that leaves such as maple and oak are acidic. Leaves that have gone through the composting process and come out as leaf mold test close to a neutral pH, or seven. In fact, no matter what kind of tree foliage, including pine needles, the final product has a pH of between six and seven. That's almost perfect for most plants. pH refers to the sweetness or acidity of a soil. Blueberries love acid soils—around a pH of five vs. most vegetable plants, which need a pH closer to six and seven. Lime and wood ashes increase the pH in your soil.

Leaves are a triple treat for the garden—as an addition to the compost pile, as mulch, or as a special organic amendment called leaf mold. They are a nitrogen source when the leaves are green and a carbon source when the leaves are brown and dry. The problem is that some leaves mat down when wet, which means if they are placed in the compost pile, they'll pack down and exclude air from the mix and shed water off the pile. Flat leaves such as sugar maples tend to mat together, and curly ones such as oaks and silver maples are an airier choice, but they all mat down to some extent when wet.

The best way to deal with leaves is to shred them with a lawn mower or leaf blower. Or pile them up and let them sit for a few years, turning the pile now and then. This follows the woodchuck principle of "Leaf It Alone." Eventually, the leaves will break down into leaf mold, which means they have decayed into rich crumbs. It's not that they're filled with lots of fungus and mold even though there is always a mixture of bacteria and a little mold with the breakdown of most organic materials.

Leaf mold occurs naturally in forests over years of the leaf life cycle. Have you ever noticed that rich dark brown stuff on the forest floor? Now you know what it's called. Some leaves contain weed-suppressing chemicals. Leaf mulch suppresses weeds, conserves moisture, attracts earthworms, protects plants from winter's freezing and eroding winds, and improves soil structure.

See the Summer section in chapter 11 entitled, *To Mulch or Not to Mulch*. Notes on maple leaves; variations in frost and the water table affect the brilliance of fall color in the maple leaves. As autumn progresses, trees withdraw food from the leaves for storage. When this happens, green chlorophyll pigments are no longer replaced and leaves change colors.

PART FOUR: WINTER

WINTER SNOW

Where do you come from

You little flakes of snow

Falling, falling softly

On the earth below?

On the trees and on the bushes

On the mountains afar

Tell me snowflakes do you come from

Where the angels are?

- Author Unknown

WINTER

CHAPTER 24

THE WINTER GARDEN

The winter garden is like no other. It takes place in the landscape itself, not in the compost pile or cold frame. Some days in midwinter the frozen, snow-covered earth is littered with solitary brown stalks and twigs, withered yellowed grasses, and a touch of red berries. The winterscape is still, hushed, and more than just bearable. A December snow falling lightly soothes the most rushed of shoppers and calms them from the stress of mall parking, gift buying, and unrealistic expectations.

Even though the sunlight begins to lengthen ever so slightly after the winter solstice (December 21st), the mood of the season still reflects an inwardness as the sun sits low on the horizon. This gives rise to contemplation, rest, and anticipation. In early December, there is the experience of change a-coming, a looking forward to something that has not yet happened. We ponder our gardens of seasons past and plan for the future. One way to stay in touch with your garden is to take some of those flowers, grasses, and herbs you grew and dried during the summer and fall seasons and fashion them into wreaths.

CHAPTER 25

WREATH MAKING

In early winter, I drove out to the rural town of Huntington, Vermont, to visit Chris Jenkins, a wreathmaker and artist; she grows all her own vegetables, herbs, garlic, flowers, and grasses and collects balsam greens in a nearby forest. The Jenkins' rustic home is adorned with wreaths, swags, drying herbs, flowers, and other of Chris's creations.

She uses grapevines, grasses, straw, silver artemisia, and sage for the base of the wreath. Sometimes she works with a wire ring and places the grasses around the wire. After the main base is completed, decorative flowers and herbs are added. Some examples are the everlasting flowers like statice, globe amaranth, and the many-colored strawflowers as well as oregano flowers, pearly everlasting, sweet Annie, silver artemisia, nigella, basil, blue globe flower, and golden yarrow.

As I walked through Chris Jenkins' home I noticed dried herbs hanging from the beams in many colors of blue, yellow, orange, white, purple, and golden brown; garlic braids filled with dried red peppers, an ornamental corn wreath, and fall swag with green sage and the long brown seeds of millet, sorghum, and garlic. Chris told me many of the colors fade with time but some of the hues remain. Outside hung a balsam wreath with dried red peppers and pine cones, and a grapevine wreath with teasel and its purplish flowers.

WREATH MAKING HINTS FROM CHRIS JENKINS

Wreath Base

The wreath base can be grown from silver king artemisia or you can collect moss, honeysuckle, grass, straw, grapevines, or birch twigs from the wild and your friends' gardens. Evergreen branches should be collected just before you use them.

Flowers

Grow flowers for color to place in the wreath like alliums, angelica, celosia, delphiniums, and goldenrod. Harvest the flowers early just as they start to bloom. Gather the stems of highbush cranberry and nigella when the pods have started to open at the top.

Hang salvia and statice in bunches to store. Attach wires to the heads of strawflowers and harvest while the centers are still tight.

The strong stems of yarrow and tansy don't require wiring.

Fragrance

Scented herbs such as rose-scented geraniums, southern-wood artemisia, thyme, rosemary, lemon verbena, and the lavenders give fragrance to the wreath.

Space

You need a large roomy workspace and a wooden table. The right supplies and tools make the craft of wreath making easier and more enjoyable.

Two Easy-to-Make-with-Kids Woodchuck Wreaths

- Begin with a grapevine base and add "everlastings" for decoration.
- Cut a piece of cardboard into a circle for the base and glue on green moss from the woods. For further decoration, glue on dried flowers and herbs.

A comprehensive book on traditional herbal wreaths is entitled *Country Wreaths from the Caprilands: The Legend, Lore and Design*, A. Simmons, World Publications, 1994. The book details basic information on wreath making and construction. It includes chapters on gathering herbs and flowers, harvesting and preparation, hanging herbs to dry, preserving herbs, herbs for wreath bases, herbs for color and fragrance, and selecting space, supplies, and tools for wreath making.

OH CHRISTMAS TREE

Besides wreath making, there is the annual collection of the greens. One of the oldest trees on earth, the evergreen has long been a symbol of hope during the coldest, grayest days of winter.

Many woodchuck gardeners keep holiday tree trimming simple by decorating fir or flowering crab apple trees in their front yard. Some years, I travel over to New Hampshire to visit my good friends Ash Eames and Deborah Stuart, who live close to the foothills of the White Mountains. They let me choose a fir tree of my liking which I cut down, tie onto the top of my car, and bring on home to Vermont. Other years, I collect evergreen boughs in the nearby forest. I hang some of the greens from the wooden beams in my home and use others for my advent garden wreath

THE ADVENT EVERGREEN WREATH

I celebrate advent in my home by gathering with friends and creating an advent garden wreath. I go into the woods and collect evergreen sprigs, being careful to pick sparingly. The first step is to place the evergreens around a special wire frame, which holds four small metal cups for candleholders. The wreath is laid on a table. The first week of December, the mineral kingdom is celebrated. Everyone finds a special stone like a crystal or a rock; each person tells the story behind the stone and places it on the wreath. The first candle is lit, accompanied by food, drink, and song.

The next week, the plant kingdom is celebrated. Everyone brings a plant or sprig, and the ritual of placing the plant on the wreath and lighting of the candle is reenacted. The third week brings the animal kingdom; children and adults bring their dogs, elephants, tigers, and animal toys to place in the advent garden. The fourth week is the celebration of the birth of the child. By now, a living wreath has been created and the creche is complete.

A SEASONAL GARDEN TABLE

A table can be created for each season of the year as has been described for advent. You can do the same for Halloween and Easter. Placement can be a habitual place in your home that reflects what's happening seasonally. In early fall, I lay out the most colorful winter squash, ornamental grasses, and some Indian corn. As you walk into my home, you are welcomed by the seasonal table.

Two books on the seasonal festivals:

- *Festivals, Family and Food* by Diana Carey and Judy Large, Hawthorne Press. 1982   A wonderful book for families and children.
- *Celebrating the Festivals with Children,* Friedel Lenz Anthroposophic Press, Spring Valley, New York (Spiritual-Christian Orientation).

Winter Continues

As winter continues her long journey, the earth freezes even deeper and ice covers ponds, brooks, and lakes. The winter sky seems more illuminated because sunset and sunrise are closer. Nature is so desolate, and the search for light continues in the northern climates. There comes a time when we all start to get a little antsy. There is a stirring hereabouts as daylight grows stronger with each passing day.

The land lies bare to the sky,
the seed buried in the earth,
all frozen and compact in its husk.
Life awaiting to be born,
a change is a comin',
but not so soon.

By the Author

Does that mean spring is just around the corner? Sorry, but winter has far to go.

One of those changes takes place in my mailbox with the abundance of mail-order catalogs. Pictures of flowers, fruits, and vegetables remind me of seasons to come, seeds to order, and gardens to plan.

CHAPTER 26

GARDENING CATALOGS OF THE NOT SO RICH AND FAMOUS

You can't be a real woodchuck gardener unless you participate in the annual winter ritual of collecting mail-order seed catalogs. Every year, gardeners discover catalogs they didn't know existed; some new ones spring forth and others drop out. The better catalogs provide information on the following:

- Days to maturity
- Frost tolerance
- The sweetest tomato
- Disease-resistant varieties
- The planting season (early, mid, or late)

- Open-pollinated or hybrid seeds
- Seeds treated with fungicides
- Organically grown seeds
- Selecting hybrid, open-pollinated, and organic seeds

If you check the better seed catalogs and notice an F1 next to the variety of the vegetable, this denotes a hybrid. Sometimes the word hybrid is used. Since most seeds are hybrids, only open-pollinated seeds are named. (Marglobe and Rutgers are open-pollinated tomato varieties, and Big Boy is a hybrid. Most of the Bell-Boy peppers are hybrids.) Most seed companies that carry organic seeds designate which ones are organic.

For the more serious gardener, it's helpful to understand a plant's soil, light, spacing, transplanting, fertilizing, and thinning requirements, as well as information on diseases, pests, harvest, and storage. The most informative catalogs are Stokes, Seed Saver's, Fedco, Southern Exposure Seed Exchange, Irish Eyes, and Johnny's.

Open-pollinated versus hybrid seeds: Hybrids are those vegetables resulting from a cross between parent stocks; they must be replanted and pollinated each year. In other words, you can't save seeds from hybrid plants because you never know what you are going to get. You can save them from open-pollinated plants because they breed true.

Some gardeners believe hybrid seeds contribute to the downfall of plant diversity and only buy open-pollinated varieties. They say the larger seed companies are reducing the gene pool by limiting the number of seed varieties. The truth is probably somewhere in the middle as hybrids play an important role in commercial and home food production. However, we don't want to lose the diversity in the plant world that comes from open-pollinated seeds. They are most appropriate for the home garden, the small farm, and Third World countries.

See Autumn chapter 18: Seed Saving in Northern Climates.

See Winter Appendix Guide 5 for a description of Seed Savers Exchange and how you as a gardener can get involved in saving rare, open-pollinated seeds.

See books on seeds, including seed saving, in Spring Appendix Guide 1.

The Winter Appendix Guide has an extensive list of seed catalogs, web sites, tools, organic controls, organic organizations, books, and magazines. Study your catalogs for more information, like maturation times and seed hardiness. Some have lots of information, like Stokes and Johnny's catalog; others don't have much. The same can be said for seed packets; you will find they are not all created equal. Many are designed these days with a flair, not a whimper, with beautiful pictures and more. Did you know seed packets were an invention of the Shaker Community?

The plain truth is that most seed company addresses are just post office boxes or call-in centers; they have nothing to do with growing the seeds they sell. The seed business is controlled by a handful of corporations. Seminis has 45% of the vegetable seed business nationwide. They own Asgrow and Royal Slvis. Seminis sells its seeds to almost all the seed catalog companies. You don't really know where the seeds come from unless the catalog company provides the seed grower's, address, which is almost never found. Two small organic seed companies, High Mowing of Wolcott, Vermont, and Turtle Seeds of Copake, New York, do provide this information.

For more information on where your seeds come from and the consolidation of the seed business, see Winter Appendix Guide 6 and 7.

With all that being said, it's fun to study catalogs and the pictures are inspiring. Come January, we all need a good dose of color photos and drawings of lovely gardens, red tomatoes, and yellow corn.

A couple of the "big boy" publications are Burpee's, Stokes, Harris, Ferry-Morse, and Parks. Specialty seed businesses offer ethnic and heirloom seeds like those found in Native American, Amish, Mennonite, Hutterite, and Cajun communities, as well as seeds from the Asian and European countries. Irish Eyes of Washington State sells 74 varieties of potatoes, along with a great description of all the spuds. The Pepper Gal lists 174 kinds of peppers. The R.H. Shumway's catalog, with its larger-than-life colored illustrations, looks as if it came out of the 1930s.

Two of my favorite catalogs are the Fedco Seeds newsprint catalog of Maine and the Stokes Seeds Company from New York State. They both provide practical horticultural information to small farmers and gardeners. When I was on the farm, I couldn't wait to take my new Stokes heavy-duty newsprint catalog out to the two-seater, a.k.a. the privy or outhouse.

One garden giant is W. Atlee Burpee, which carries mostly hybrid seeds but also a fourth edition of heirloom varieties. These include a 1901 tomato named Quarter Century and a breakfast radish brought over from France in the 1880s by Burpee himself. By the way,

Lyman Wood, marketer of rototillers and garden carts.
Photo from Country Home Products, Vergennes, Vermont.

Burpee's has been bought and sold many times over by multinational corporations.

THE TOP TOOL AND SUPPLY COMPANIES

A number of garden companies sell garden tools, organic controls, season extenders, seed-starting supplies, machines, and supplies.

The most extensive tool catalog for organic farmers and gardeners comes from Peaceful Valley Farm Supply in California. Their selection ranges from hand tools to market garden equipment, to organic aids and controls. Fedco and Johnny's, both from Maine, also have tools and organic supplies but nowhere near the selection of Peaceful Valley. Lehman's in Ohio carries everything from coveralls to kerosene lamps to tools for the farm. Many Amish families purchase from Lehman's because they only carry nonelectric items. Country Home Products of Vermont markets rototillers, garden carts, trimmers, and mowers, all appropriate to the small farm and large garden. Their machines have large rubber tires, good balance, dependable motors, and will turn on a dime. Gardener's Supply of Burlington, Vermont, is one of the largest garden catalog companies in the country. They carry a mix of tools, greenhouses, fertilizer, irrigation and germination supplies, garden carts, and compost bins.

YUPPIE CATALOGS

Then there is the parade of stylized gardening catalogs for the rich and famous that are chock full of designer bird baths, yard ornaments, and teak benches. Gardening is big business. In fact it is America's No. #1 hobby, bringing in billions of dollars. The upscale Martha Stewart catalogs have a lot to do with looking good. How many woodchuck gardeners can afford an indoor grow-light garden system on wheels for $419? I don't have the gelt for a natural cedar compost bin for $115. I prefer to follow one of the woodchuck principles of "making do" by building my own compost bins with scrap lumber and wooden pallets.

It's hard to know which of the 1,000 mail-order gardening suppliers in the U.S. and Canada to choose from. Some woodchuck gardeners don't use catalogs but wait for garden and farm store sales in May and June. They also buy seeds in bulk in the spring and fall at the stores.

See Winter Appendix Guides 1-14 for Ron's Favorite Seed catalogs along with a comprehensive list of addresses, phone numbers, and more information on seeds, fruit, plants, tools, and supply companies as well as seed saver groups, organic organizations, and garden web sites.

CHAPTER 27

WOODCHUCK TECHNOLOGY

The typical American gardener uses the same hand tools as the pilgrims did in 1620. The shovel, rake, hoe, shears, and wheelbarrow are still in wide use, as they were over 200 years ago. Two additions for the small farm and garden are the rear-tined rototiller and the garden cart, an improvement on the wheelbarrow because it takes the weight off your back and makes it much easier to move loads around the garden.

Most woodchuck gardeners use "the big three" when they work

in the garden: a pointed shovel, a heavy-duty hoe, and a strong rake, all of which are long handled and don't break in a season or two. I use the shovel, hoe, and rake to build all my slightly raised beds.

See Ron's Vermont Planting Tips in Chapter 4 for information on how I use the shovel, hoe, and rake to build raised beds.

In addition to "the big three," a couple of other hand tools come in handy, like the stirrup hoe and the three-tined cultivator, a good tool for heavy surface weeding and cultivating. A number of new long-handled, sharp hoes allow you to stand straight up because the blade is parallel to the ground. The 7" sharp blade is made of high quality Swiss steel that keeps its edge. The 60" handle is American hardwood. These hoes come in many shapes and sizes. I suggest you visit different farm and garden stores and feel out the hoes and other tools to see which fit best in your hand. Also, check out your friends' tools.

TWO HOE RON

Use a sharp hoe for cultivating and weeding in the long rows because it has a very sharp edge and can cut weeds close to the plants. The other hoe I work with has a large, square head on it. It's rather dull, and I use it for hilling plants in rows and removing the larger weeds. *See Chapter 4, Ron's Vegetable Planting Tips, and Winter Appendix Guide 4 for tool and small farm catalogs under Tools, Machines, Nursery Products, and Supply Companies.*

DUCT TAPE AND GARDENING

Besides shovels, rakes, and hoes, other woodchuck garden items are practical, cheap, creative, and efficient.

The Phenomenal World of Plastic

Plastic has its uses for gardeners: milk crates, 5-gallon buckets, and 1-gallon milk jugs all come in handy.

Plastic milk crates: Use them to store just about anything or to support a potting bench. To build one, stack three milk crates and do the same with another set of crates. Place a 2" x 12" plank of wood between the crates and you've got a workbench on which to repair lawn mowers, chainsaws, and so on. You can find milk crates on back roads, at recycling centers, at the dump, and at yard sales.

Five-gallon plastic buckets: These are great because you can carry wood, water, potting soils, vegetables, and apples. You can store carrots in sand in them in the cool parts of the cellar. Even turn the

Woodchuck paraphernalia: 5-gallon buckets, flats, and milk crates.
Photo by Robert King at his garden.

buckets upside down and put down a plank between them to hold trays of seedlings. You can brew your own liquid manures and nettle teas in them or punch holes and start your own container garden. They are efficient for moving perennials around...and the list goes on. Dunkin Donuts sometimes sells them and sometimes gives them away. Food stores and home builders throw them out. Keep your eyes open and check the dumpsters.

A book called *The Five-Gallon Bucket Book* (by Jim McKenzie, Andrews McMeel, 1999) describes 105 uses for this ultimate recyclable.

One-gallon plastic milk jugs: I visit the recycling center every couple of years and pick up a bunch of 1-gallon jugs. I cut the bottoms off and place them over young tomato, cucumber, squash, and pepper plants from mid-to late-May. Water the plants by simply pouring water through the spout. If the temperature heats up, punch holes in the sides and make sure to check the young plants on a regular basis. If it gets too hot, take them off. You can also use the cut-off bottoms to hold water for your clay pots or use the tops for funnels. Fill the entire jug with water and leave them in your cold frames for a solar heating effect. When I am finished with the milk jugs, I take them back to the recycling center or string them up and store them for next year.

Another method for storage is to place them one on top of the other on a long tomato stake.

MORE WOODCHUCK PARAPHERNALIA

TWINE: Take a ball of twine and place it in one of those cut-off milk jug funnels, thread the free end of the twine through the bottleneck, nail the jug upside down to the barn or garage door and you will have a nifty way of pulling twine out as you need it.

You can use bailing twine that has been removed from bales of hay. Check at a farm supply store for the large round rolls of baling twine, which sometimes are broken and can be purchased more cheaply. Place extra rolls in a 5-gallon plastic bucket to keep them dry; they store for years—and you never run out of twine. Or look around for old bales of hay with discarded twine. I don't like the plastic twine because it doesn't break down in the garden and leaves a mess.

NEWSPAPERS: They are cheap and safe. Twenty-some years ago, printers' ink contained heavy metals like lead, and toxic solvents were used to spread the ink on paper. Bad news for any garden. The good news is today's solvents are soy-based and biodegradable, and heavy metals have been eliminated from the pigments for both black-and-white and color printing. Newspapers make a good mulch for vegetable and flower beds. Cover the newspapers with more traditional organic mulches, like hay, lawn clippings, shredded leaves, or bark to give your beds a more natural appearance.

PENCILS: Pencils can be used for placing seeds in germinating trays or for transplanting small seedlings.

WOODEN POTTING LABELS can be used like a miniature trowel or cultivator. Or go to Ben and Jerry's Ice Cream and pick up free wooden spoons and forks, along with a scoop of not-so-cheap woodchuck crunch.

LEAVES: Leaves can be used for mulch and in compost. If you happen to have one of those machines that blows leaves around, they have a vacuum attachment that shreds leaves into a perfect mulch. Your garden beds will look just as good using shredded leaves as buying those expensive peat or bark mulches.

WOODCHIPS: Sometime flag down a truck full of wood chips. If you catch haulers in the right mood, they will dump them off for you at little or no cost—or a six-pack of Bud. Use wood chips around shrubs and bushes or create a garden bed of lilies or ferns by simply spreading the chips out and planting. It's best to dig up the soil before you lay down the wood chips, but it's not necessary if you let the chips fall as they may for a year.

There is no end to the possibilities of ingenuity and invention. Use your imagination, live simply, and follow the lead of this cheap woodchuck gardener to create your own garden tchotchkes.

P.S. If you're still wondering what possible connection can be found between duct tape and gardening, it's simple. Duct tape is a metaphor for low-and no-cost woodchuck technologies. I use duct tape to keep the freezer door on my refrigerator closed, on holes in screens and shower curtains, and, of course, to cover holes on my car to pass inspection.

CHAPTER 28

WOODCHUCK TIPS FOR HOUSEPLANTS

For those experiencing the post-epiphany blues, winter is a good time to care for houseplants. Indoor gardening has never been one of my specialties. I basically water the plants on a regular basis, feed them with compost once a year, take most of the plants outside in a partially shaded spot to live in the summer, and repot them from time to time. First, I give them a bath by sprinkling the leaves and running a slow trickle of water through the soil. This can be done in the bathtub, shower, or the kitchen sink. Over time, salts build up on the surface of the soil and you need to flush them away. While you're at it, snip unwanted and diseased leaves.

You might find mealybugs-round, white fuzzy critters that hide on leaf stems or in the axis; aphids-small, soft green, reddish or black insects clustered on new growth; scale-hard, oval or round-shelled insects attached to stems or leaves; or whiteflies-small white insect specks that feed on the leaves.

Check out a good garden book at the library or bookstore for pictures of these critters or write for a pamphlet from your local agricultural extension agent.

To repot or not to repot is often the question most asked during "March Madness." A spider plant packed to the point of brown-tipped leaves is definitely in need of a change. Geraniums wintered over and grown for the third year in the same soil need renewal. March is the time to consider giving houseplants a new home, because most are beginning to grow active in response to longer days and warmer temperatures.

Repotting is not necessarily a yearly affair for any plant, and some, like amaryllis, angel-wing begonia, and many ferns produce best when their roots are crowded. I am sure your grandmother grew the same plant in the same pot for two generations; it may have been starved, miserable, and deprived—but it survived a long time. And if you believe plants have feelings, that doesn't bode well for your grandmother's karma in her next life.

MORE TIPS

Wash the plant thoroughly in the sink or tub. If the plant is covered with insects, you might have to use a soapy cloth or toothbrush to clean it. If the plant is small, turn it upside down in a pail of lukewarm water for a few minutes.

Allow the plant to dry in a shaded location, never in the sun.

If using an insecticide, try an insecticidal soap like Safer's brand, which contains fatty acids that help kill insects. They are safe to use indoors and will not harm pets. As with any insecticide, read the directions. Be careful when using insecticidal soap on houseplants such as ferns, jade plants, and palms; test a small portion of the plant first if you aren't sure.

For delicate plants such as angel-winged begonias, try dabbing the pests with a cotton swab soaked with rubbing alcohol and then rinse the plant with water.

Well folks, it feels good to do a little indoor gardening while the snow covers the earth. I hope you will try to care for a couple of houseplants. Another activity that's fun is to force the "Woodies" like forsythia.

CHAPTER 29

BRINGING IN THE WOODIES

Some gardeners' melancholia drives them to fill the void with masses of greenery and blossoms inside their home. After removing the Christmas tree and Chanukah paraphernalia, they have more space and light and now need some color. One old woodchuck trick is to "Bring in the Woodies." Even in midwinter, you can take cuttings of forsythia, shad, lilac, and quince bushes, bring them inside, and place in a vase of warm water. In about 7 to 10 weeks, you may have midwinter blossoms adorning your home, but

it doesn't always work. To increase your chances, cut the stems at an angle, beat them lightly with a hammer, remove the bark of the lower stems, and place them in water.

The forsythia produces small yellow flowers, and quince has large sprays of blossoms in different colors, like pink and salmon. They, like forsythia, can be started in February or later. White shad, shadblow, or what some call serviceberry is the first to blossom in the Vermont woods and is a sure sign spring is here. After the shad come the pin and chokecherries and then the apple blossoms.

You can also force lilac stems. The Druids cut lilacs on January 1st and plunged them into water. How well the leaves sprouted determined that year's good will and growth.

The woody most people are familiar with is the pussy willow. The common pussy willow (*Salix discolor*) is a shrub or small tree, 10-18 feet high, that is one of the first to blossom in spring. Female catkins are the familiar pussy willow blossoms that are easily forced by bringing them into a warm room.

Some florist shops sell almond, plum, quince, shad, forsythia, crab apple, pussy willow, witch hazel, magnolia, and other woody stems already budded out. They take little time to blossom.

As the sun stops its retrograde motion and our light-deprived lives begin to quiver, it's time to force the woodies into action. Remember to cut the stems when the moon is waxing rather than waning. The expansive action of the moon enhances leaf and flower development. See information on the cosmic forces in the Summer section in Chapter 10: *Let the Force be With You.*

Besides the woodies, you can force bulbs to bloom and brighten winter's gloom. Paper-whites (narcissus) and amaryllis are among the easiest bulbs to force. The idea is to trick them into behaving as though they've finished winter. Place about three paper-white bulbs (about 89 cents per bulb) in a 5-inch-wide clay pot full of loose soil. Refrigerate for about two weeks. Leave about one-fourth of the bulb above the soil line and water them once a week to keep the soil moist. Remove the pot and place it in direct sunlight in a cooler room. The more light they have, the longer they will bloom and stand strong.

Amaryllis are the rich person's bulb, costing as much as $10 per bulb, but they can last for years with proper care. Place one bulb in a deep, narrow pot. They don't need any refrigeration and if placed in direct sunlight will bloom in five to six weeks. Make sure to let the flowers die off, allowing it to produce a full set of leaves that last about five weeks. Let the leaves wither some before placing the bulb in the garden soil. Dig the plant up in the fall and store the bulbs over the winter in a cellar or cool, dark room before forcing them again in the spring. Clip all the leaves, feed with compost, and in about six weeks, you'll have blooms again.

Tulip and daffodil bulbs are more difficult to trick into blooming. They need to be refrigerated in soil for 10-15 weeks. If they're started too late, they bloom when the bulbs are flowering in your front yard. Water the bulbs once a week until they make three-to four-inch sprouts. Place in direct sunlight and they should bloom in about five weeks.

As you can see, gardening never ends, even in winter, when you are really into it. There is always something to learn and do, like making wreaths, ordering seed catalogs, planning the garden, caring for houseplants, or forcing woodies and bulbs.

CHAPTER 30

WINTER APPENDIX GUIDE

Winter Appendix Guide Number One

A REVISED LIST OF

Seed companies in alphabetical order.
Garden Tools, Machines, Nursery Products & Supply Companies.
Heirloom Seed Saving Businesses & Fruit Catalogs
Organic Organizations
Gardening Addresses & Web Sites
Information on Master Gardening
Information on Farm & Garden Training & Apprenticeships
All Purpose Organic Gardening Books & Pamphlets
Gardening Magazines and Publications

Winter Appendix Guide Number Two

SEED COMPANIES IN
ALPHABETICAL ORDER

W. ATLAS BURPEE AND CO., Warminster, PA 18974; (800) 333-5808; *www.burpee.com*. Sells bulk seeds to commercial growers, which come in a separate catalog from the one sent out to home gardeners. Burpee's also carries a catalog of organic seeds.

COOK'S GARDEN, P.O. Box 535, Londonderry, VT 05148. Good for salad greens plus and mesclun mixes. Some unique organic/vegetable seed varieties. (800) 457-9703; *www.cooksgarden.com*. Cook's Garden pioneered the concept of pre-mixed salad greens including the use of mesclun and cold, hardy lettuce and spinach. These greens can be grown under the right conditions in the cold frame and greenhouse during late fall, winter and early spring. Cook's Garden, located in Londonderry, Vermont sells over 40 varieties of lettuce as well as other vegetables and unique flowers. They are a subsidiary of Park Seeds, a large family owned business of South Carolina.

ETHNOBOTANICAL CATALOG OF SEEDS, c/o J.L. Hudson, Seedman, Star Route 2, Box 337, La Honda, CA 94020. Rare varieties of seeds.

EVERGREEN Y.H. ENTERPRISES, P.O. Box 17538, Anaheim, CA 92817. Oriental vegetable seeds.

FEDCO SEEDS, P.O. Box 520, Waterville, ME 04903. Great Organic Growers Supply Catalog. Seeds, tools, supplies, books, information. (207) 873-7333; *www.fedcoseed.com*. Attempting to grow more organic seeds. Organic seeds are labeled in catalog. 5% of seeds grown in Maine, 10% organic. This low-cost organic grower's supply company is one of my favorites. Fedco is a Maine cooperative whose consumers own 60 percent and whose workers own 40 percent of the business. The catalog is full organic information. It has extensive garden seed choices, a selection of Maine Moose Tubers (onion sets, potatoes and shallots), heirloom varieties, cover crops and green manure seeds, grains, soil amendments, as well as tools and books. Fedco also carries an ornamental and professional growers catalog.

HARRIS SEEDS, 60 Saginaw Drive, P.O. Box 24966, Rochester, NY 14624; (800) 548-7928. Large commercial seed company. Sells bulk seeds to market gardeners as well as seeds and supplies to the home gardener. They also sell untreated and organic seeds in a separate catalog. *www.harrisseeds.com*.

HIGH MOWING ORGANIC SEED FARM, 813 Brook Road, Wolcott, VT 05860; (802) 888-2480. High Mowing specializes in heirloom and open-pollinated varieties, biodynamic & organic vegetable seeds, flowers, medicinal & culinary herbs & grains. The seeds are grown at High Mowing and biodynamic & organically certified seed farms in Vermont, Oregon and California. High Mowing lists the seed farms where the crops are grown.

HORIZON HERBS, LLC, P.O. Box 69, Williams, OR 97544; (541) 846-6704; *www.horizonherbs.com*. This is strictly a medicinal catalog filled with seeds, plants, live roots and more. It's very informative with a fascinating introduction and from what I've heard, the germination rate on the seeds is high.

IRISH EYES INC. AND GARDEN CITY SEEDS, P.O. Box 307, Thorpe, WA 98946; (877) 733-3001; *www.irisheyes.com*. A merger of Ronnigers Potato Seed Company with a garlic and garden seed business. 95 potato varieties and 26 different garlics along with shallots, onions, alliums, and vegetable seeds.

They carry a large number of organic seeds. A must catalog for serious gardeners.

JACKSON AND PERKINS, 85 Rose Lane, Medford, OR 97501-0703; (800) 292-4769; *www.jacksonandperkins.com*. Specialize in flowers and perennials.

JOHNNY'S SELECTED SEEDS, 310 Foss Hill Rd., Albion, ME 04910; (207) 437-4301; *www.johnnyseed.com*. Seeds, tools, and supplies. One of my favorite all-around seed catalogs. Johnny's is known for publishing a catalog so useful it's a basic garden course in itself. Detailed information on the seed packets includes number of days to maturity, germination percentages, number of seeds, cultural information, depth and distance, transplanting guidance, harvest tips, and disease and organic pest control. Johnny's sets up seed trials for seed growers and breeders. They sell tools, organic aids, and they both organic and conventional seeds.

LE JARDIN DU GORMET, P.O. Box 75, St. Johnsbury Ctr., VT 05863-0075; (800) 659-1446. Herb plants and seeds, beans and pea seeds from France, other European countries and South Africa. Also sells leeks, garlic and rocambole.

NICHOLS GARDEN NURSERY, 1190 North Pacific Highway, Albany, OR 97321; (614) 928-9280. Many kinds of herbs, garlic and rare seeds. Have been in the seed business for many years.

PARK SEED COMPANY, 1 Parkton Ave., Greenwood, SC 29647 (864) 223-7333; (800) 845-3369; *www.parkseed.com*. One of the "Big Boy" catalogs.

PEACEFUL VALLEY FARM SUPPLY, P.O. Box 2209, Grass Valley, CA 95945; (888) 784-1722; *www.groworganic.com*. Great selection of organic seeds for gardener and farmer. See more on Peaceful Valley in Garden Tool Section.

PINETREE GARDEN SEEDS, Box 300, New Gloucester, ME 04260 (207) 926-3400; *www.superseeds.com*. Offers good quality seeds to folks with small gardens. Their packets contain small but adequate quantities and are priced right. This makes trying out a new variety less painful. Pinetree also categorizes some of their seeds according to ethnic origins. The catalog is large and comprehensive. Many of the seeds are tested in Maine.

RENEE'S GARDEN. Seeds are available at garden centers. (888) 880-7228; *www.reneesgarden.com*. Founder Renee Shepherd is the queen of the "rainbow packet," a mixed pack of seeds in different colors.

SEEDS OF CHANGE, P.O. Box 15700. Santa Fe, NM 87506; (888) 762-7333; *www.seedsofchange.com*. Offers 500 varieties of seeds. Unique organic Native-American corn, amaranth and pepper varieties. It is a colorful catalog you can give your friends for Chanukah. 100% certified organic, open-polli-nated, GM-free seeds. Owned by Mars Inc., the international candy, food, and pet-food conglomerate. The grandson of Mars founder Forrest Mars Sr., Stephen Badger is now the president. Besides organic seeds, Mars has invest-ed heavily in the natural foods market.

SEEDS OF DISTINCTION, P.O. Box 86, Station A (Etobicoke), Toronto, Canada, M9C4V2; (416) 255-3060; *www.seedsofdistinction.com*. An interesting catalog of distinct seeds and a challenge for the advanced gardener.

SEED SAVER'S EXCHANGE, 3076 North Winn Rd., Decorah, IA, 52101; (563) 382-5990. *www.seedsavers.org.* *(See description of SSE in #5.)*

R.H. SHUMWAY'S, P.O. Box 1, Graniteville, SC 29829-0001; (803) 663-9771. The pictures in the catalog are a throwback to the turn of the century. Shunway's is in its 129th year. They offer bulk seeds to farmers as well as seeds to home gardeners. It is chock full of history and plant information.

SELECT SEEDS, 180 Stickney Hill Road, Union, CT 06076; (860) 684-9310; *www.selectseeds.com* An antique flower catalog with stylish annuals and tender perennials. Great drawings.

SOUTHERN EXPOSURE SEED EXCHANGE, P.O. Box 460, Mineral, VA 23117; (540) 894-9480; *www.southernexposure.com*. A wide selection of corn, garlic, onions, shallots and peas. Large, colorful, informative catalog.

STOKES, Box 548, Buffalo, NY 14240; (800) 396-9238; *www.stokesseeds.com*. Quality seeds since 1881 – vegetable, flower, herb, bulbs, plants, supplies. One of the best information catalogs on the market. One of the old-est and most reliable seed companies in the U.S.

TURTLE TREE SEEDS, Camphill Village, Copake, NY 12516. 1-800-620-7388. These open-pollinated seeds come from a number of experienced biodynamic seed growers throughout the United States. They include root, leafy and fruiting vegetables, herbs, flowers and farm, feed and cover crops. They offer some of the best seeds on the market.

TERRITORIAL SEED COMPANY, P.O. Box 158, Cottage Grove, OR 97424; (541) 942-9547. A large catalog with conventional, organic and biodynamic seeds and many products. *www.territorialseeds.com*

VESEY'S SEEDS LTD., P.O. Box 9000, Calais, ME 04619; (902) 892-1048.

WHITE FLOWER FARM, 30 Irene Street, Torrington, CT 06790; *www.whiteflower.com*. (860) 482-3638. Other seedsmen follow White Flower Farms lead with new varieties. This use to be Shepherd's Seeds.

WILD GARDEN SEED, P.O. Box 1509; Philomath, OR 97370; (541) 929-4289. Questions – *frank@wildgardenseed.com*. Orders - orders@wildgardenseed.com. A fascinating seed catalog from a master seedsman. A must-see for organic gardeners for greens and herbs.

Winter Appendix Guide Number Three

THE SAFE SEED PLEDGE

Some seed companies like Johnny's, Cook's Garden, High Mowing, Southern Exposure, Fedco and Turtle Seeds that carry organic seeds have taken the Safe Seed Pledge which states that do not knowingly buy or sell genetically engineered seeds or plants. More research and testing is necessary to further access the potential risks of genetically engineered seeds. Moving DNA from one cell to another (gene splicing) is too much of a risk. The reader can check their seed catalogs to see of the Safe Seed pledge is included. Keep informed. This is one of the most controversial subjects of our time, especially for the organic gardening and farming movement.

Winter Appendix Guide Number Four

GARDEN TOOLS, MACHINES, NURSERY PRODUCTS, AND SUPPLY COMPANIES

A.M. LEONARD, PO Box 816, Piqua, OH 45356. Gardening tools and supplies.

CARTS VERMONT, 1890 Airport Parkway, S. Burlington, VT 05403. (800) 852-2340. Gard-way carts and parts.

COUNTRY HOME PRODUCTS, Meigs Road, P.O. Box 25, Vergennes, VT 05491; (800) 446-8746. A good selection of trimmers, mowers, rototillers and garden carts.

FEDCO SEEDS, PO Box 520, Waterville, ME, 04903; (207) 873-7333. *www.fedcoseeds.com*. Good selection of tools for the home garden & small farm.

GARDENER'S SUPPLY, 128 Intervale Road, Burlington, VT, 05401; (800) 863-1700; *www.gardeners.com*. Supplies for the home gardener.

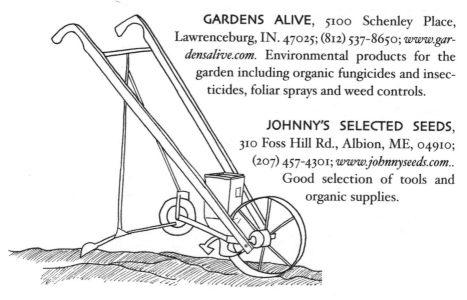

GARDENS ALIVE, 5100 Schenley Place, Lawrenceburg, IN. 47025; (812) 537-8650; *www.gardensalive.com*. Environmental products for the garden including organic fungicides and insecticides, foliar sprays and weed controls.

JOHNNY'S SELECTED SEEDS, 310 Foss Hill Rd., Albion, ME, 04910; (207) 457-4301; *www.johnnyseeds.com.*. Good selection of tools and organic supplies.

LEHMAN'S, PRODUCTS FOR THE FARM, 1 Lehman Circle, P.O. Box 41, Kidion, OH, 44637; (888) 438-5346; *www.lehmans.com.* All nonelectric items.

MELLINGER'S, 2310 W. South Range Rd., North Lima, OH, 44452. Nursery products and plants.

MUSSER FOREST INC., P.O. Box 340, Indiana, PA, 15701. Trees, plants, and tools.

PEACEFUL VALLEY FARM SUPPLY, P.O. Box 2209, Grass Valley, CA, 95945; (888) 784-1722; *www.groworganic.com.* Tools, supplies and a large selection of environmental supplies for organic farming and gardening, including organic insecticides, fungicides and sprays. Carries BSA rototillers and Planet Junior seeders and implements.

RABUN PRODUCTS INC. P.O. Box 8, Tiger, GA 30576; (706) 782-4224. Mole chasers.

Winter Appendix Guide Number Five

SEED SAVER'S EXCHANGE

Smaller seed catalogs attract customers to the open-pollinated varieties. Every month more than a thousand gardeners across North America trade, sell or donate the seeds of 12,000 fruits and vegetables that have been in their families for generations. They do this annually with Seed Savers Exchange of Decorah, Iowa, a non-profit organization established in the 1970s to reverse the alarming declines in the number of heirloom varieties available to consumers.

These old varieties are often unique to certain regions of the country, brought there decades ago by immigrant farmers. They were eclipsed by supermarket hybrids, bred for longevity and mechanical harvesting, or home garden varieties more uniform in shape with higher productivity. They are not necessarily as tasty, colorful or nutritious as the older varieties. Heirloom seeds are part of our heritage, handed down from father to daughter, or grandmother to grandson.

If you are one of those faithful gardeners who has been saving seeds of a favorite vegetable from harvest to harvest because you know you can't buy them from seed companies anymore, contact the Seed Savers Exchange (SSE).

SSE maintains a list of seed-savers, and the seeds they are saving, and it puts seed-savers and would-be-seed-savers in contact with each other.

SSE runs a grower's network the goal of which is to build an inventory of outstanding varieties that are protected and maintained. SSE just completed a computerized list of all non-hybrid seed varieties available from mail-order companies in the U.S.

They provide information to growers on preserving seeds and a plant-finder service for locating seeds. SSE says it's network of growers maintains varieties of over 2,000 beans, 600 tomatoes, 200 squash, 100 corn, 100 potatoes, and others. If you are interested in learning more or participating, write to: SSE, 3076 North Winn Rd., Decorah, IA 52101; (563) 382-5990; *www.seedsavers.org.*

Their catalog is full of historical anecdotes on the origins of different seed varieties.

SSE also produces the Garden Seed Inventory, an inventory of seed catalogs listing all non-hybrid vegetable seeds available in the United States & Canada. A monumental work. 808 pgs. paperback $26.00

Winter Appendix Guide Number Six

BURSTING THE BUBBLE:
THE POLITICS OF SEEDS

There is rapid consolidation occurring in the seed industry. The seed business has changed dramatically since W. Atlee Burpee offered seeds in his first catalog 125 years ago. Multi-national conglomerates are buying out family-owned seed companies, dropping their collections of standard vegetables, and replacing them in many cases with hybrids and patented varieties. For example, Cook's Garden is owned by Park Seeds, Gurney's Seed, Henry Fields Seeds & Nursery, Stark Brothers Nurseries, Spring Hill, the Vermont Wildflower Farm, and nationalgardening.com are all part of mySeasons.com owned by Foster & Gallagher. J.W. Jung Seeds owns Seymour Select, Totally Tomato, and R.H. Shumway's.

The top ten garden seed companies in the world control 30% of the market or $24 billion a year. That's just the tip of the iceberg, as most seed catalog companies buy their seeds from large breeders, commercial seed growers and wholesalers such as Seminis, Pan American Seed or Sakata. In other words, most of the seeds you see advertised in seed catalogs don't come from the companies that sell them. Most garden companies purchase the exact same seeds and then package them with different company's labels.

Winter Appendix Guide Number Seven

SEED STATISTICS

Only 10% of the seed business are garden seeds and 10% of garden seeds are sold via catalogs. Most of the seeds that are sold are corn, soybean, rape (canola) and grass seed for use on the farm, in the garden and for the lawn. A high percentage of these are genetically modified (GM) seeds. This means that a lot of the food you purchase in the supermarket is grown with (GM) seeds. There is currently a strong movement in Europe and U.S. against (GM) foods. In fact, 60 seed companies have taken – The Safe Seed Pledge not to buy or sell (GM) seeds. The pledge was mentioned above after the alphabetized list of seed catalogs. Check out your seed catalogs for the Safe Seed pledge.

Winter Appendix Guide Number Eight

OTHER HEIRLOOM
SEED-SAVING BUSINESSES

EASTERN NATIVE SEED CONSERVANCY, 222 Main Street, Box 451, Great Barrington, MA 01230.

FEDCO, see their catalog for more information on seed saving.

MAINE SEED-SAVING NETWORK, P.O. Box 126, Penobscot, ME 04476.

TURTLE TREE SEEDS (also listed above under seed companies) Camphill Village, Copake, NY 12516.

Winter Appendix Guide Number Nine

FRUIT CATALOGS

W. ATLEE BURPEE AND CO., Warminster, PA 18974; (800) 888-1447; *www.burpee.com*. Carries fruits and berries.

CUMMINS NURSERY 4233 Glass Factory Bay Rd, Geneva, NY 14456; (315) 789-7083.

ELMORE ROOTS NURSERY for the coldest hillsides in Vermont, 631 Symonds Mill Road, Wolcott, VT 05680; (800) 42-PLANT; *www.elmore-roots.com*. Carries fruit trees, berries, flowering shrubs, roses, hedgerows, nut trees, roots, and herbs.

FEDCO TREES. PO Box 520, Waterville, ME 04903-0520; (207) 872-8317; *www.fedcoseeds.com*. Good selection of fruit trees, small fruits and berries, conifers, nut and shade trees.

MILLER NURSERIES. 5060 West Lake Road, Canandaigua, NY 14424; (800) 836-9630. Specializes in apple trees. Also carries berries.

NOURSE FARMS, 41 River Road, South Deerfield, MA 01373; (413) 665-2658. Specializes in small fruits and berries.

ST. LAWRENCE NURSERIES, 325 State Hwy 345, Potsdam, NY 13676; (315) 265-6739; *trees@sln.potsdam.ny.us; www.sln.potsdam.ny.us*. Hardy fruit & nut trees.

*For fruits and berries, I prefer to buy from regional and local fruit nurseries where you can see the plants and speak to the nursery managers.

Winter Appendix Guide Number Ten

ORGANIC & FARMING ORGANIZATIONS

THE BIODYNAMIC FARMING AND GARDENING ASSOCIATION,
25844 Butler Road, Junction City, OR 97488; (541) 998-0105; e-mail: *biody-namic@aol.com.*; Web site: *www.biodynamics.com.*

Biodynamic gardening and farming is referred to throughout the book. For specific information, see summer chapters on Companion Planting and Planting Astrologically. The Summer Appendix Guide #8 has more information on how to obtain the quarterly BD magazine, a list of pamphlets and books, training programs and more. The BD Resource Guide covers most of this information. Call toll free (888) 516-7797 for a copy.

NORTHEAST ORGANIC FARMING ASSOCIATION (NOFA), 411 Shelton Rd., Barre, MA 01005; (978) 355-2853. Has a quarterly magazine called *The Natural Farmer* and summer conference.

NOFA VERMONT, P.O. Box 697, Bridge Street, Richmond, VT 05477; (802) 434-4122; *www.nofavt.org.* Has an annual winter conference and organic gardening and farming workshops throughout the year. Also, sells the most complete book list I am aware of and organic products including soil amendments. Other programs include: apprenticeships for young farmers, certification of organic farms and educational programs in the schools.

MAINE ORGANIC FARMERS AND GARDENERS ASSOCIATION, MOFGA, See fedco catalog. PO Box 170, Unity, ME 04988; (207) 568-4142.

NEW HAMPSHIRE NOFA, White Farm, 150 Clinton St., Concord, NH 03301; (603) 899-2806.

NEW YORK NOFA, 661 Lansing Rd., Fultonville, NY 12072; (518) 922-7937.

CANADA ORGANIC GROWERS, Box 116, Collingwood, Ontario, L9Y 324; (705) 444-0923; *www.gks.com/cog.*

ORGANIC TRADE ASSOCIATION OF NORTH AMERICA, (413) 774-7511. List of organic brokers, suppliers, growers and associations.

NORTHEAST SUSTAINABLE AGRICULTURAL WORKING GROUP, P.O. Box 608, Belchertown, MA 01007. (413) 323-4531. *nesawg@smallfarm.org* *www.smallfarm.org*

THE COMMUNITY FARM, 3480 Potter Rd., Bearlake, MI 49614; (231) 889-3216. A Voice for Community Supported Agriculture.

THE ROBYN VAN EN CENTER FOR CSA'S in the Northeast c/o Center for Sustainable Living, Wilson College 1015 Philadelphia, PA 17201; (717) 264-1578. Information and materials and a good website on Community Supported Agriculture. *www.csacenter.org*

VICTORY GARDEN PROJECT, RR 1, Box 6025, Athens, ME 04912. An organization for political and social change using organic food production and distribution as the primary tool.

Winter Appendix Guide Number Eleven

GARDENING ADDRESSES AND WEB SITES

Information on Organic Gardening and Organic Issues:
ORGANIC GARDENING, 33 Minor St., Emmaus, PA 18090; (800) 666-2206; *wwworganicgardening.com. Newfarm.org*

Information on Community Gardening:

AMERICAN COMMUNITY GARDENING ASSOCIATION, 100 North 20th St., Philadelphia, PA., 19103-1495; (215) 988-8785; *www.communitygarden.org.*

THE HARMONY GARDEN, Hennessey and Martin, a 71-page handbook on community gardening and greening. Excellent information for new and beginning gardeners. For handbook write to: M. Leugers, City of

Burlington, Department of Parks and Recreation, Pine St., Burlington, VT 05401; (802) 862-0123.

Information on Saving Seeds:

SEED SAVERS EXCHANGE, 33076 North Winn Road, Decorah, IA, 52101; (319) 382-5990; *www.seedsavers.org.*

Children and Gardening including resources, organizations, books, grants, and pamphlets:

DIGGING DEEPER: INTEGRATING YOUTH GARDENS INTO SCHOOLS AND COMMUNITIES. Joseph Kiefer and Martin Kemple. Common Roots Press.1998.

FOOD WORKS, 64 Main Street, Montpelier, VT 05602; (800) 310-1515. THE COMMON ROOTS PROGRAM Reconnecting Schools to the Natural Heritage of their Community, a project of Food Works (pamphlet).

THE NATIONAL GARDENING ASSOCIATION (NGA), 1100 Dorset Street, S. Burlington, VT 05403; (802) 863-5251 or (800) 538-7476; Web site: *www.kidsgardening.com;* e-mail: *nga@garden.org.* Provides information on children and gardening through classroom and education projects such as the Grow Labs Program, youth garden grants, and a Gardening with Kids catalog.

Gardening Web Sites (not alphabetized)

NATIONALGARDENING.COM great site: includes information on gardening resources, regional reports, Q&A library, How-To-Projects, Pest Control Library, Zone Finder, Dictionary, Food Garden Guide, Online Courses and Buyer's Guide.

WWW.NYSAES.CORNELL.EDU The Cornell University site provides a myriad of data on gardening topics with an emphasis on growing vegetables.

WWW.HORTICULTURE.COM, headlines horticulture industry news including current horticulture references to other web sites.

WWW.UCSUSA.ORG a site of the Union of Concerned Scientists on the genetic engineering issue.

WWW.HEDGEROWS.COM

WWW.THEHUNGERSITE.COM hunger and food security issues.

WWW.BERKSHIRE.NET/ENSC a site on saving seeds from the Eastern Native Seeds Conservancy.

WWW.GARDENWEB.COM very informative garden website includes forums.

HTTP://GO.COMPUSERVE.COM/GARDENINGFORUM a site where you can chat with over 50,000 other gardeners. People from diverse backgrounds share an abiding interest in gardening. This information may be more immediate and applicable than gardeners receive from current magazines, books, and newspapers.

Why not check these out as well on google:

Garden.org   TheGardenHelper.com
Gardenguides.com   Plantcare.com

Also check out LifeWKR@aol.com - on GE

*Many garden web sites have gone under recently due to competition and corporate takeovers and it keeps on changing.

Winter Appendix Guide Number Twelve

INFORMATION ON MASTER GARDENING

Most states have a Master Gardener's Program where beginning gardeners can take a course on how to become master gardeners. These programs are coordinated out of the University Agricultural Extension services. **VERMONT MASTER GARDENER PROGRAM,** UVM Extension , P.O. Box 53010, Burlington, VT 05405. Contact: Nancy Hulett (802) 656-9562; *http://pss.uvm.edu/mg/mg*

Winter Appendix Guide Number Thirteen

INFORMATION ON FARM AND GARDEN TRAINING AND APPRENTICESHIPS

UNIVERSITY OF VERMONT CENTER FOR SUSTAINABLE AGRICULTURE, 590 Main Street, Burlington, VT 05405; (802) 656-8874. Sets up internship programs for students to work on farms that practice sustainable agriculture.

Other states have similar programs. Check with your state university and Agricultural Extension Office.

See also Winter Appendix Guide 10 for NOFA VT and the Biodynamic Association for apprenticeship and training information. Most organic organizations have apprenticeship and training programs.

Winter Appendix Guide Number Fourteen

ALL PURPOSE ORGANIC GARDENING BOOKS AND PAMPHLETS

THE VEGETABLE GARDENER'S BIBLE: WIDE ROWS, ORGANIC METHODS, RAISED BEDS, DEEP SOIL. Edward C. Smith. Storey Books 1999. This book focuses on the home gardener and extending the growing season.

FOUR-SEASON HARVEST. Elliot Coleman. Chelsea Green Publishing 1992. Focuses on northern gardeners through the four seasons along with techniques and tips on how to start plants earlier in the spring and extend the growing season in the fall. Elliot Coleman is considered the guru of the organic gardening movement. Also wrote *The New Organic Grower,* Chelsea Green Publishing 1995.

COLD-CLIMATE GARDENING. Lewis Hill. Garden Way Publishing. How to extend your growing season by at least 30 days.

HOW TO GROW FRUITS AND VEGETABLES BY THE ORGANIC METHOD, RODALE'S ALL NEW ENCYCLOPEDIA OF ORGANIC GARDENING. Rodale Press.

THE PFEIFFER GARDEN BOOK, AN INTRODUCTION TO GARDENING THROUGH BIODYNAMICS. The Biodynamic (BD) Association. The Biodynamics Association publishes a large number of gardening and farming books. Information on the BD Association is listed above under Organic Organizations.

The publishers with the most books on organic gardening and farming: CHELSEA GREEN, STOREY, RODALE, BIODYNAMICS, AND GARDEN WAY. Books on seeds and seed saving are in spring appendix guide.

Winter Appendix Guide Fifteen

GARDENING MAGAZINES AND PUBLICATIONS

THE AMERICAN GARDENER, 7931 East Boulevard Dr., Alexandria, VA 22308; (703) 768-5700; *www.ahs.org*. This magazine is a publication of the American Horticulture Society. When you subscribe, you also receive the membership's free seed exchange, free admission to garden shows and public gardens, access to a gardening information service, and web site exclusives.

THE AVANT GARDENER, Box 489, NY, NY 10028. Published monthly. More like a newsletter than a magazine; very informative. Each issue focuses on a particular topic like pruning.

TAUNTON'S FINE GARDENING, P.O. Box 5506, Newtown, CT 06470; (203) 426-8171. This magazine is for the serious flower and design gardener. The photographs are outstanding. The gardener can actually see the design elements in the pictures.

HORTICULTURE: THE MAGAZINE OF AMERICAN GARDENING, 98 North Washington St., Boston, MA 02114; (617) 742-5600, *www.hortmag.com*. The oldest gardening magazine in America.

ORGANIC GARDENING, 33. E. Minor Street, Emmaus, PA 18098; (610) 967-5171; *www.organicgardening.com*. A monthly magazine published by Rodale and considered the best overall organic gardening magazine in the country.

PEOPLE PLACES & PLANTS GARDENING MAGAZINE, P.O. Box 6131, Falmouth, ME 04105; (800) 251-1784; *www.pplants.com*. The only magazine dedicated to gardening in New England.

NEW GARDEN MAGAZINE'S PRACTICAL GARDENER, 31633 120th St Cedar Falls IA 50613; (319) 266-1548; *www.thepracticalgardener.com*. Promises to emphasize timesaving and money-saving ways to garden and includes gardener-to-gardener contact. Advertising is restricted to 25%.

THE GARDENER, 30 Irene Street, Torrington, CT 06790; (877) 257-5268; *www.thegardenermagazine.com*. No advertising. The charter issue included the first in a series on making a perennial garden work year-round. Check it out.

Organic Nonprofit Farm and Garden Magazines
THE NATURAL FARMER, 411 Shelton Rd., Barre, MA 01005. NOFA Massachusetts publishes four times a year for the Northeast.

NOFA NOTES, POB 697, Bridge St, Richmond, VT 05477. NOFA Vermont puts this out for farmers in the Northeast. See Winter Appendix Guide 10, Organic Organizations, for more addresses.

BIODYNAMICS: FARMING AND GARDENING FOR THE 21ST CENTURY, 25844 Butler Rd., Junction City, OR 97488, (541) 998-0105. *www.bio-dynamic@aol.com*. The Biodynamic Association publishes six times per year.

ACRES USA: A VOICE FOR ECO-AGRICULTURE P.O. Box 91299, Austin, TX 78709; (512) 892-4400; e-mail: *info.acresusa.com*. An organic farming monthly newspaper that has been around for many years with a proven track record of informative material on organic farming.

FOOD ROUTES.ORG Farm issues by Alan Gilbert. Quite interesting and up-to-date.

NEW FARM.ORG A farmer-to-farmer issue oriented website from the Rodale Institute.

CHILDREN AND
GARDENING

It's healthy for children to follow the whole cycle of nature: to plant pumpkin seeds and nurture the young plants to large orange globes; to cut out jack-o-lantern faces and help make pumpkin pies, roast seeds, and save some for next year's planting. Kids want to be connected, not feel isolated from their environment.

Today, children's gardens are in. There are the ones with an archway filled with overhanging giant gourds or a sunflower house with climbing blue morning glories. Why not a bean tepee where the young ones can hide and rest from the hot summer sun. Or small theme plots: maybe a salsa garden with hot peppers and tomatoes, or a Native American garden with corn, beans, and squash. I even heard of a Beatrix Potter garden starring Peter Rabbit. The ideal children's garden is filled with flowers to smell, herbs to crush, vegetables to eat, butterflies to enjoy, and life cycles to observe like watching lettuce go to seed. How could I forget wind chimes, worm bins, frog ponds, hummingbird areas, or an old apple tree with a swing where we can all be kids again.

Onward to the future gardeners and caretakers of the earth.

PART FIVE: CHILDREN AND GARDENING

Children under umbrella. Photo by Jim Flint at Children's Discovery Garden at the Ethan Allen Homestead in Burlington, Vermont.

THE FOUR SEASONS: A PREVIEW

This final section of The Woodchuck's Guide to Gardening follows kids through the four seasons. We commence with an overture called The Healing Circle. The music begins in early fall with a group of kindergarten children nurturing healing herbs in JoAnne Denne's classroom. We follow their journey through the winter, spring, and summer.

The other major movements of the children's garden symphony continue along the garden path with The Potato Lady and The Good Witch on the Hill who greet us in late winter and early spring. Sabrina Milbury, The Potato Lady, teaches children how to germinate seeds, grow plants, and start a plant business—all in the confines of her urban classroom. The Good Witch on the Hill, Margaret Daniel, brings wild plants into class and mixes elixirs in the rural heartland of Vermont.

During the season of the sun we discover how two young girls, Posey and Katharine King, garden on a hill farm in Putney, Vermont. They don't need a curriculum guide. In autumn, Marcy Summers teaches her kindergarten class how to press apple cider, grind grains, bake bread and make butter. Winter blesses us with the "Ideal Gardening Curriculum" grades (1-8). So hang on to your skivvies; gardening with children is a real workout.

PART FIVE
CHILDREN & GARDENING

CHAPTER 31

THE HEALING CIRCLE

JoAnne Dennee has been a kindergarten teacher and gardener for 28 years and a Waldorf kindergarten teacher for the last eight years. Let's visit her healing circle at the Lake Champlain Waldorf School in Shelburne, Vermont.

A Basket of Healing Herbs

When the children arrive at school in September, the healing herb garden is waiting for them. It comprises echinacea, lemon balm, calendula, chamomile and red clover, which grows wild in the lawn.

JoAnne deadheads the chamomile and calendula plants in summer, which allows the blooms to make a reappearance in early fall. Thus, the children are welcomed by a myriad of flowers.

Their first activity is to pick the chamomile flowers and dry them for winter teas. Calendula flowers are harvested at Michaelmas (September 29) and combined with beeswax to make a healing salve called "Courage." Comfrey and plantain leaves are also added to the mix. Thus, a healing basket full of salves is available in case someone gets hurt. Each child takes a jar home for their family.

SLEEPING SEEDS

After the first frosts, some of the healing plants are deadheaded and others like calendula are allowed to go to seed. Calendula, sometimes called pot marigold, is a prolific self-seeder. JoAnne shows the children how to pick calendula seed. They watch how the seed pods curl into tight crescent moon shapes, brown up, and dry. The children learn to tell the difference between the dried pods and the fleshy young green ones.

The dried seeds are brought inside in pouches dyed in onion skins at Michaelmas. They are placed in a treasure box, protected by a blanket of leaves, and stored under the nature table. JoAnne tells the children this is the time when Mother Earth is retreating into her cave under the nature table—and when gnomes guard the seeds and roots in the earth.

THE HIDDEN SPARK

At Martinmas, November 11th, the children make lanterns for the lantern walk. This festival is a symbol of the last spark of the summer sun, which is diminishing but still shines bright just as there is a spark hidden in a deep mysterious place inside the seed.

While the seeds are stored away, the harvested dried herbs of echinacea roots, calendula, chamomile, red clover flowers, and lemon balm leaves are set aside in a jar on the herb shelf. Once a week, the children make bread and brew up hot tea from the dried herbs.

THE HEALING BROTH

JoAnn tells the children a story in their morning circle of how the gnomes grind the crystals deep in the earth into fine powders in late winter. When the warm spring rains come, the seeds are bathed in a mineral soup. It's like a healing broth for seeds and roots. This is when the green life of the plant kingdom begins to reemerge from the earth. This is also the time to take the seeds out from the treasure box and begin the germination process.

THE SHARING OF THE GIFTS

The cycle continues. The seeds are sprouted. The leftover herbs are crumbled up, placed into little white cotton tea bags, and given out on Mother's Day. The children then begin to work in the healing garden, digging up the German chamomile and calendula, rearranging them, and taking the extra plants home to create their own gardens with their parents.

RENEWING THE CIRCLE

The children continue to work in the garden in early summer, cleaning up the debris, transplanting the healing herbs into beds, and rebuilding the garden paths. Inwardly, they may recall what happened the previous year and reestablish their connection to the summer season. During midsummer, they are welcome to come pick calendula and chamomile flowers with their family. By this time, the children have developed a deep connection to the cycles of the year and the changes that take place through the four seasons. Nature lives within them.

CHAPTER 32
SPRING

THE POTATO LADY

Sabrina Milbury teaches gardening at the Orchard School in South Burlington, Vermont, where she is called "The Potato Lady." This is because she likes to make starch from potatoes at the Orchard School. It all started when her daughter's fourth grade teacher asked Sabrina if she would set up a Grow Lab program in the school. The south-facing windows in the classroom didn't provide enough light to grow plants in late winter and early spring. Because of the lack of winter light in high northern latitudes, plants need a boost and Grow Labs can help.

Grow Labs are like small greenhouses. They use 40-watt cold and hot fluorescent bulbs or special full-spectrum bulbs called grow lights. Most setups have three levels with two lights each and fixtures supported on a wooden or metal frame. The Grow Lab program at Orchard School is sponsored by the National Gardening Association of South Burlington, Vermont. NGA works with thousands of schools throughout the country to foster an appreciation for gardening through practical activities such as Grow Labs.

Word spread around the school how well the Grow Lab was working, and other teachers wanted Sabrina Milbury's help. Sabrina said, "The first year, I created the curriculum as I went along because I had never taught gardening with kids. I only had a garden at my home. I started working with the Grow Labs and then with potatoes because I spent summers on my grandfather's potato farm in Aroostook County, Maine. We made starch from potatoes, and potato prints."

Sabrina also produced salad gardens in the second through fourth grades by using the Grow Labs to produce an assortment of greens. They learned a salad is more than iceberg lettuce—which Sabrina calls "inconveniently packaged water."

She said, "In the spring, we grow different greens with varied colors, flavors, and textures: mustard and turnip greens, leaf lettuces, and arugula and flowers of nasturtiums and even small cherry tomatoes and cucumbers. The tomatoes and cukes take a long time to ripen in the Grow Labs. The kids are thrilled when they get tomatoes to ripen with 40-watt fluorescent bulbs. Cool weather plants, like spinach, radishes, carrots, and some lettuce, don't do well at all because the classrooms are too warm, but this year carrots were successful. The kids unanimously agreed they are better than what you buy in the store."

Since the gardening program is self-supporting, students started a May election day plant sale last year at the Orchard School. They sold annual and perennial flowers, herbs started from seed and cuttings. Favorite cuttings were German ivy and spider plants. Students began the work in March by planting ageratum, alyssum, marigolds, coleus, daisies, zinnias, dwarf snapdragons, chives, basil, marjoram, thyme, dill, and others. They learned how to plant the seeds, then how to transplant, thin, and pot up individual plants. Each student also had to research the plants to understand their growth requirements and needs for sun and water. This information was then shared with customers. Sabrina withheld the information on the seed packets so students could learn how to use books, seed catalogs, indexes, and tables of contents.

Sabrina believes the real benefit of the gardening program is to connect children with their environment. She said 90% of children learn about the environment sitting in classrooms or watching TV. They have almost no direct interaction. "If we are going to shift the way the world is going and keep living on this planet, we need to bring kids back to these connections. The food chain is not seen in the aisles of the supermarket. These little green plants grow and then animals eat the plants and then we eat the animal or we eat the plant directly. That's closer to the food chain."

Spring Continues: The Good Witch on the Hill

Margaret Daniel, whom I call The Good Witch on the Hill, travels from her home high on the mountain down to the valley at the Whitcomb Elementary School in Bethel, Vermont. There in the rural heartland of Vermont, she teaches second graders about wild spring plants and gardening. The children can't wait to see her arrive with baskets full of healing herbs and natural juices in spring. She never tells the children what's in the basket because if she did they might not try it out. In April, the children drink white birch sap with some natural fruit juice. They are inquisitive wanting to know what is in the drink. When Margaret tells them, they grimace at first—then ask for more.

Later in spring, Margaret gathers her own salad greens from dandelions, nettle, mustard and turnip greens, winter cress, and violets. She adds her homemade salad dressings and her famous vegetable powders. Once the children have tasted the salad, Margaret tells them the names of the wild greens, how they are collected, and their medicinal value.

CHAPTER 33

SUMMER

OF FIRE FAIRIES AND FROG PONDS

There is no better place to visit in summer than the garden of Posey and Katharine King, who grew up on a hill farm in the 1970s in the town of Putney, Vermont. When Katharine was three, she told her father Robert she wanted more flowers in the garden. So they planted more and more flowers. Soon they ended up as flower gardeners who coincidentally grew vegetables. They took great joy in creating a children's flower circle of calendulas, asters, and snapdragons. As more flowers joined the garden, Katharine spent lots of time there by herself, laughing and talking to the fire fairies and other elemental beings.

When Posey King needed money to buy a violin, her father planted a 70-foot double row of flowering sweet peas, trained on a 6-foot chicken wire fence. Every day, Posey would pick and gather the white, blue, and pink flowers into bunches. She and her mother Linda took the sweet pea blooms to the Putney Food Co-op where they sold them. Within one summer, with a little help from her parents and the flowers, Posey was playing the violin.

Sweet peas are tricky when it comes to germination. They do best when planted as early as possible because they don't like warm weather. If you get poor germination, try it again. I plant mine an inch to two inches under the soil. If the soil is sandy, plant them deeper, and if it is clay, plant them closer to the top. The best way to ensure good germination is to save your own sweet flowering pea seed, but be careful: They pop out of their pods once they are ripe. That's why those packets of sweet peas cost so much.

Gardening has a magical quality for children like Katharine and Posey. A sturdy young tomato plant is a wonder for anyone to behold, but for a child, it unveils a new world.

Above all, gardens should be fun places for children. It's not so important to give gardening lessons, or hope kids will eat lots of broccoli. Katherine and Posey were never forced to work in the garden, but were left free to participate as much as they wanted.

Even though they are now grown up and not gardeners, I believe gardening played a role in developing their values and preparing them to live creative, caring lives.

CHAPTER 34
FALL

MARCY'S KINDERGARTEN

Marcy Summers has been a Waldorf kindergarten teacher for 15 years. She loves to celebrate the autumn season with her children. In fall, the children prepare for the long winter months by grinding grains and making bread, churning butter, and making apple sauce and apple pies.

CIRCLE TIME AND FARMING

The autumn circle time focuses on songs and stories related to farmers, haying, grains, apples, and bread making. As the songs are sung, the teacher and children make gestures of sowing seeds in the earth.

On a Monday morning

sunny Monday morning

we sowed the seeds

Tatus and I

sowed them when the sun was high

sowed the seeds, Tatus and I

sowed them when the sun was high.

Tatus is a Polish term of endearment for father. This song comes from *Let's Form a Ring: An Acorn Hill Anthology of Poems and Songs,* from the Acorn Hill Waldorf Kindergarten and Nursery in Silver Springs, Maryland. The songs continue through the week:

On Tuesday, we mowed the hay
On Wednesday, we dried the hay
On Thursday, we raked the hay
On Friday, we gathered the hay
On Saturday, we sold the hay
On Sunday, we bowed our heads.

Hay and grasses, which include the grains of wheat, rye, oats, and barley are placed on the nature garden table. The garden is a reflection of what is going on seasonally. On Tuesdays of every week throughout the year, the whole process of bread baking is reenacted. Whole wheat grains are ground with a hand-cranked grinder. The flour is mixed with water, honey, salt, and yeast, and the dough is kneaded and baked golden brown in the oven. The kids with the most energy love to grind the grain. Marcy bought a butter churn in North Hero, Vermont, last summer; it looks like an egg beater in a jar. On Mondays, cream is churned into butter for the bread on Tuesdays. After weeks of singing songs and hearing stories about farmers, sowing seeds and harvesting grains, classes move on to the next theme of autumn, which is a subject dear to our hearts in the Green Mountains. You guessed it folks, apples and cider!

A POEM, A SONG, AND A STORY

A Poem

Down in the orchard it is harvesting time,
and up the tall ladder the fruit pickers climb.
Among the green branches that sway overhead,
the apples are hanging all rosy and red.
Just ripe for the picking, so juicy and sweet,
so lovely to look at and wonderful to eat.

A Song

Shake, shake the apple tree

Apples red and rosy

Shake shake the apple tree

Apples red and rosy

One for you, one for me

Shake, shake the apple tree

The apple tree song was arranged by Christoff Jasske. It comes from *Rhythms, Rhymes and Games: Aids to English Teachers in Waldorf Schools.*

A Story

THE THREE APPLES
BY CAROLYN BAILEY AND CLARA LEWIS

In the school garden, Marcy and the children sit under the old knurled apple tree, and she tells them a story about a tree with only three apples left. The shortened version goes something like this:

A boy walks along and picks the first apple, eats it, and throws the core away. A little girl comes along and she picks the second apple, but it's so beautiful she doesn't want to eat it, so she tucks it away in a special hiding place. A third child comes along and takes the last rosy red apple home to his mother. She tells him there is a secret inside the apple. She cuts it in half, shows him the star that one finds in every apple and the dark seeds used to grow another apple tree. Together, mother and child plant the seeds.

The story is part of a book, *Favorite Stories for the Children's Hour*, 1955, Clatt & Monk, Inc., NYC.

After the story, the children make apple pies and applesauce and, of course, save seeds, sometimes scavenging them anywhere they are found and stuffing them into their pockets. They use a new green shiny apple peeler and corer from Hackett's Orchard in South Hero, Vermont. Harvesting and saving prepares kids for winter. Marcy tells them how the seeds are going to sleep in the earth and how the trees

Charlotte and Verity Watts, of London, England and their friends Cassie and Weenie Marie.
Photo by Robert King at his garden in Putney.

lay down their leaves like a blanket to keep them warm.

THE COMPOST PILE

While all this is going on there are chores to do; one of the children's favorites is going to the compost pile. At the end of the day while everyone is cleaning up the room, three children are selected to take the bucket down to the compost pile. It's a treat. A wooden bin with a cover holds the compost bin; the ever-present mice cause great excitement. But the children are more on the lookout for the compost gnomes, which they see from time to time. Sometimes they leave special treats for them. They are fascinated by the compost smells and how it all breaks down into food for the garden.

CHAPTER 35

WINTER

THE IDEAL GARDENING CURRICULUM

While winter still has us within her grasp, let's dream of the ideal school gardening program where the garden, farm, and natural world are woven into the very fabric of the school. For children who live in rural areas, gardening and caring for animals is part of their everyday life. But for most young people, a comprehensive gardening curriculum is needed. Many schools include some gardening programs, but few integrate gardening throughout the growing season from grades 1-8. As soon as a child climbs the doorsteps to the first grade and even before in kindergarten, the gardening world is introduced. Let's travel with them.

FIRST GRADE

In the first grade, children sing songs and listen to nature stories and poetry tied in to the seasons of the year. They play in a small outside garden and take nature walks down to the river. The children work in the little school garden, but it is not a very conscious activity. The idea is to have a place for free outside play. In the fall, the children plant bulbs and take geranium cuttings to grow over winter for gifts on Mother's Day. They play and hear stories about elemental helpers such as the flower fairies and Brother Sun and Sister Wind.

SECOND GRADE

In the second grade, they do more of the same and also hear Native American stories. They have a little harvest and Thanksgiving festival complete with corn blessings to the four directions: east, west, north, and south. In the spring, they clear the earth, prepare the soil, and plant wheat, corn, beans, and pumpkins for the coming year. The class visits a small farm and presents a gift of three apple trees, which they help the farmer plant. Throughout the year, they bake bread once a week in class and also make butter from cream.

THIRD GRADE

In the third grade, gardening goes big time. The wheat is harvested along with the corn, beans, and pumpkins which had been planted the previous spring. The wheat is threshed and winnowed and saved for grain which is ground into flour. Each student weaves a corn dolly from the grain straw and buries some grain back into the earth as a gesture of thanks. The third grade makes seven-grain world bread from the wheat they grew along with rye, barley, corn, and oats. They also pick apples on a local farm and make apple cider using an antique press.

They again go to the small farm, but this time they stay over at the farm for two nights and have real work days where they help out in the gardens, build compost piles, and milk the cows. After all the harvesting and cooking of their meals, they sleep soundly in the barn.

FOURTH GRADE

The fourth grade again visits the farm in the fall and helps harvest pumpkins, squash, potatoes, and corn. A local Native American storyteller comes to the farm to tell them tales. An old woman in her 80s reminisces of the days when her family had a small farm where they grew all their food. The children continue to work in the school garden and plant trees in a local county forest.

FIFTH GRADE

The children begin to do more practical work at the school: repairing and building new fences, fixing the rock walls, and doing regular garden chores. Gardening in the school garden is combined with the study of the botany and geology of the area. The class goes on mushroom walks, hikes the Appalachian trail, and watches Canada geese fly south for the winter.

SIXTH, SEVENTH, AND EIGHTH GRADES

The class starts a business called Earth's Garden Nursery. Seedlings are grown in the school greenhouse and sold to friends, parents, and the community to raise money for trips. The students run the business, keep the books, and learn how to start plants from seeds and other methods of propagation. In the seventh grade, the class runs a composting program at the school and begins a flower gardening project in the town common.

In the eighth grade, the school raises funds to send the class to Costa Rica to study the rain forest, build nature trails, hike, and study. Students experience the diversity of the plant, animal, and mineral kingdoms and the relationships and symbiosis of the three. The highlight of the trip to Costa Rica occurs when the class sees Volcano Arenal erupt.

Students appreciate and learn from the natural world when they grow up close to nature and are schooled in gardening, science, and nature study from the first grade on. Those eight years of study live on in a much deeper way than anyone can imagine. An inherent wisdom is found in the healthy work of horticulture. Children serve as true witnesses to this eternal cycle of the year.

Monica Marshall, a teacher at the Monadnock Waldorf School in Keene, New Hampshire, provided the material for the ideal gardening curriculum. She has been teaching for over 18 years.

Winter Appendix Guide 11 has information on Children and Gardening.

CHAPTER 35

CONCLUSION

It pleases me to end this gardening journey with mention of the front cover of a young woman planting hearts. The mural provides a backdrop for how important gardening is to all of us, especially children. My wish is that all children will grow up as did the young woman in the painting, planting hearts into the earth.

If young children are free to dig, touch, smell, run, climb, and explore the world of gardening, their chances of becoming lovers of the earth and the plant kingdoms are strengthened. As the young ones move from kindergarten to elementary and on to middle school and beyond, a gardening curriculum can become an integral part of their learning. Small green thumbs can grow into larger thumbs that can heal the earth.

Of course, our children aren't the only ones who need help. How about our current generation of grownups who are unaware of how fresh fruits and vegetables are produced, and from where they come. This is not the case with past generations. Our dependence on processed and convenience food isolates us from the land and deprives us of the joys and responsibilities of growing, preparing, and sharing food together. Gardening bridges this gap by giving us a sense of season, place, and community.

Just in my lifetime, the tradition of growing food is being lost. What happens when all we do is watch people garden on television? Henry David Thoreau wrote in his book *Walking*, "In wildness is the preservation of the world." I feel the same about gardening with children: Gardening with children is the preservation of the world.

AFTERWORD

We have traveled a long way through the four cycles of the year — from seed to seed. I realize after spending eons of time writing *The Woodchuck's Guide to Gardening* I have only touched lightly on the garden path. There was so much I didn't cover...but then no garden book ever could. One thing is for sure: The more I garden, the more I become aware of how little I really know. Just the other day while weeding down at my plot at the Tommy Thompson Community Garden, the youngest daughter of the Mai family, who immigrated from Vietnam, brought me some salad greens I had never tasted. The world of horticulture goes on ad infinitum. The gardening well is deep. There is so much to learn.

I hope I have given you a taste of northern gardening. My wish was to offer spirit and soul to the plant kingdom. You're the judge on this account. And a good gardening to you.

Photo of author by Jamie Mittendorf, Tommy Thompson Community Garden.

GLOSSARY OF
COMMON GARDENING TERMS

ACID & ALKALINE SOILS: These words refer to pH, an index denoting acidity or alkalinity. The scale runs from 0=acid to 14=alkaline with 7 being neutral. Most plants grow well in a range of 5.5 to 7.0. Blueberries and other acid-loving plants like azaleas need a garden acid soil close to 5. Sulphur will acidify the soil.

You can find very acid soils are in bogs. Corn and many vegetables like soils closer to a pH of 6 and 7. These are called alkaline or sweet soils. Strong alkaline soils are found in the deserts. Adding lime and wood ashes sweeten your soil (increase alkalinity).

ACTINOMYCETES: This refers to a group of soil microorganisms that produce an extensive thread-like network throughout the soil. They look like the soil molds but resemble bacteria in size. Actinomycetes are important in the decomposition and humus formation of organic matter. Actinomycetes produce antibiotic substances in the soil.

ANNUAL PLANT: A plant living one year or less. The plant grows, blooms, produces seeds, and dies. (e.g., beans, sweet corn).

BARE-ROOT: A bare-rooted plant does not have soil on its roots. Many rose plants are bare-rooted when you purchase them from a nursery or mail-order catalog.

BIENNIAL PLANTS: These plants require two years or part of two years to complete there life cycle (e.g., beets, carrots, cabbage), which usually produce seed the second year.

BIOLOGICAL CONTROL: This term refers to pest control by natural means, such as parasite/predators instead of chemicals. For example, using lacewing larvae in a garden to control aphids instead of spraying malathion, a poisonous insecticide. Herbicides, insecticides and fungicides are chemicals used to kill weeds, insects, and fungus diseases.

BLANCHING: This is a method of preventing sunlight from striking a plant part. As a result, the part is white in color, as with celery. For this result, hoe soil around the green stem of the celery plant.

BOLTING: The production of a seed stalk by vegetable plants such as lettuce and spinach. Bolting occurs when days are long and hot. Some gardeners use the term, *going to seed.*

BULB: This refers to a plant structure made up of a short fleshy stem, containing a growing point or flower bud. The stem is enclosed by thick, fleshy scales. Many gardeners plant daffodils and tulip bulbs in the fall and dahlias and gladiolus in the summer. The tender summer bulbs need to dug up in the fall and stored over the winter. Fall bulbs are hardier and don't need to be dug up. They continue to produce bulbs year after year.

COLD FRAME: This refers to an enclosed wooden structure used to grow plants and harden off young plants before placing them in the garden. Glass or poly frames are used to cover cold frames.

COMPOST: The breakdown of organic matter (manure, leaves, mulch hay, vegetable wastes), into a dark, brown, crumbly substance, which is used to feed the soil.

COVER CROPS, GREEN MANURES AND CROP ROTATIONS: Cover crops are the same as green manures. These refer to plants grown and then turned under, usually within one gardening season. Their purpose is to increase organic matter as well as prevent erosion. If you plan on leaving the cover crop in over the winter, it's a good idea to plant a grass and legume mix like rye and clover. Cover crops include oats, buckwheat, white and yellow clover, rye and rye grass. Planting cover crops can be done after vegetable harvest time or earlier by planting between vegetable rows.

A four-year crop rotation on a farm might be corn, oats, clover, wheat, in four fields of similar size. A legume (clovers, alfalfa, beans or peas) is advised as a soil builder.

GARDEN SOILS: There are three basic classes of garden soils: Sands, silts and clays. All soils are composed of particles which vary greatly in size. Clay consists of fine particles and is high in nutrients. Silt falls between clay and sand. Sand includes about 20 percent silt and clay. It's particles are large and irregular in shape. Sand has good drainage, warms early and is lower in nutrients. Loams can be described as a combination of sand, silt and clay. There are gravely sands, fine sands and loamy sands or sandy, silty or clay loams or heavy clays or silty clays.

You can get a good idea of your soil's texture and class by rubbing it between the thumb and the fingers or in the palm of the hand. Sand particles are gritty; silt has a talcum powder feel when dry and is moderately plastic when moist; clay is harsh when dry and very plastic and sticky when wet. In addition to clay, silt, and sand, there's also organic matter, which comprises about 2 to 5% of the soil.

Compacted soils are heavier soils that have been packed or worked too wet and are hard. A hardpan is a hard layer of soil a few inches under ground level, which results from constant plowing at the same depth. Soil crusting forms when a thick hard layer of soil on the surface is created from the impact of many rain drops during a heavy rain fall.

GENUS AND SPECIES: The whole system of how plants are classified for the general public is confusing. If you want to reach the pinnacle of correctness, use the Latin or botanical name for the plant. The Latin name clears up any confusion about using multiple names for the same plant and the same name for different plants.

As far back as 1753, the botanist, Linnaeus, devised the system which assigns each plant or animal species two names, usually in Latin. The first name is the genus or larger grouping; the second is the species which is the most specific classification. For example the carrot is *Daucaus carota*. The potato is *Solaum tuberosum*. We already know many flower garden plants by their Latin genus names: *Delphinium, Dahlia, Gladiolus* and *Zinnia;* however most of the time the names we give fruits, herbs and vegetables are simplified from the Latin. For example, Detroit Dark Red is a beet variety and Red Cored Chantenay is a carrot cultivar. (Generally, variety is a common generic term used to classify a wide number of plants and cultivar is a more formal, technical term.)

If you want the whole enchilada, pick up a book like *The Dictionary of Plant Names*. By the way, the largest classification beyond genus is the word *family* like for orchids, *Orchidacea*. One can even go further out like orchids are monocots. Other monocots are grasses and grains, lilies and irises.

HARDENING OFF: This refers to shifting plants from a more-to-a-less sheltered environment to a less-protected one. This helps the plant adapt to an outdoor location and increases it chances for survival.

HUMUS: Humus is organic matter in a more advanced stage of decomposition in the composting process. In a compost heap, some of the organic matter turns into humus and the remaining fraction completes the decomposition process in the soil. Humus transforms the nutritive elements in soil into soluble substances which in turn feed the finer feeder roots of the plant. By solubility is meant the ability of a substance to dissolve in water. Humus also keeps the activity of bacteria in the soil at a high level, adds to general fertility, and improves soil structure.

HYBRID: This term describes a plant derived from the crossing of parent plants differing in one or more gene. Seed from hybrid plants will usually not "come true," that is, grow identical parents, so they are not saved for another year. Most modern vegetable seeds are hybrids. By law, hybrid seed must be identified as such in catalogs. Plant hybrids aim to increase productivity, flavor and disease resistance. Open-pollinated / heirloom seeds maintain their original characteristics.

IPM (INTEGRATED PEST MANAGEMENT): A method of controlling pest populations by monitoring: that is, timing pest treatment to be most effective and least damaging to natural controls; it also refers in some cases to using selective, not-broad spectrum, pesticides.

LEGUME: A member of the plant family Leguminosae, characterized by their ability to fix nitrogen from the air with their nodule bacteria. Legumes are the best soil building and forage crops. They have more protein and calcium and vitamins A and D per acre than any other roughage. Some examples of legumes are alfalfa, peas, beans and clover.

MULCH: Mulch describes a layer of material spread around plants over the soil to lessen evaporation, maintain even temperature, and keep down the weeds. Mulches can be organic: Grass, hay, leaves, wood chips provide organic matter to the soil. Or mulches can be inorganic like black plastic, which add nothing to the soil.

PERENNIAL PLANTS: Plants that normally live for an indefinite number of years. Examples of edible perennials are asparagus and rhubarb. The term usually refers to herbaceous plants or plants with no persistent woody stem above the ground. There are some not-so-hardy perennial herbs and flowers which are grown just as annuals and others which continue to grow year after year. Hardy is a term to describe plants able to winter over without artificial protection.

PESTICIDE: Any one of a number of deadly chemical sprays used to kill insects and weeds. The use of pesticides is not condoned in the organic method because of the indiscriminate harm done to beneficial insects and soil life, and because of the potential threat to human health. (Herbicides and insecticides are considered broad classes of pesticides.)

PHOTOSYNTHESIS AND GLOBAL WARMING: As soon as the plant has a root and green leaves it can start to make its own food. This usually takes from ten to thirty days. The root takes up the water and minerals. These raw materials are carried in the stream of water or sap up to the green leaves, where they are made into plant food. The water and minerals in the soil, carbon dioxide in the air, and light must come together in the green leaf before they can be used by the plant as food.

The green color in the leaf is caused by chlorophyll, which has the ability to transform the water and minerals into starch (sugars and carbohydrates) in the presence of light. This is called, photosynthesis, the dynamic principle which lays the basis of all plant life. Plants are the respiratory system of the earth, taking in carbon dioxide and giving off large amounts of oxygen.

We need to be mindful of this dynamic principle and take action to reverse the use of fossil fuels which produce large amounts of carbon dioxide, which increase the temperature on Earth. This is even more critical today due to recent imbalances in nature caused from the destruction of the rain forests coupled with the increase in fossil fuels. Global Warming is like a canary in a coal mine. The Arctic region is taking the first blows. The number of 40-below days is now half what it was in the 1950s. This means the permafrost is warming and the sea ice is shrinking as well as the populations of sea lions and seal pups. Other effects are dying Salmon in the North Pacific, the loss of Coral reefs and the cloud forests of Costa Rica. Global Warming is real and is threatening our existence on planet earth.

POLLINATION: Pollination is a necessary part of the fertilization process, whereby pollen from the stamens, the male flower parts, is transferred to the pistil, the female flower part. This is accomplished naturally by the wind, bees, and other insects.

Some plants have both male and female organs on the same plant like cucumbers and others do not.

ROOT CROPS: Any crop whose edible portion is taken from under the ground is commonly called a root crop. Popular gardens root crops are beets, carrots, parsnips, and turnips. Onions are bulbs and potatoes are tubers.

SIDE DRESSING: This refers to applying fertilizers such as compost along the side of plants after they are established and growing.

TRANSPLANT: A plant produced from seed germinated in a favorable environment for later planting in an area where the plant is to grow for maturity. Example: a young tomato seedling started from seed in your home which grows into a young tomato plant. A seedling is a young plant emerging from a germinating seed.

Another definition of transplant refers to those people who move to Vermont from who knows where.

TUBERS: The short fleshy underground stem which becomes thickened with the accumulation of plant materials. The potato is an edible starchy tuber. The sweet potato is tuberous root related to the morning glory family whereas the white potato is related to the nightshade family.

WINDBREAKS: a screen of living trees which help to hold down soil against heavy winds and keep snow from drifting. A wide plank wooden fence can also be used as a windbreak. It will keep the soil warmer on one side of the plank fence and allow the gardener to plant earlier. Cold frames can be used on the warmer side away from the wind to start seeds in spring and grow plants in summer, fall and winter.

THE EASY-TO-USE
WOODCHUCK'S INDEX GUIDE

Photo of Alison Flint, by Jim Flint